"This path-breaking study on comparative public law confirms that the globalisation of debates about the relationship of law and religion allows today a profound, sensible re-assessment of plurality-conscious 'justice as discourse'. Truly liberal theories of justice can indeed be reformulated and contextually applied to include Muslim concepts. An argumentative masterpiece!"

Professor Emeritus Werner Menski, SOAS University of London, UK

"In a time of political Islamic reductionism, when the plural experience of Islam is at risk of being reduced to a dogmatic monolith, Jamal's book invites Muslims to engage with liberal theories of justice not as the passive recipients of Western ideas, but as the active innovators of the local and global polity."

Professor Marco Ventura, University of Siena, Italy

"This is a highly commendable and fresh contribution to the debates on the relationship between Islam and the Modern State, proposing a much needed third way apart from a theocracy or an anti-religious secular state. A well researched and highly recommended read."

Professor Mashood A. Baderin, SOAS University of London, UK

Islam, Law and the Modern State

Within the global phenomenon of the (re)emergence of religion into issues of public debate, one of the most salient issues confronting contemporary Muslim societies is how to relate the legal and political heritage that developed in pre-modern Islamic polities to the political order of the modern states in which Muslims now live. This work seeks to develop a framework for addressing this issue. The central argument is that liberal theory, and in particular justice as discourse, can be normatively useful in Muslim contexts for relating religion, law and state. Just as Muslim contexts have developed historically, and continue to develop today, the same is the case with the requisites of liberal theory, and this may allow for liberal choices to be made in a manner that is not a renunciation of Muslim heritage.

Arif A. Jamal is Associate Professor at the National University of Singapore, Faculty of Law where he teaches comparative law, legal theory, law and religion, and Islamic law. He has studied and researched in law, politics and Islamic studies in Canada, the UK and the USA, and writes on issues of law and religion, comparative law and law in Muslim contexts.

ICLARS Series on Law and Religion

Series Editors:
Silvio Ferrari, University of Milan, Italy, Russell Sandberg, Cardiff University, UK, Pieter Coertzen, University of Stellenbosch, South Africa, W. Cole Durham, Jr., Brigham Young University, USA, and Tahir Mahmood, Amity International University, India

www.routledge.com/ICLARS-Series-on-Law-and-Religion/book-series/ICLARS

The *ICLARS Series on Law and Religion* is a new series designed to provide a forum for the rapidly expanding field of research in law and religion. The series is published in association with the International Consortium for Law and Religion Studies, an international network of scholars and experts of law and religion founded in 2007 with the aim of providing a place where information, data and opinions can easily be exchanged among members and made available to the broader scientific community. The series aims to become a primary source for students and scholars while presenting authors with a valuable means to reach a wide and growing readership.

Other titles in this series:

Islam, Law and the Modern State
(Re)imagining Liberal Theory in Muslim Contexts
Arif A. Jamal, National University of Singapore, Singapore

Religious Freedom and the Australian Constitution
Origins and Future
Luke Beck, Western Sydney University, Australia

Free Exercise of Religion and the United States Constitution
The Supreme Court's Challenge
Mark P. Strasser, Capital University Law School, USA

Law and International Religious Freedom
The Rise and Decline of the American Model
Pasquale Annicchino, European University Institute, Italy

Proportionality, Equality Laws, and Religion
Conflicts in England, Canada, and the USA
Megan Pearson, University of Southampton, UK

Islam and Women's Income
Farah Deeba Chowdhury, Queen's University, Canada

Blasphemy, Islam and the State
Stewart Fenwick, University of Melbourne, Australia

Islam, Law and the Modern State

(Re)imagining Liberal Theory in Muslim Contexts

Arif A. Jamal

Routledge
Taylor & Francis Group
LONDON AND NEW YORK

First published 2018
by Routledge

2 Park Square, Milton Park, Abingdon, Oxfordshire OX14 4RN
52 Vanderbilt Avenue, New York, NY 10017

Routledge is an imprint of the Taylor & Francis Group, an informa business

First issued in paperback 2019

British Library Cataloguing-in-Publication Data
A catalogue record for this book is available from the British Library

Library of Congress Cataloging-in-Publication Data
Names: Jamal, Arif A., author.
Title: Islam, law, and the modern state : (re)imagining liberal theory in Muslim contexts / by Arif A. Jamal.
Description: Abingdon, Oxon [UK] ; New York : Routledge, 2018. | Series: ICLARS series on religion and law | Includes bibliographical references and index.
Identifiers: LCCN 2017048591 | ISBN 9781138205482 (hardback)
Subjects: LCSH: Justice, Administration of (Islamic law) | Justice, Administration of. | Islam and justice. | Religion and law.
Classification: LCC KBP1572.J36 2018 | DDC 340.5/9—dc23
LC record available at https://lccn.loc.gov/2017048591

ISBN: 978-1-138-20548-2 (hbk)
ISBN: 978-0-367-89372-9 (pbk)

Typeset in Galliard
by Apex CoVantage, LLC

For my parents

Contents

Preface xii
Acknowledgements xiii

Introduction 1
The challenge 1
The structure 3
The approach 5
The contribution and the argument 5

1 Developing the concept of 'justice as discourse' 7
The challenge of diversity: liberal theory's normative commitment 7
Liberal and theological responses 9
Rawls' political liberalism 10
Responses to and critiques of Rawls 13
Alternatives to Rawls' theory 19
Theologically-oriented positions 19
Wolterstorff's consocial position 21
Habermas' refinement 22
Weithman's two propositions 26
Ladd's critique of liberal absolutism 29
Gaus: public justification and expanding public reason 30
Constructing a theory: justice as discourse 30
Justice as discourse versus some alternatives 34
Bader's 'priority for democracy' 34
An-Na'im's 'civic reason' / 'public reason' 35
Expanded public reason 37
Conclusion 38

2 Justice as discourse in application 40
Justice as discourse and classical liberal theory 40
Diversity 40
Neutrality 42
Limits 44

Justice as discourse and the secular 45
Secularism 45
Secularisation 47
Non-Western secularisation 48
Justice as discourse 49
Implementing justice as discourse: the axes of state, law, civil society and politics 51
Executive, bureaucratic and judicial authorities 51
Legislative provisions 53
Civil society: community organisations, NGOs 53
Political reasons 54
Conclusion 55

3 Muslim contexts I: history and heritage 58
Why use the term 'Muslim contexts'? 59
What is the same, and what is different, about Muslim contexts? 62
Navigating liberal ideas and theories past colonialism 65
The politico-legal legacy 67
Muhammad, the prophet, the leader and the lawgiver 67
After the prophet: power, law and religion 69
The development of the law: the schools, the fiqh *and* usul al-fiqh *73*
Power, law and religion: the ongoing dynamic 78
Conclusion and lessons from the heritage 81

4 Muslim contexts II: contemporary contexts 84
Reworking the law: replacement, codifications and etatization *87*
The nexus of Din, Dunya *and* Dawla*: religion, politics and the state – divided? 91*
Contemporary opinions in Muslim populations 95
Prospects for democracy? 99
Conclusion 101

5 Terms of engagement: (Re)imagining religion, law, state and society for Muslim contexts 103
Challenges to the uses of liberal theory 104
Issues and challenges from the paradigm of liberal theory 104
Challenges arising out of the heritage of Muslim contexts 109
The macro challenges: pluralism and sovereignty 117
Transitional character of Muslim contexts 120
Defining a practical political model 121
Constitutional law 121
Non-constitutional law 123
Political debate 124

Judges, state executives and civil servants 124
Bader's models revisited 125
The bridge from politics to law: Menski's kite 126
The overall argument and conclusion 127

Conclusion 130

Bibliography 134
Works cited 134
Works consulted 142
Websites 144
Index 146

Preface

Within the global phenomenon of the (re)emergence of religion into issues of public debate, one of the most salient issues confronting contemporary Muslim societies is how to relate the legal and political heritage that developed in pre-modern Islamic polities to the political order of the modern states in which Muslims now live.

This work seeks to develop a framework for addressing this issue by drawing upon two sources. The first is an interpretative understanding of the history of Muslim contexts, emphasising, in particular, the diversity of views about what Islam mandates that have always been a part of Muslim experience and the distinction between political and religio-legal authority that developed in practice in these environments. The second source is a variety of contemporary liberal theory which this work develops and calls 'justice as discourse'.

The central argument is that liberal theory, and justice as discourse in particular, though it may have emerged in a different social and cultural milieu, can be normatively useful in Muslim contexts for relating, religion, law, state and society. It is argued first that Muslim contexts are facing issues similar to those out of which liberal theory emerged. Additionally, it is argued that both Muslim contexts and liberal theory are dynamic and continually developing, and that this shared dynamism means that there may be space for convergence of the two. Just as Muslim contexts have developed historically (and continue to develop today), the same is the case with the requisites of liberal theory and this may allow for liberal choices to be made in a manner that is not a renunciation of Muslim heritage.

Acknowledgements

This work owes much to many.

This book emerges out of my doctoral thesis and I thank my supervisors, Alison Diduck (primary supervisor) and Cécile Laborde (secondary supervisor), for their advice and guidance. Alison, in particular, had the wisdom to know when, and in what measure, to guide, to challenge and to support. My thanks to her are enduring.

I also thank numerous friends and colleagues at University College London, the School of Oriental and African Studies and, especially, the National University of Singapore (NUS) Faculty of Law whose input, advice and encouragement have been so important. Jeremiah Lau (NUS Law 2015), Thaddaeus Aaron Tan (NUS Law 2019) and Hee Jinn Wong (NUS Law 2019) all provided valuable research assistance at different stages for which I express my gratitude. Their work was supported by grant WBS R-241-000-108-133 from NUS.

I must also acknowledge the generous scholarship support I received from the Institute of Ismaili Studies, London for my doctoral studies, and especially thank its former Director, Azim Nanji, for his encouragement. I also thank the Islamic Legal Studies Program at Harvard Law School for affording me the opportunity to spend a very enriching academic year at Harvard at the beginning of my PhD work and especially thank Roy Parviz Mottahedeh of the Harvard faculty for his time during that year.

My greatest thanks is owed to family.

To my parents, brother and sister-in-law, and my two darling nieces, I am nearly at a loss for words to express my deepest gratitude for all that they have done. Their hopes, dreams and prayers have meant so much. And always will.

And finally, from the bottom of my heart, I thank my wife, who has believed in me every step of the way and whose support and love helps to sustain me and gives me succour.

To borrow a line from Vikram Seth, "To these I owe a debt past telling."[1] I only hope that I have been able to do them some measure of justice.

1 See the dedication in Vikram Seth, *A Suitable Boy: A Novel*. New York: Harper Collins Publishers, 1993.

Introduction

The challenge

Among the most prominent issues facing contemporary Muslim societies is how to relate the legal and political heritage that developed in pre-modern Islamic polities to the political order of the modern states in which Muslims now live. This challenge arises from a number of different factors. On the one hand, Muslim contexts have witnessed the rise of so called 'political Islam'[1] in movements that have sought to re-shape the state, society and politics along what have been asserted to be 'Islamic' lines (as this is understood by the putative reformers themselves). These movements often call for the establishment of 'Islamic states' and the rule of 'Islamic law' and thus propose a dominating, even domineering, role for religious outlooks in the polity. The Iranian Revolution headed by the Ayatollah Khomeini in 1979 and its legacy in the current Iranian regime, and the Taliban regime that existed in Afghanistan and more currently the so-called 'Islamic State' (otherwise referred to as ISIS or Daesh) serve as examples of this trend that achieved, for some time and to some extent at least, their political ends. Alternative perspectives, however, question not only the desirability but also the means by which an Islamic identity can be projected.

Second, as several states of the Muslim world emerged out of the old colonial empires their evolution has seen them seek out new forms of political identity and legitimacy, a process which has, for some, led them to re-consider the role of Islam in the polity. Moreover, both from within and outside Muslim contexts, hard questions are being asked about how Islam interacts with human rights doctrines and norms, about religious pluralism, both intra-Muslim and, more generally, about rights of non-Muslim minorities within majority Muslim populations and, conversely, about the Muslims living as minorities among majority non-Muslim populations. Issues arise about what it means in practical terms to live in accordance with Islam, in terms, for example, of personal law, banking or community relations. These questions arise both in Muslim majority situations as well as where there are Muslim minorities. While the full gamut of these questions is beyond the scope of any one treatment, the fact that these issues are percolating within Muslim societies indicates that Muslims are facing a challenge. Put simply, it is the challenge of relating Islam – however interpreted and understood – to the contemporary life and society of Muslims. One critical aspect of this challenge is the relationship of religion, the state and the public sphere. This challenge is reflected, more concretely for example, in the discussions about the appropriate role for religion in national constitutional structures. For instance, in both Afghanistan's

1 The discussions of this are legion but one might look for example at Ayubi (1991) or Roy (1994).

new constitution[2] and Iraq's constitution,[3] to give just two prominent examples, the issue of the place of Islam, and the role of Islamic law, was a much-debated topic.

This book seeks to participate in these discussions by developing a framework for structuring the relationship between religion, the state and public discourse, with a focus on what I will call 'Muslim contexts', and, in particular, these contexts in countries of Muslim majority. This means that I will focus on the place of Islam in the 'public sphere' the conceptualisation of which owes much to the work of Jurgen Habermas.[4] Charles Taylor has explained that the public sphere is:

> a common space in which members of society are deemed to meet through a variety of media: print, electronic, and also face-to-face encounters; to discuss matters of common interest and thus to be able to form a common mind about these. . . . It's a kind of common space . . . in which people who never meet understand themselves to be engaged in discussion and capable of reaching a common mind.[5]

Crucial to the construction of any such framework also will be the need to reflect upon and address issues which may be considered generally under the rubric of 'law and religion' and, in this respect, they are relevant to all societies, be they Muslim or not. A focus on Muslim contexts, then, is merely a type of case study, although, as with any case study, it yields particular factors that must be taken into account.

One of the salient issues that arises is, broadly stated, how society should deal with a diversity of views. This is the 'simple-to-state-but-difficult-to-address' challenge of pluralism: the challenge of society needing some basic principles in order to function while recognising that with great diversity of opinions and values held by individuals, finding the points of agreement will be difficult at best. Religious beliefs and commitments will, of course, be one clear source of diversity of outlooks and values among individuals and groups. Indeed, religious beliefs might be especially important in this regard because they can be constitutive of a comprehensive sense of 'the good life' for their adherents and thus impact outlooks on a wide spectrum of social issues. Thus, religious beliefs can be firmly linked to different conceptions of public good that must be brought into some *modus vivendi* for any society to function.

A second related question is what the appropriate *role* for religion is in public discourse as a source of different conceptions of the good life in public discourse. It is one thing to recognise that religious beliefs are a source of diversity and that diversity must be brought into a sort of social *modus vivendi*, but this might be achieved by regulating, and relegating, religious commitments to the margins of social life. But this is only one alternative, and herein lies the question: can religion be brought into discussion on public issues or is it, as Stephen Carter has wondered, "something you should leave behind when you come to serious public debate or into the workplace; something that you should be willing to split off from yourself if you want to be taken seriously?"[6]

The ultimate aim of this work, then, is to propose a model that will be both appropriate and useful in Muslim contexts to structure the relationship between religion, the state and

2 See http://president.gov.af/en/afghan-constitution-2/ for the English translation of the Afghan Constitution.

3 See www.wipo.int/edocs/lexdocs/laws/en/iq/iq004en.pdf for the English translation of the Iraqi Constitution.

4 See Habermas (1989).

5 Taylor (2007) at 185 and 187. See also Taylor (2004) at 83 and 85.

6 Calder (1993) at 18.

the public domain: appropriate inasmuch as it will be sensitive to the particular characteristics of Muslim contexts and useful in that it will provide a fresh perspective on an issue of contemporary importance.

The study is based on a few key premises and animating ideas. The first is that there has been an unfortunate and ultimately misleading dichotomy that has become prevalent in Muslim contexts suggesting that the only options available to society with respect to a public role for religion are between becoming a theocracy on the one hand, or a kind of anti-religious secular state on the other. This dichotomy is false because the available options are not necessarily diametrically opposed and presenting them as such deals too simply with the idea of the secular, which, while it is not always a clear concept (and perhaps easier to identify than define), offers much more by way of possibilities than simply being defined as 'anti-religious'. Indeed, by looking at the development of the term 'secular' we will see that, while it may define an 'areligious' space, this does not mean it defines an '*anti-religious*' space. A secular context within which religion might operate robustly is a viable option.[7] And it has reasons to commend itself. Indeed, what will be advanced here is a pluralistic space including a variety of religious perspectives.

Second, it will be argued that Muslim contexts have particular characteristics derived from a mixture of their historical evolution as well as conceptions of the role and place of Islam and its relationship to social and political affairs that distinguish them from other contexts, notably from Western Europe and North America. This means that, as noted above, a framework developed for these contexts must take account of these features especially in the *presentation* of options and ideas. However, this does *not* mean that some of the principles and even structures developed in other societies, including in the 'West',[8] are of no value and relevance in Muslim contexts. Indeed, quite the contrary is the case, as this study will show that, though mediated through different cultural lenses and historical experiences, there is a substantial commonality of concerns, values and aspirations with respect to the relationship of religion, the state and the public life in and between Muslim contexts and those of the West (and, indeed, perhaps of other societies as well).

Thirdly, this work assumes that the law plays a critical role in defining the relationship between religion, the state and public discourse. This is because it is through law that these relationships will be determined. For example, constitutional law governs the establishment of an official religion and the extent and impact of such an establishment; it also determines the provision or limits of rights of freedom of thought, conscience and religion, and freedom of speech, expression or assembly all of which may impact religious expression or practice in private and public spheres or in state structures such as legislatures and courts. In short, any framework that is constructed will have its beams made of legal timbers.

The structure

This study proceeds in three parts. The first part constructs the theoretical framework for the role of religion in public discourse. I call this framework 'justice as discourse'. Justice as discourse owes much to the work of John Rawls and in particular his *Political Liberalism*,

7 See Lægaard (2013).

8 I use the term the 'West' to denote Western Europe and its 'successor' civilisations in North America and Australasia, etc. While common enough, this is a problematic term as it implies a certain essential and consistent character across this range of countries that is difficult to establish. As such, I embrace the term only grudgingly. At the same time, if there is as I argue below something to the idea of 'Muslim contexts' and a sense of 'family resemblance', then the same might be said of the West.

a work that has become a 'classic' in positing how we may deal politically with diversity. In many respects, justice as discourse follows the general contours of a 'liberal' outlook for which Rawls is considered a major theorist. Liberal theory, however, has many more voices than just that of Rawls and, in the end, I do not adopt a fully Rawlsian perspective but rather consider responses and critiques of Rawls, notably, but not exclusively, those of Jurgen Habermas and Paul Weithman in the formulation of the position of justice as discourse. The essential departure of justice as discourse from Rawls (and also from Habermas) is that it removes the restrictions that each of these thinkers would apply – albeit in different ways – on reasoning coming from a religious basis in public debate and discussions. On the contrary, justice as discourse, while conscious of the challenges that arise with unshared reasons confronting each other in public deliberations, argues that it is only in embracing the right of all reasons to be expressed in their own terms, no matter how divisive they may be, that we can fully realise our plurality – a key goal of liberal theory, as will be elaborated later. The discussion of these issues takes place in Chapter 1. Chapter 2 continues to elaborate justice as discourse, though now not against the other theoretical alternatives but rather conceptually and, in particular, with respect to the concept of the 'secular', which is discussed at some length. As this chapter makes clear, justice as discourse does rest on having a secular state, but the secularity that it invokes must be understood in a way that is different from its most common association of being 'anti-religious'. Chapter 2 also describes the non-secular politics that justice as discourse envisages, and the space it allows for religiously-based reasons and discussions to impact decision-making and general political exchanges.

With the theoretical framework constructed, the second part of this work, Chapters 3 and 4, then turns to an elaboration and analysis of 'Muslim contexts'. This term is somewhat unusual and indeed the very idea of looking at Muslim contexts *per se* requires elaboration and some justification. I begin by explaining what I mean by Muslim contexts and why this category of analysis – which, after all, encompasses a vast diversity of peoples and societies – makes sense. Most of the effort of these chapters, and especially of Chapter 3, however, is devoted to an interpretive and analytical reading of the history of these contexts and, in particular, the religio-legal heritage which permeates Muslim contexts based on the work done by historians. Significantly, a distinction is made between the loci of religio-legal authority and political authority in Muslim history, and the interpretational diversity which has characterised Muslim history since its early days is emphasised. As these chapters illustrate, the consequences of these two observations, in short, is that attempts to speak in 'Islamic' terms are disingenuous at best and misleading at worst and, thus, any theorising for Muslim contexts must recognise as central to their heritage the *de facto* separation between political and religio-legal authority on the one hand and the plurality of religio-legal opinions on the other hand. In Chapter 4, the largely historical analysis is brought into a more contemporary focus as the discussion explores attitudes in Muslim communities today.

Finally, the third part of the study seeks to illustrate how and why the liberal framework of justice as discourse is useful in light of the heritage and contemporary reality of Muslim contexts. While the overall argument that justice as discourse, *qua* a variety of liberal theory, represents a desirable model for Muslim contexts is developed and suggested throughout Chapters 1 through 4, it is in Chapter 5 that I try to finalise the argument. I emphasise here how and why the theory of part one fits the contexts elaborated in part two. This uniting chapter thus both completes the analysis and concludes the argument. The ultimate argument presented in this work can be stated simply: a framework built from within liberal theory is the appropriate model for structuring the relationship between religion, the state and the public sphere for Muslim contexts because it both suits the division between religio-legal and political authority which has developed in these contexts as well as, and more importantly, the plurality of interpretations in these contexts. At the same time, a particular version of liberal theory is emphasised, which gives due space and scope to the expression of religious reasons in public discourse, which, it is argued, is important for societies with a Muslim heritage.

The approach

All of the above enables the construction of a model that, it is hoped, will be seen as appropriate to Muslim contexts in particular (though it may have relevance for other contexts as well). The framework creates a discursive space that will allow the expression of religion (whether Islam or any other) and respect its importance to individuals and to communities in a way which allows open discourse between those of faith (in all their varying interpretations), and those of no faith. I locate this discursive space in politics writ large, by which I mean national political debates and processes, whether in parliaments, the media, the academy or civil society where public issues are discussed and debated – in short, in the public sphere. In this way, the approach defended in this work neither succumbs to the marginalisation and exclusion of religious voices, nor, on the contrary, allows public life to be driven entirely by religion. At the heart of the enterprise is a similar process: a discursive political sphere open to foundational and normative input coming from various sources, including religion, while the state stands independent from any particular religious tradition. Religion is allowed to express itself politically in the public sphere, but is kept separate both formally and institutionally, from the state and the state's capacity to act coercively.

The contribution and the argument

Some may ask if the formula advanced in this study covers any new ground. Is it not the case, it might be claimed, that existing structures already allow this? If we look at the United Kingdom, for example, is it not the case that we have a secular state on the one hand as well as a public sphere that is open enough to a range of voices, including for those who wish to raise the voice(s) of religion? Indeed, might the same not be said for several societies in Western Europe, or for Canada, the US, and Australia? Is it then the case that what is merely being done is to ground this model in a Muslim framework, to make explicit that its threads are also found, or at least findable, in Muslim experiences?

In light of the challenges articulated above that face Muslim contexts, elaborating a theory that will fit these contexts and analysing the heritage of these contexts to make this argument is, however, to make a contribution. I refer in the title of this book and below to a (re)imagination and I use this phrase deliberately to make two points: first, that what this study is doing is not presenting these issues for the first time in Muslim history but rather considering them in a fresh way and in light of contemporary discourses. Second, that what is proposed here is a possibility for re-imagining Muslim contexts which has much to commend itself practically, even if it is not reflected in current reality. This contribution also points to the limits of this work. The framework and principles articulated here are developed in general terms, not in terms of a specific country, and their particular application will require a nuanced and sensitive adjustment to the specific circumstances of any one country or society. Just as liberal theory is a moving form, so also is the digestion of the heritage of Muslim contexts, and this points to the on-going evolution of political land legal norms in these contexts as well as outside of them. That, however, is as it should be.

Fundamentally, what is presented here is an argument that proposes a possibility. The argument rests on a few basic premises. First is that liberal theory, and indeed a liberal theory such as presented here that is inspired by – but not identical with – that of John Rawls, is not hostile or inimical to religion or religious voices. Rawls and liberal theory more generally are sometimes characterised as a poor fit for environments in which religion is important, as in Muslim contexts, because of the exclusion or limitations that they apply to religion. I see Rawls and theories that draw from him as being more open to religion than some of his critics may claim.[9] Secondly, that one of the main emphases in Rawls' theory and in liberal perspectives in affinity with his is an acceptance of diversity or plurality not just as a fact but also as valuable. Finally, the third premise is that Muslim contexts have been and continue to be sites of profound plurality in interpretations and practices. Thus, although there are basic sources of reference for Muslim contexts, there has not been one 'Islamic' understanding that has emerged. Rather, Muslim contexts are characterised by a multiplicity of responses to Islam.

9 As Tom Bailey and Valetina Gentile say: "Indeed in our view, his [Rawls's] exclusion of religion is extremely limited and qualified, such that he provides for extensive accommodation of religions in political life." See 'Introduction' in Bailey and Gentile (2015) at 7.

1 Developing the concept of 'justice as discourse'

This chapter seeks to develop a theoretical perspective that can be a useful normative framework for identifying the role of religion in public political discourse and its impact on the making of law in Muslim contexts. This perspective will be a type of 'liberal theory'. I put this term in quotations because, as will be seen later, this phrase represents not so much a position as a range of positions, albeit a range that might be viewed to be united by certain concerns and normative principles and, more loosely, by certain specific views. The first part of this chapter thus critically discusses a range of liberal outlooks to distil and construct from them a version (since it can only be *a* version) of liberal theory upon which I will rely for the remainder of this work: a set of principles which I call 'justice as discourse'.

In the next chapter, I draw out the implications of these principles for the relationship of religion to the state, to civil society, to and for general political discourses, and in relation to law and law-making. Justice as discourse also implies a version of a secular state to a certain extent and what this means will also be discussed in the next chapter. Together, these two chapters provide the theoretical framework for my project. In subsequent chapters, I explain and justify why I believe a framework based on liberal theory is an appropriate framework for political and legal realms Muslim contexts.

The challenge of diversity: liberal theory's normative commitment

John Rawls noted that a modern society:

> is characterized not simply by a pluralism of . . . comprehensive doctrines but by a pluralism of incompatible yet reasonable comprehensive doctrines. No one of these doctrines is affirmed by citizens generally. Nor should one expect that, in the foreseeable future, one of them, or some other reasonable doctrine, will ever been affirmed by all or nearly all citizens.[1]

By 'comprehensive doctrines', Rawls means doctrines that cover "all recognized values and virtues within one rather precisely articulated system".[2] In other words, it is Rawls' contention that we live in modern societies defined by a diversity of worldviews or basic outlooks.

1 Rawls (1993) at xvi.

2 Rawls (1993) at 152, n17. The definition of comprehensive doctrines in n17 goes on to say: "whereas a doctrine is only partially comprehensive when it comprises a number of non-political values and virtues and is rather loosely articulated."

One of the key sources of comprehensive doctrines is religion. Indeed, it is religious (as well as philosophical and moral) doctrines that Rawls has in mind when he talks about comprehensive doctrines. While for analytical purposes religious comprehensive doctrines may be treated in the same manner as other comprehensive doctrines, the discussion later will focus on religious convictions and differences for two reasons; firstly, because to talk about Muslim contexts is to talk of contexts defined in religious terms and because of a religious heritage. In the chapters that follow I discuss the problems of such definitions and why I believe, notwithstanding these problems, that one can reasonably talk about 'Muslim contexts'. The second reason for focusing upon religious comprehensive doctrines is because Muslim communities today face critical issues of the place in their societies of religious outlooks and religious law.

While seemingly stated as a matter of descriptive fact, Rawls' characterisation of a modern society also contains a challenge. The challenge is one of recognising pluralism, which Christopher Beem has called the central political problem for liberal-democratic regimes. Recognising pluralism means, as Beem notes, that society can no longer be organised around any one conception of the good.[3] The launching point for liberal theory is the fact of our diversity as to matters of values and principles, and a willingness to accept this diversity.

Thus, the central liberal question is, as Rawls has stated:

> How is it possible that there may exist over time a stable and just society of free and equal citizens profoundly divided by reasonable religious, philosophical and moral doctrines? This is a problem of political justice, not about the highest good.[4]

As a short hand, we might refer to this as the *challenge of diversity*.

The importance of the challenge of diversity arises especially because Rawls notes that the fact of reasonable pluralism is an assumed permanent fact in the political culture of a democratic society being an inevitable outcome of free human reason.[5] As we will see later, Rawls' theory is not about the elimination of this fact but can be seen as embracing it. As Tom Bailey and Valentina Gentile have said: "he [Rawls] is concerned simply with how shared principles for the narrow 'political' realm can be elaborated from among the diverse moral values of a society in mutually respectful ways."[6] In this respect, we can see Rawls as certainly wanting to address the means by which we deal with our reasonable pluralism but as not hostile to this pluralism – instead, looking for ways to respect it. This attitude is consistent with related strands in liberal theory that also emphasise a respect for diversity as part of a normative commitment.

The first step in addressing this challenge of diversity is recognising the fact of the irreducible pluralism of comprehensive doctrines. A democratic polity must find a way of choosing a course to follow from among the range of different principles, perspectives, values and opinions coming from comprehensive doctrines that may exist among its people. The question is how this might be done, given that the outlooks of citizens may be based on incompatible comprehensive doctrines. In other words, how can we seek to develop some consensus out of possible incompatibility? And, if we cannot develop consensus, then how should decisions be made and directions chosen?

3 See Beem (1998) at 16.
4 Rawls (1993) at xxv.
5 Rawls (1993) at 35–36.
6 'Introduction' in Bailey and Gentile (2015) at 10.

More directly for our purposes, we may ask how and to what extent different outlooks coming from different religious traditions should be allowed to influence decisions about public policy. This is an issue of particular relevance at this moment because, as José Casanova has demonstrated, the (re)emergence of religion into issues of public importance and of public debate, and of political choices, is a widespread phenomenon. It is Casanova's thesis, in fact, that religions are no longer accepting their confinement to the private realms of life and are seeking to play a more robust role in public affairs. Casanova calls this the deprivatisation of religion and finds examples of it in different locations around the world.[7]

Robert Audi and Nicholas Wolterstorff have also identified the question of religion's political role as both fundamental and intractable in contemporary societies. They say:

> The relation between religion and politics is a perennial concern of political philosophy, but it has never been more important than it is now. . . . There is a growing conviction that religious ideals should play a larger role in leading modern societies through the crises of our age, and there is – sometimes among the same people – a widespread fear that the religious zeal of some may abridge the freedom of others.[8]

Incompatibility is not, therefore, restricted to the incompatibility of different religious doctrines or convictions, though it does include different religious convictions as sources of comprehensive doctrines, but includes also the potential incompatibility of religion with secular space. Religion may, thus, be seen as a particular genre of comprehensive doctrine and addressed as such.

Liberal and theological responses

Audi and Wolterstorff have outlined two broad approaches to identifying the role of religious convictions in public debate. One view they call the 'liberal' view; the other they call the 'theologically-oriented' position. Each of these will be discussed in turn, beginning with the liberal view.

It is simple but not inaccurate to say that at the heart of the liberal view is the idea that religion and politics should be separated institutionally.[9] This is not to say that citizens of religious conviction must resist those convictions impacting their political views, but rather it asks for citizens' public political participation to be separated from their (by implication, private) religious convictions.

The mainstream liberal answer to the question of diversity, therefore, is essentially two-fold. On the one hand, doctrines that are unreasonable because they are socially deleterious must be excluded. More interesting, however, is the case of diversity of reasonable doctrines. Here, standard form liberalism takes the position that in the face of diversity it is not reasonable to expect others to support reasons (let alone positions) coming from one's own religious tradition and, therefore, these arguments need to be excluded from public political debate.[10] There are, as we shall see, different institutional models that seek to give expression to the liberal theory's normative commitment to pluralism. Not all of these are always

7 Casanova (1994). See generally and at 3 and 66.

8 Audi and Wolterstorff (1997) at ix.

9 This view of liberalism is expressed, for example, by Kause (2008) at 1–2.

10 Though there is variation on how broad these limits are. The debate may be just on constitutional essentials and matters of justice (themselves contested definitions) or more-general issues.

described as 'liberal', because they do not all, or always, share the view of mainstream liberalism that arguments from religious convictions should not be made in public political debate, or at least they moderate such requirements. In spite of these practical differences, (most) alternatives to the mainstream position, and certainly the alternatives that we will consider herein, still share liberal theory's normative commitment to pluralism and to allowing the full diversity of our thoughts and opinions to be expressed, though, because of the limits that are applied, not necessarily to shape *all* of our public decisions. It is in this important sense that 'liberal theory' can encompass a variety of different institutional positions, which, nonetheless may still be labelled as liberal because of their shared 'committed-to-pluralism' perspective. Audi and Wolterstorff's distinction between liberal and theological positions is thus a distinction not between the normative commitments which underlie these positions but rather with the institutional forms that these positions assert.

In its mainstream institutional position, the liberal outlook owes much to the particular challenge that religious diversity poses to a modern state. In his *On the Jewish Question*,[11] Karl Marx saw what he called 'political emancipation' as the solution to the tensions that arise when a confessional state has within it religious adherents of another faith tradition (in this case, German Jews within a Christian state). Political emancipation would emerge when ". . . the state as state emancipates itself from religion by emancipating itself from state religion – that is to say by the state not professing any religion, but on the contrary asserting itself as a state." In saying this, Marx further recognised, "It is possible for the state to have emancipated itself from religion even if the overwhelming majority [of the population] is still religious. And the overwhelming majority does not cease to be religious though being religious in private." In this situation, "Religion is not the spirit of the state. . . . Religion has become the spirit of *civil society*, of the sphere of egoism, of *bellum omnium contra omnes*. . . . Political emancipation is thus the reduction of man, on the one hand, to a member of civil society, to an egoistic, independent individual, and, on the other hand, to a citizen, to a juridical person." The goal of this process of political emancipation is limited to the political sphere, it "neither abolishes the real religiousness of man, nor strives to do so".

Writing in response to earlier theoretical works, Marx's work presages two important elements of contemporary liberal theory. First, it identifies the tension that can arise in a situation of religious diversity within a population, on the one hand, and religious commitments by the state *qua* state, on the other. It then distinguishes the solution for resolving these tensions from having to affect individual, private, religious belief, which can happily remain intact. In so doing, Marx's work also makes the point that the solution occurs at the 'political' level – i.e., the level of our public affairs – by separating out individual religious convictions from state religious convictions. As we will see next, contemporary liberal theory draws much from these Marxian lines in recognising tension that religious diversity can engender vis-à-vis the state and positing a 'political' level solution to this tension.

Rawls' political liberalism

Perhaps the most prominent contemporary work which discusses, and in fact establishes, the liberal position as a theory of public reasoning is John Rawls' *Political Liberalism*.

In answering the liberal question posed above, it is Rawls' contention that:

> we are to appeal only to presently accepted general beliefs and forms of reasoning found in common sense, and the methods and conclusions of science when these are

11 See text available at http://marx.eserver.org

> not controversial . . . we are not to appeal to comprehensive religious and philosophical doctrines – to what we as individuals see as the whole truth – or to elaborate economic theories of general equilibrium, say, if these are in dispute.[12]

This outlook has been called the 'standard approach'[13] of liberalism.

Rawls argues that we need to rely on a particular type of reasoning in public life that he calls 'public reason.' Since our comprehensive doctrines are various and varied, Rawls posits that they cannot be endorsed by citizens generally and as such cannot serve as the basis for our decisions. What we need instead is a way to determine another basis for society, and for this we require a type of reasoning that does not rely on our comprehensive doctrines. This is the core element and distinguishing feature of 'public reason'. Public reason would deal with matters that are public inasmuch as they would be matters that have broad effect. For Rawls, these matters include what he calls constitutional essentials and basic questions of justice, including the basic structure of a society's main political, economic and social institutions and how they fit together.[14] Public reason would address these public matters through principles and values that are independent from comprehensive doctrines, and that are principles and values that all citizens can endorse.

Rawls explains that public reason is public in three ways: (i) it is the reason of citizens as such, and thus the reason of the public; (ii) its subject is the public good; and (iii) its nature and content is public being given by society's conception of the public good and conducted on an open basis.[15] At the heart of the idea of public reason is the understanding of the democratic premise that all citizens have the right to participate equally in deciding the directions of the polity. As Rawls says, "public reason is the reason of equal citizens who as a collective body exercise final political and coercive power over one another in enacting laws and in amending their constitution".[16] Rawls' public reason applies to citizens when they are engaging in public fora and advocating politically or to those, such as candidates for public office, who engage in public political debate. The demands of public reason do not encompass considerations of political questions that we might undertake personally or those that are conducted by members of an association, or in universities or religious organisations (Rawls refers to 'churches' but this would, of course, apply to other religious organisations as well). In all of these elements of 'civil society', as it is known, it is perfectly acceptable to use non-public reasons and Rawls recognises and acknowledges that these non-public reasons will exist as the basis of actions. Public reason is thus a particular type of reason that Rawls would have us use when we engage in political discussions touching on subjects in the 'domain of the political' when we discuss these in public fora.

The boundaries of public reason are drawn in this manner because of the concern about how we make decisions in common and with decisions that affect us collectively. Where the line is drawn between actions that affect and do not affect others is, of course, highly contestable. In an apparent effort to allow as much of our different and very particular views of the good life to be realisable in how we live on a day-to-day basis, Rawls circumscribes the boundary around the 'political' at a minimal level. He does not mean to restrict us holding preferences or acting out of particular motivations when these do not have general impact and general effect on others. Thus, we can have our associations and our communities and

12 Rawls (1993) at 224. See also Rawls (1997).

13 This is a phrase used by Paul Weithman. See Weithman (2002); and also see Eberle (2015).

14 Rawls (1993) at 11.

15 Rawls (1993) at 213.

16 Rawls (1993) at 214. See also Rawls (1993) at 217.

act within them and out of motivations that, on Rawls' theory, we should not be allowed to bring into the political level. This, in turn, means that Rawls' theory seeks to allow, as much as it deems possible, for our plurality – especially in our diverse conceptions of the good life – to be given wide expression at many levels of our existence. It is thus a pluralism-enhancing theory inasmuch as we must constrain ourselves only when we seek to make claims that are applicable to all of us collectively. Thus, Rawls presents public reason as a mechanism for achieving what he calls a political conception of justice which rests on the above two noted vectors, namely: (i) it is political because it applies to political, social and economic institutions, and (ii) it is freestanding because it is not presented or derived from a comprehensive doctrine. To these, Rawls adds a third vector, which is that (iii) the content of the political conception is expressed in terms of certain fundamental ideas seen as implicit in the public political culture of a democratic society.

In fairness to Rawls' argument, and for analytical purposes, it is important to note here that Rawls is addressing himself to a modern constitutional democratic society and a modern democratic state, indeed some may say particularly to the United States. The question of the generalisability of Rawls' framework – and of the liberal position more generally – to other contexts that may not reflect the standards of a modern constitutional democracy is not something that he explicitly addresses.

Rawls' framework is premised on ascribing to people two moral powers: first, a capacity for a sense of justice, and, second, a capacity for a conception of the good. These two moral capacities make it important to recognise and respect each other's individual sovereignty and rights of participation in political deliberation – precisely because we all have the capacity for a sense of justice and a conception of the good. That is to say that Rawls' ascription provides a philosophical grounding and explanation for the equal sovereignty through equal political participation that democracy provides for all of its citizens. This connects to the concern about comprehensive doctrines in that, as we shall see more fully below, because we all have these moral powers, Rawls believes that we must all be allowed to exercise them by being able to understand public political speech, and we can only do this if it is not premised on comprehensive doctrines that we do not share or fully understand. Rawls' claim here is ontological: it is about human nature and a moral capacity inherent in humans as such. This would apply across human societies and cultures and is, therefore, universal even if this capacity is not recognised or indeed nurtured by the political order.

Another important element of Rawls' argument concerns the realms in which decisions must be made. Rawls distinguishes a well-ordered democratic society from both an association and a community. He posits that democratic societies are closed entities that one enters by birth and leaves by death. Democratic societies are not like associations, Rawls asserts, because they are not directed to any final ends or aims. At the same time, a democratic society is also distinct from a community in the Rawlsian sense of the term, in that unlike a community it has no shared comprehensive doctrine.[17] So, democratic society is a significant, but not encompassing, part of our social life and our life-in-common with others. And Rawls wants to create rules for decision-making that will apply in this sphere but not necessarily in associations or communities, notwithstanding that these are also important parts of life. This is a sphere where citizens do not affirm any one reasonable political, religious, philosophical or moral doctrine. The conception of justice, therefore, must be restricted to what is outside of the zones of comprehensive doctrine. Rawls calls this the

17 On the distinction Rawls draws between an association and a community, see Rawls (1993) at 40 n43.

'domain of the political'. Through public reason, we would develop values for the domain of the political – that is to say for the constitutional essentials and questions of basic justice, including questions such as 'Who has the right to vote?' and 'Which religions should be tolerated by the state?'

At the heart of Rawls' theory is this: since we take for granted that in a democratic society people can hold a variety of reasonable comprehensive doctrines which would inform their political views and their conceptions of justice and the good, and since we further acknowledge that these comprehensive doctrines, though reasonable, may be incompatible, therefore we must not use reasons stemming from any of these doctrines (which we can now see as having a 'personal' or 'private' character) to take political decisions, because these reasons are not shared by all citizens. It would be unfair to rely on reasons in public fora to which all citizens did not have access, precisely because they did not share the comprehensive doctrine(s) that are the basis of these reasons. Public reason, therefore, requires us to limit ourselves, when we engage in political discussion in public, to using only those reasons to which all may have access; these may not be our only reasons for our political convictions, indeed, there seems to be a *prima facie* case for saying that they will not be, but they are the only ones we should discuss publicly. Political liberalism, which has at its heart the idea of public reason, declares that political power, with its potential to coerce us as individuals, is only justifiably exercised when it is exercised according to a system which "all citizens may reasonably be expected to endorse in light of principles and ideals acceptable to them as reasonable and rational".[18] This, Rawls declares, is the *liberal* principle of legitimacy.

Clearly, the Rawlsian position and its limitations imposed by public reason entails a restriction on the use of religious reasons in public discussions. Rawls acknowledges this. Knowing that they hold a variety of reasonable but different (to the point of possible incompatibility) doctrines, citizens should be willing to explain the basis of their actions or convictions in the domain of the political to each other in a language that others might understand and endorse. This, for Rawls, is the duty of civility.[19] The duty is really nothing more than the duty to articulate public reasons for our political views, as distinct from the many non-public reasons that may otherwise govern our various civil society communities, organisations and associations. The duty of civility is connected to the basis of political legitimacy that requires, in Rawls' formulation, that on matters of constitutional essentials, public policies are justifiable to all citizens.

This further means that in a democratic system, we must accept that our public political life can never be guided by the 'whole truth' as we see it, as these larger conceptions would come from our various comprehensive doctrines. So, Rawls' theory is *not* about how we might choose among, and deliberate about, what we see as ultimate ends – or the 'whole truth' – but only about how we might reasonably and fairly choose workable principles to govern our political interactions and the essentials of our political organisation. It is, to use Rawls' term, therefore only about 'political justice'.

Responses to and critiques of Rawls

Paul J. Weithman[20] elaborates in sharper detail the implications of Rawls' framework specifically for the role of religion in the public sphere. Philosophical liberals who

18 Rawls (1993) at 217.
19 Rawls (1993) at 218.
20 Weithman (1997) and see also Weithman (2002).

advocate the standard (Rawlsian) view see religion as a threat to political stability, having the capacity for both political and social disruption, as well as for actual political violence. Given these concerns, advocates of the standard approach idealise a well-ordered society of civility and mutual respect. To achieve this end, they seek to isolate a set of values and principles that reasonable citizens could willingly and publicly endorse. Religious values and principles (*qua* comprehensive doctrines) are not, as such, members of that set of values, because we recognise that these are not shared by everyone in our pluralistic political orders.[21] Weithman calls this framework the 'liberalism of reasoned respect', which demands that citizens cooperate on the basis of reasons they can publicly endorse to one another – that is to say, that are not dependent upon a comprehensive doctrine. It demands that public reason is conducted on this basis so that each citizen can understand and, therefore, respect the arguments made by others as well as the conclusions, in the form of policy and principle that result from deliberations conducted in this way. Liberalism of reasoned respect posits that respect for each other requires social cooperation based on terms that citizens can accept based on their *common* reason.[22] To argue from any position or perspective that a fellow citizen cannot reasonably be expected to support is not to respect other citizens, and there is a concern that a lack of respect may result in political and civil strife and imperil a well-ordered society. Given the fact of plurality, it is not reasonable to expect others to support reasons (let alone positions) coming from one's own religious tradition and, therefore, these arguments should not be made in public political debate. This, as Weithman says, is liberalism's conclusion. Nicholas Wolterstorff describes liberalism as not being one position but rather a family of positions, but agrees with Weithman that all of the positions within the family propose a restraint on the use of religious reasons in deciding and deliberating about political issues in public.[23] What distinguishes the individual positions in the family from one another is the severity and scope of the restraint that they impose. In this sense, Rawls' concern to impose the restraint only for 'constitutional essentials' and matters of basic justice, is a more moderate version of the restraint compared to other possibilities.[24] According to Weithman, the form of liberalism/liberalism as reasoned respect described above has a basis in the philosophies of Immanuel Kant and Jean-Jacques Rousseau, with the idea that citizens should treat each other as free and equal co-holders of power.[25]

The Rawlsian liberal position thus described has, of course, been subjected to critiques, especially in how it treats those who have religious convictions. Broadly speaking, these evaluations fault the liberal position as being politically undesirable, pragmatically unworkable or impractical, and finally as imposing a differential burden upon those who have religious views compared to those who do not.

21 Weithman (1997) at 4.

22 Weithman (1997) at 6.

23 Audi and Wolterstorff (1997) at 75.

24 Among the varieties of restraint that Wolterstorff mentions are positions that would apply the restraint to private as well as political decision-making, a ban on the use of religions reasoning at all, and a position that allows religious reasons only so long as there are other non-religious reasons in support of the same position.

25 Weithman (1997) at 11.

On undesirability, the liberal position is found to be too restrictive and too restraining on those who have deep commitments to comprehensive doctrines, of which religious convictions are the prime example. Jean Bethke Elshtain has expressed this critique:

> One enters political life as a citizen. But if one also has religious convictions, these convictions naturally will inform one's judgement as a citizen. My religious views help to determine who I am, how I think, and what I care about. This is as it should be . . . it makes no sense to ask people to bracket what they care most deeply about when they debate issues that are properly political.[26]

Jeremy Waldron similarly argues that, with proper recognition, religious convictions should not be restricted from public life and discourse:

> So long as there is due recognition of the multi-faith and secular aspects of our society and due recognition of the constitutional structure that responds to that, *there is no particular reason for church people to refrain from participation in public life on the basis of their values*, provided this is accompanied by a willingness "to grant all citizens of every worldview and moral conviction the legitimacy of their own faith-based participation in American public life."[27]

Waldron echoes Christopher Eberle's expression of such an inclusivist position, that a "citizen is morally permitted to support (or oppose) a coercive law even if she enjoys [only] a religious rationale for that law".[28] Especially in pluralistic societies, all religious views and values ought to be permitted for participation in public life.

On this line of argument, it is not right that we should force people to leave their deeply held convictions, religious or otherwise, aside when it comes to political matters. And yet this 'idling' of convictions is exactly what the liberal position requires.[29] In fact, liberalism forces us to, as it were, 'abstract' ourselves as political actors.[30]

Our convictions define what we care about and think – and what we think and care about is relevant to our political deliberations and choices. As such, a framework that asks us to bracket these cares when we debate and discuss the terms of how we live together would lead us to an impoverished politics and, thereby, a less-informed range of policy options.

Since religious convictions are the example *par excellence* of comprehensive doctrines, the critiques from undesirability can lead easily into a critique of unfairness because it imposes a greater burden on those who hold convictions stemming from comprehensive doctrines than on those who do not. Those who have religious convictions would be required to fashion an independent 'artificial' self, cut off from their real cares and concerns, in order to interact in the public area. Those who do not have religious convictions (or convictions coming from another form of comprehensive doctrine), however, will not have to create a sort of public alter ego separated from their real beliefs and selves. This results in a 'dignity harm' befalling those of religious conviction, as they may feel silenced because they are only

26 Elshtain (2003) at 79.
27 Waldron (2012) at 4 (emphasis added).
28 Eberle (2002) at 10. See also March (2013) at 523–524, for a thorough overview of the inclusivist position.
29 Audi and Nicholas Wolterstorff (1997) at 73.
30 See Sandel (1984).

able to present truncated forms of themselves in the public arena.[31] Forcing this truncation has been described as rights violating[32] since, as Weithman says:

> It belongs to the religious convictions of a good many religious people in our society that *they ought to base* their decisions concerning fundamental issues of justice on their religious convictions. They do not view it as an option whether or not to do it.[33]

As Jurgen Habermas says reinforcing the point: "A devout person pursues [his or] her daily rounds by ***drawing*** on belief. Put differently, true belief is not only a doctrine . . . but a source of energy . . . and thus nurtures his or her entire life."[34] The truncation that is demanded of those with religious convictions does not affect those without religious beliefs (or convictions derived from another type of comprehensive doctrine) because there is nothing to truncate; there is no part of them that is cut off. However, it is doubtful that such a category of people exists.

Another facet of this same line of critique is that the above-described liberal position goes too far to achieve its ends: that its remedy is too draconian for the desired outcomes. If the liberal concern is that an argument will not be assented to by everyone because of the plurality that is manifest in society, or to put it more strongly that some might be coerced or duped into accepting an argument that they do not understand because of the diversity of comprehensive doctrines, then would it not be enough to accept difference without restricting its expression? Sanford Levinson casts this critique in terms that specifically address arguments coming from a religious basis when he says:

> why doesn't liberal democracy give everyone an equal right, without engaging in any version of epistemic abstinence, to make his or her arguments, subject, obviously, to the prerogative of listeners to reject the arguments should they be unpersuasive? . . . [I]t seems enough for those of us who are secular to disagree vigorously with persons presenting theologically-oriented views of politics. To suggest as well that they are estopped from presenting such arguments seems gratuitously censorial rather than wise.[35]

The critique presented here is that the need for reasonable debate and deliberation of public political matters should not necessitate the eradication of religious speech (*qua* speech from a comprehensive doctrine) in public life, as this too hastily precludes the possibility of an intelligible public discourse *including* religious speech. In fact, what happens is that this possibility is adjudged untenable before it is tried. The restriction is too strong in two senses: first, because it imposes, in advance, a limitation on those of religious conviction that may be more than what is required for intelligible public political debate; and second, because it may thereby overly constrain and censor our public political life

31 See the discussion of 'dignity harm' in Perry (1991) and in Sanford Levinson's review of this work in Levinson (1992) at 2077.
32 See Audi and Wolterstorff (1997) at 116.
33 Weithman (2002) at 157 (emphasis in original).
34 Habermas (2006a) at 8 (emphasis in original).
35 Levinson (1992) at 2077.

generally – this type of censorship being anathema whose imposition should be permitted only when strictly necessary.[36]

The classical liberal response to this three-fold critique is itself three-fold. To the claim that public political debate is being undesirably constrained, the liberal retort is that it is not reasonable to expect that arguments coming from religion, or more likely from any one any particular religious perspective, will be accepted by others not sharing this perspective, or that they will be comprehensible in a way that would allow for meaningful public political debate and engagement with the issues. To the charge that religious reasons are being unfairly singled out for particular restriction and, thus, that a special burden is being placed on those of religious conviction, Rawls would also add another defence, namely that public reasons are not equivalent to secular reasons. Reasons from non-religious comprehensive doctrines, e.g., philosophical comprehensive doctrines, could be without any religious basis but they would not be public reasons, precisely because they rest on comprehensive doctrines.[37] So, suggesting that the classical liberal position accepts all secular reasons and only excludes religious reasons would be an unfair charge based on an erroneous understanding of the claim. Indeed, liberalism's 'censorship' that Levinson talks about is broader, but it must be made clear that it is not based on a purging of the religious in favour of the secular in a simplistic way. The liberal position may purge (or censor) but it does this to reasons derived from religious and secular comprehensive doctrines alike. Finally, to the argument that it is impossible or at least impractical for those holding religious views to leave these aside when they come to public political debate, the response is that this is necessary under ideal conditions to make these reasons accessible to all.

These critiques highlight potential problems in the balance that Rawls' theory sought to achieve between our diversity on the one hand, and a generally comprehensible public political debate on the other. They suggest, in short, that when it comes to religious convictions a more fine-tuned balancing will be required – and one more accommodating of religion's public role.

The previous arguments do not, however, exhaust the range of concerns about Rawls' theory. Another major concern with the Rawlsian liberal position is that the social threat that this position sees from religious speech being allowed into the public square is exaggerated, or at least is not worth defending with the types of restrictions that the liberal position requires.

We can recall that a chief concern of the liberal position is social stability in the face of the divisive potential of diversity. Focussing on religious language, this critique argues that it is wrong to see religious language as (any) more threatening to the social order than language coming from other sources about which people may disagree. Wolterstorff points out that there has been, and continues to be, political passion expressed in arguments over the welfare state. He might also have added that such passions have certainly been divisive. Moreover, in terms of actual political violence, the twentieth century has seen great brutality stemming from the non-religious doctrines of nationalism, communism and fascism, so it can hardly be said that religious doctrines represent a greater threat or indeed that they are especially marked out as zones of political violence. On the other hand, abolitionists in the US as well as the US civil rights movement, both of which had strong faith-based components and

36 As Lawrence Solum has stated: "There is wide agreement that government should not censor public debate about politics, at least not without very good reasons." Solum (1993) at 729.

37 Rawls (1997) at 775.

faith-based leaders have contributed to creating the human rights focus and rights-based anchors of modern liberalism, as have other faith-based movements resisting communism (e.g., Solidarity in Poland) and apartheid in South Africa. Of course, there has also been political violence which has come with religious motivations. We can recall with a shudder the so-called 'ethnic cleansing' that took place in the former Yugoslavia, where mainly Catholic Christian Croats, mainly Orthodox Christian Serbs and mainly Muslim Bosnians turned on each other, as well as the attacks that have been and are perpetrated by the entity or entities that operate under the banner of al-Qaeda or Daesh/Islamic State. This, however, only shows that political violence can emerge from a variety of sources, religious and non-religious. This suggests that there is no particular risk from religiously inspired political violence as opposed to non-religiously inspired political violence. And this, therefore, further suggests that there is no special or particular threat that religion poses to peaceful political stability.

Of course, defenders of the liberal position may point out that their concern is not with religion to the exclusion of other comprehensive doctrines. If, for example, communism is an example of a philosophical comprehensive doctrine, then citing the risks it poses in terms of political violence, or pointing out that it can engender the same types of risk as religious-based doctrines, only strengthens the argument that *all* of these types of comprehensive doctrines should be kept away from public political debate – precisely what the Rawlsian liberal model proposes. Such a defence is vulnerable to the same logic behind the 'undesirability' critique: namely that it would leave us with an over-sterilised politics that, in turn, would limit the range of policy choices that are generated.

A final line of critique attacks the liberal position from the other end. The restraint imposed on reasons from comprehensive doctrines – and the very idea of public reason – posits that by excluding comprehensive doctrines, we might develop a reasoning that is accessible to all citizens and thereby that forms a reasonable, and indeed the only fair, basis for public political debate. Through this one will achieve free and willing assent to a political consensus – what Rawls called an 'overlapping consensus' – and, therefore, to a stable society.[38] By an overlapping consensus, Rawls means a consensus that is at the same time affirmed by holders of different, opposing religious, philosophical and moral doctrines,[39] but that is not formulated in terms of general, comprehensive religious, philosophical or moral doctrines but rather in terms of certain fundamental intuitive ideas viewed as latent in the public political culture of democratic society.[40] Importantly, Rawls does not see an overlapping consensus as simply a ***modus vivendi***. He argues that it is a moral conception even though those who produce it may do so from different (philosophical, moral and religious) grounds.[41] However, in recognising the fact of plurality, we have recognised that we have fundamentally different understandings of the 'whole truth' and visions of the good life. How then can we be so confident that we can develop out of this diversity common accessible reasons? As Weithman points out, the claim that we *can* have common accessible reasons stems from a conviction that we share common rational capacity, and the claim that we *must* have common accessible reasons stems from the conviction that it is this common capacity that gives us our dignity. In short it "answers our desire for community within pluralism" inasmuch as it supposes that we can be held together by mutual respect for one

38 See Rawls (1987) at 4–5, and the discussion of what an overlapping consensus consists of in Rawls (1997).
39 Rawls (1987) at 1.
40 Rawls (1987) at 6.
41 Rawls (1987) at 11.

another's reasons.[42] Laudable and comforting as this desire may be, it rests on a contradiction in proposing that out of (a potentially incompatible) plurality of doctrines, we can find a commonly accessible reasoning. Weithman argues that accessibility is hardly self-explanatory and, indeed, that accessible reasons cannot plausibly be set out, such that:

> The pluralism to which I have pointed throughout the book entails that there are unlikely to be shared grounds for the *faith in liberal democracy* and common humanity that Rawls hopes to vindicate. . . . In a pluralistic society, citizens will also have very different reasons for believing that human beings have a moral nature. Yet they may have little to do with the possibility of an overlapping consensus or citizens' responsiveness to public or accessible reasons.[43]

If indeed we cannot hope to find shared grounds out of, or precisely because of, the very plurality that liberals acknowledge, then it is doubtful that we can find a fair (might we even say workable?) method of deliberation on public political issues. Absolute certainty, however, eludes us here, as we cannot be sure whether we will be able to achieve accessible reasons or not. Rawls conceded: "Whether justice as fairness (or some similar view) can gain the support of an overlapping consensus so defined is a speculative question."[44] It is thus worth distinguishing between the reasons that may be brought to public reasoning, which Rawls and classical liberal theory restrict, and the deeper moral values that engender commitment to the political order. The latter may indeed arise from comprehensive doctrines, including religious influences. A believer may thus have deep reasons for her political values but can only appeal to the 'thin', non-religiously grounded reasons in public discussion. If we are not certain about the possibility of realising actual reasons out of this process, we are also not sure that we cannot and, thus, we have to guard against Weithman's scepticism as well. Doubt, however, does no favours to principles that advocate social and political arrangements.

The critiques of Rawls' theory suggest that noble though its goals are, the theory has not fully realised it aims with respect, in particular, to religious convictions. Out of a desire for a neutral and shared public reason, the Rawlsian answer has so curtailed the capacity of religious convictions to speak that those who hold them may not find a respectable place in public political debate from which they feel they actually can participate. Without this being attained Rawlsian liberalism becomes exclusionary and limiting, rather than pluralism enhancing. On the other hand, the hope that we might find community in pluralism seems to be too uncertain a prospect; it remains a hope but its practical achievability admits of no guarantees. Other options, however, have been presented that either rest on different principles to Rawls or that seek to reconstitute 'liberal theory' to overcome the critiques of Rawls.

Alternatives to Rawls' theory

Theologically-oriented positions

Just as there are varieties of the liberal position, so that Wolterstorff could describe it as not so much one position but as a 'family of positions', there is also a family of positions

42 Weithman (2002) at 6–7.
43 Weithman (2002) at 216–217 (emphasis added).
44 Rawls (1997) at 15.

in the alternative. As we noted above, Audi and Wolterstorff refer to the alternative as the 'theologically oriented' position, or we might now say, family of positions. Using the term 'theological' may, however, be less than ideal, as it suggests that the alternatives are connected to the complexities of theology (as this exists within many religious traditions). That is not really the case. The alternatives are not about a particular theological position nor do they argue from any particular theological principles or sources. Instead, we might see the alternative to the liberal position as 'religiously-oriented' or even more modestly as a 'more religiously oriented' position than the classical or standard liberal position(s).

In these "theological alternatives", the 'problem' we are trying to solve remains the same. The issue is the challenge of diversity within a democratic framework and how we can go about making decisions about political principles and practices confronted with a plurality of views about fundamentals. In this, the theological position shares the essential liberal concern to respect and embrace our diversity. It is important to keep in mind that we are addressing the same challenge and *not* that the religiously oriented position is seeking to advance the concerns of any particular religious tradition or theological stand to change our political structure. There may be more concern with how those of religious conviction can participate in politics, and for the appropriate role that religious believers can play, but this is a political concern, not a theological concern *per se*. It remains a question of what is politically fair. Indeed, we may frame our question in these terms. Rawls asked: "How is it possible that there may exist over time a stable and just society of free and equal citizens profoundly divided by reasonable religious, philosophical and moral doctrines?", to which we may add, "And what is the appropriate place for religious convictions as part of answering this first question?" This position is concerned to relax or to even remove the restrictions that the Rawlsian liberal position places on the use of religious argument in public political debate and deliberation. There does not, however, seem to be one *locus classicus* of the alternative 'religiously oriented' position like Rawls' *Political Liberalism* is for the liberal position. This may be because the religiously-oriented position has developed as a response to the liberal position, and perhaps especially to Rawls' articulation of it. We will, therefore, proceed by examining different variations of the 'theological' (or, perhaps better, religiously-oriented) position.

Before examining some these alternative models, however, we must first explore one idea that may divide the classical liberal and alternative positions. This has to do with how democracy is conceived. The liberal model laid great emphasis on democracy being a relationship of free equals and was concerned, as we saw earlier, that a theory of political deliberation maintained our mutual equality and freedom vis-à-vis each other. Thus, anything that compromised our capacities to interact with each other in freedom (for example, any coercion), or equitably (for example, any argument that we could not understand as well as others) was *prima facie* anathema to the liberal position. Rather, liberal theory is often about justifying coercion but on the basis of a respect of the free and equal nature of others. Democracy so conceived rests on these free and equal interactions and through them fulfils its promise of decisions being made by and for the people. Ultimately then, democracy is about how we co-operate in reaching political decisions.

However, there is a different view of democracy as aggregative that sees democracy as a competition of interests in which different ideas are floated by individuals or groups seeking to achieve interests they believe in or desire. It is these beliefs and desires that are pursued as the ends, not a situation of freedom or equality. On this view, I would be concerned about whether you accepted my point of view morally, but, ultimately, what matters is that we freely agree on outcomes, not reasons. Of course, this does not licence actual coercion, such as physical coercion, or an overt violation of equality, like giving some citizens less of a vote than others, but it does treat individuals as having to, and by implication being able to, fend for themselves in a competition of interests. So, ideas and principles will be articulated in a 'self-interested' way inasmuch as their advocates will want these ideas to be realised and these principles to be accepted. This may be for reasons that are personal and parochial or, more generously, because the advocates of the ideas will genuinely think these ideas would be best for society. In any case, however, the ideas would be put out into public political debate and in that forum would have to compete with all the other ideas. As people will be able to choose or reject the ideas, by supporting or rejecting their advocates for office, say, or supporting or rejecting a proposition in a referendum, only those ideas and principles that the majority of the people favour will receive democratic sanction. To win support, advocates of ideas and principles will of course have to be pragmatic and present their views in ways that are attractive to at least a plurality of the voters.[45] Thus, the principle of political legitimacy is the acceptance of an idea or principle by a majority of citizens through a fair electoral process, rather than political legitimacy resting on the idea of the co-sovereignty of free equals. The liberal position was concerned with the potential instability that an unregulated competition might engender and the risk of social tension that might result, and sought to mitigate these risks through a process that removed the greatest source of these tensions from public political debate, particularly at the level of 'constitutional essentials' which it would want to be defined by 'overlapping consensus'. The competition framework more readily embraces this potential tension and, therefore, responds to one of the critiques we saw earlier, namely a (too strong) concern with stability. It also embraces possibilities of argument that the liberal model's basic principles would not admit, because of their concern with political justice.

Wolterstorff's consocial position

Not every alternative to the liberal position is based on a competition-of-interests model of democracy. Wolterstorff, for example, presents what he calls the 'consocial' position that shares the concern with political justice. It departs from the Rawlsian liberal position on two points, however. First, it gives up the idea of finding an independent source for our political language and removes, entirely, the restraint on the use of religious language in political deliberation. Second, it interprets the requirement of the coercive state being neutral towards particular religious views to mean not a separation of state and religion (à la the classical liberal position), but rather that the state must be impartial to any particular religious tradition – that the state must treat them all equally:

> What unites these two [above described] themes is that, at both points, the person embracing the consocial position wishes to grant citizens, no matter what their religion or irreligion, as much liberty as possible to live their lives as they see fit.[46]

Wolterstorff contends that a limitation on the expression of religious convictions and reasons in the 'public square' effectively limits freedom of religion and, therefore, the liberty of the religious. This allies itself with the critique we saw earlier about the supposed neutrality of the liberal position:

> the liberal assumes that requiring religious people to debate and act politically for reasons other than religious reasons is not in violation of their *religious* convictions. He assumes, in other words, that although religious people may not be in the *habit* of

45 Though, of course, this may not necessarily be to a plurality of the eligible electorate, depending on voter turnout.

46 Audi and Wolterstorff (1997) at 115.

> dividing their lives into a religious component and a non-religious component, and though some might not be *happy* doing so, nonetheless, their doing so would in no case be a violation of their religion. But he is wrong about this.[47]

Wolterstorff's consocial position, while asserting a similar aim to the liberal position, namely political justice (rather than a debate over the 'whole truth'), finds the restraint that the liberal position imposes on the use of religious language in the public square (which, of course, the liberal position extends to language coming from other comprehensive doctrines, as well) to be rights *violating* instead of rights affirming. His call is then for a dramatic departure from the Rawlsian liberal position, viz. lifting all constraints off the use of religious language in the public square.

This alternative is, therefore, the mirror image of Rawls: we neither look for an overlapping consensus nor do we, to facilitate such a consensus, impose any limits on religious reasoning expressing itself in public. Yet, the consocial alternative shares the seminal liberal goal – namely *political* justice. What it does not answer, however, is whether its unrestrained voices can resolve themselves into any sort of socio-political harmony, or whether the failure to do this is a matter of concern. Rawls worried about our capacity to develop political justice if we cannot understand each other. The legitimacy, or lack thereof, of this concern must be addressed.

Habermas' refinement

Jurgen Habermas also presents an alternative to the Rawlsian liberal position, though one that might still be considered to hew closer to the Rawlsian rubric because it maintains a modified sort of constraint on the use of religious language in the public square.[48] Habermas points out that the Rawlsian idea of an ethic of citizenship rests on an epistemic basis in which:

> for all their on-going dissent on questions of world-views and religious doctrines [read: 'comprehensive doctrines' in Rawls' language], citizens are meant to respect one another as free and equal members of their political community. . . . And on that basis of mutual respect when it comes to contentious political issues citizens owe one another good reasons for their political statements.[49]

This is the context in which Habermas notes that Rawls speaks of the duty of civility and the 'public use of reason' that were outlined above. The epistemic implication of this position is that there can be good reasons that are shared and accessible. However, as we saw earlier, this claim is not uncontroversial. Weithman, for one, questioned a common base of human reason that would lead to the potential for the development of accessible public reasons. Laying this objection to the side for a moment, Habermas draws out a further implication of the Rawlsian framework, namely that it implies a secular state. He says: "The assumption of a common human reason is the epistemic base for the justification of a secular state which no longer depends on religious legitimation,"[50] since, "In a secular state only those political

47 Audi and Wolterstorff (1997) at 116 (emphasis in original).
48 Habermas (2006a).
49 Habermas (2006a) at 7.
50 Habermas (2006a) at 5.

decisions are taken to be legitimate as can be justified in light of *generally accessible reasons*, vis-à-vis religious and nonreligious citizens and citizens of different religious confessions alike."[51] As was seen, Rawls himself would argue that his objection was not to religious reasons *per se* and that he did not accept all secular reasons, since any secular reasons from comprehensive doctrines would also be restrained on Rawls' theory. What Habermas appears to be getting at, however, is that because for Rawls public political reasons should not include reasons derived from religion there would necessarily be a non-religious, and in this sense secular, basis for the constitutional fundamentals of the state.

However, in his essay subsequent to *Political Liberalism*, Rawls seems to relax his position by saying:

> reasonable comprehensive doctrines, religious or non-religious, may be introduced in public political discussion at any time, provided that in due course proper political reasons – and not reasons given solely by comprehensive doctrines – are presented that are sufficient to support whatever the comprehensive doctrines are said to support.[52]

This furnishes the so-called 'proviso' in Rawls' theory for the use of non-public, including religious, reasons. Let us note that although Rawls' position here seems broader than the restriction he articulated in *Political Liberalism*, because it allows the expression of reasons that may have been under a blanket ban, it is not allowing these reasons to stand alone and, indeed, still appears to find these reasons unacceptable, or inadmissible, without their being supported by 'proper political reasons' which must be reasons of a qualitatively different order because they must be 'reasons [not] given solely by comprehensive doctrines', including, of course, religious doctrines.

It is from here that Habermas proceeds to put some clear distance between his position that of Rawls, even Rawls with the proviso. Habermas says:

> We cannot derive from the secular character of the state an obligation for all citizens to supplement their public religious contributions by equivalents in generally accessible language. The liberal state must not transform the requisite institutional separation of religion and politics into an undue mental and psychological burden for all those of its citizens who follow a faith . . . it must not expect them to split their identity in public and private components as soon as they participate in public debates.[53]

Rawls' theory, however, even with the proviso, would require a certain split inasmuch as citizens would have to come up with other 'properly political' reasons for the position they take in public discussions. Habermas' wider scope for the use of reasons coming from religious convictions does not, however, compromise the institutional separation of religion and the state – i.e., the state as secular – for which Rawls' theory provides the epistemic basis. For Habermas, only secular reasons will count "beyond the institutional threshold that divides the informal public sphere from parliaments, courts, ministries and administrations." Yet, he argues that "This awareness need not deter religious citizens from publicly expressing and

51 Habermas (2006a) at 7 (emphasis added).
52 Rawls (1997) at 783–784.
53 Habermas (2006a) at 10.

justifying their convictions by resorting to religious language."[54] To this, Habermas adds no proviso for additional justification by other reasons.

What motivates Habermas is a desire to open up political discussion in this informal sphere. This is not entirely inconsistent with Rawls, because Rawls's exclusions would not apply to the informal sphere.[55] Yet, one can still discern in Rawls a worry about instability and social tension that could result from plurality, while Habermas sees a potential benefit in diversity. The liberal state, Habermas argues:

> has an interest of its own in unleashing religious voices in the public political sphere, for it cannot know if whether secular society would not otherwise cut itself off from key resources for the creating of meaning and identity. Nor is there a good normative reason for an overhasty reduction of any polyphonous complexity.[56]

Importantly, then, Habermas does not add a proviso like Rawls' requiring other non-religious (and non-comprehensive doctrine-based) justifying reasons in public political debate. Yet Habermas does share the concern that the institutional state should not be given over to any one religious view. Thus, Habermas imposes a requirement of 'translation' such that: "The truth content of religious contributions can enter into the institutionalised practice of deliberation and decision-making only if the necessary translation already occurs in the pre-parliamentary domain, i.e., in the political public sphere itself."[57] This burden, however, does not just fall on those who would use religious reasons. Habermas insists that non-religious citizens must likewise "open their minds to the possible truth content of those [religious] presentations and even enter into dialogues from which religious reasons then might well emerge in the transformed guise of generally accessible arguments."[58] This distinguishes Habermas' view from that of Wolterstorff. Wolterstorff's position drops the Habermasian translation requirement, a fact that Habermas himself points out.[59]

The translation requirement seeks to prevent the possibility that principles will be decided on the basis of the religious convictions of the ruling majority in any state, and the coercive power of the state then being made the agent of this majority. Translation then would ensure a "fair deliberation" preceding a vote on any particular issue, the fairness resting on the fact that, through translation, any religious reasons being presented in the institutional setting, i.e., the parliament or legislature, will be available to those who do not share the religious convictions the underlie them.

Habermas conceives of the translation requirement involving effort being made by both those of religious conviction as well as those without:

> Religious citizens had to learn to adopt epistemic attitudes toward their secular environment, attitudes that secular citizens enjoy anyway, since they are not exposed to similar cognitive dissonances in the first place. However, secular citizens are not spared

54 Habermas (2006a) at 10 (emphasis added).
55 Rawls (1997) at 443–444, n(13). For Rawls, the informal public sphere would include newspapers and other media as well as, presumably, other forms of dialogue with the background culture of a society.
56 Habermas (2006a) at 11.
57 Habermas (2006a) at 11–12.
58 Habermas (2006a) at 12.
59 Habermas (2006a) at 12.

> a cognitive burden, because *secularist* consciousness does not suffice for the required co-operation with fellow citizens who are religious.[60]

Habermas, thus, wants to open our public cognitive horizons to include a "self critical assessment of the limits of secular reason," which, he asserts, imposes complementary learning processes on *both* religious and non-religious citizens.[61] This new cognitive horizon is a "post-metaphysical thought" that "is prepared to learn from religion while remaining strictly agnostic" and that "refrains from the rationalist temptation that it [rationalism] can decide which part of the religious doctrines is rational and which part is not."[62] It is also a thought for what he calls "post-secular society". This form of society:

> does more than give public recognition to religious fellowship in view of the functional contribution they make to the reproduction of motivations and attitudes that are socially desirable. The public awareness of a post-secular society also reflects a normative insight that has consequences for the political dealings of unbelieving citizens with believing citizens. In the postsecular society, there is increasing consensus that certain phases of the 'modernization of the public consciousness' involve assimilation and the reflexive transformations *of both secular and religious mentalities.* If both sides agree to understand the secularization of society as a complementary learning process, then they will also have cognitive reasons to take seriously each other's contributions to controversial subjects in public debate.[63]

Thus, Habermas' theory wants to inject into our political deliberations potential normative challenges that come from taking religious reasons seriously, and indeed the potential epistemic shifts in our cognitive horizon that may result from this process. He believes that this requires both religious as well as non-religious citizens to engage in an opening of their minds to new possibilities and arguments. As part of this process, Habermas would allow religious reasons to enter into some public political debate, without the Rawlsian proviso that they must then be accompanied by other reasons not resting on the same sources that justify the point for which they are arguing. Through the translation requirement, however, Habermas' theory continues to impose some restraint on the use of religious reasons including in the 'pre-parliamentary' public sphere, but only so as to preserve a difference between our institutional and non-institutional political worlds. The difference is that Habermas draws the line of constraint in different place from Rawls. Therefore, we can still see in Habermas' theory a focus on the limited zone of 'political justice'. Habermas must surely believe that the requirement of translation can preserve the essential point(s) of the positions that are translated. In this sense, translation is merely a facilitative requirement that acts to make the translated points of view accessible to those who do not share them. Inasmuch as translation would engender the better mutual understanding between religions and non-religious citizens, it may be seen as positive. Although this may be the case in some circumstances, we might nonetheless critique Habermas' requirement as failing to recognise that the process of translation may itself do violence to the positions that have to be translated because translation is not simply a mechanical and entirely content-preserving

60 Habermas, (2006a) at 16 (emphasis in original).
61 Habermas (2006a) at 17 and 18.
62 Habermas (2006a) at 20.
63 Habermas (2006b) at 46–47 (emphasis added).

process.[64] For example, it difficult to imagine that the full range of symbolic and affective meanings that a religious believer will have towards their own faith tradition will be translatable to someone outside of that faith tradition, any more than the linguistic form and beauty of a poetic work would be fully translatable into another language. Our whole truth world views may be subject to similar restrictions on translatability. Habermas may be willing to accept that translation may not be perfect and might entail some loss of meaning, because he may view the general access to positions that translation will engender to be a greater good for which some sacrifice of meaning may be an unfortunate necessity. This point of view, however, is by no means obviously correct on the one hand and, on the other hand, there might be other viable political alternatives, as we will see below.

Habermas' outlook, like Rawls', may be seen to follow the institutional position of the 'standard approach' of mainstream liberal thought because it also insists on a restraint in the public use of religious reasons. But there is a crucial difference between the theories. Habermas is concerned that we at least open our 'whole truth' frameworks – be they secular or religious – to cognitive challenges and that we do not dismiss any arguments – again whether we are religious or not – without due consideration. The demand to expose our whole truth frameworks to challenges is beyond the Rawlsian position and may be seen to represent a different ethical conception absent (at least explicitly) in Rawls.

Weithman's two propositions

Paul Weithman's work on religion in the public sphere seeks to defend propositions that are less restrictive than those of Habermas. Weithman argues for the following two propositions:

> Citizens of a liberal democracy may base their votes on reasons drawn from their comprehensive moral views, including their religious views, provided they sincerely believe that their government would be justified in adopting the measures they vote for.

and

> Citizens in a liberal democracy may offer arguments in public political debate which depend upon reasons drawn from their comprehensive moral views, including their religious views, without making them good by appeal to other arguments – provided they believe that their government would be justified adopting the measures they favour, and are prepared to indicate what they think would justify the adoption of such measures.[65]

64 Paolo Flores d'Arcais makes a related point in his 'Eleven Theses Against Habermas' (Flores d'Arcais (2009); accessible at www.the-utopian.org/2009/02/000062.html) when he says (at 3) "that the expected translation [of religious reasons into] secular-democratic terms is often impossible. Such expectation is nothing but wishful thinking." Habermas replies (Habermas (2009) at 4; accessible at www.the-utopian.org/2009/02/000063.html):

> It is certainly true that any translation of a thought from a religious to a secular *language must entail a loss of connotations.* To render the idea that human beings were made 'in the image of God' as 'human dignity' is to lose the original connotation of man having been 'created'. Nevertheless, the core of the semantic content need not be lost. (emphasis added).

Even if we accept Habermas' defence, his concession to the 'loss of connotations' weakens his position and the viability of translation.

65 Weithman (2002) at 3.

These two propositions are Weithman's conditions of responsible citizenship.

We can immediately see some of the similarities and differences between Weithman's responsible citizenship and Rawls' duty of civility. Like Rawls, there is a concern not to be too parochial, and thus a requirement that any measures that are proposed are considered worthy of government policy generally and, even more importantly, that those who would advocate policies or reasons based on (for example) religious views are willing to justify the adoption of such policies. Weithman allows the reliance on and expression of religious views without these needing to be 'made good' by an appeal to other, non-religious, reasons. In contrast to Rawls, however, Weithman allows the entrance of reasons drawn from comprehensive doctrines, including religious doctrines, to enter public political debate and for these reasons to stand alone. There is no Rawlsian proviso inasmuch as there need not be any other non-comprehensive-doctrines-based justifying reasons that citizens must offer. In addition, there is no requirement that reasons offered must be accessible. To these two differences, Weithman adds a third. His first two statements, he claims, allow religion to play a much more prominent role in political decision-making than does the standard Rawlsian, liberal approach. In so doing, they allow for a type of engagement of religion in the public square that proponents of the standard liberal approach would find unacceptable as a violation of the duty of citizenship (expressed above as the duty of civility).[66] Neither does Weithman impose any Habermasian translation requirement on reasons coming from religious doctrines or other comprehensive doctrines. Here, Weithman is more accommodating than Habermas in allowing *voting* on the basis of comprehensive doctrines reasons, and thereby allowing them directly to influence policy and law, without the need to be 'translated' first.

We can also see a continuing Kantian influence in the second part of both of Weithman's propositions. In both cases, citizens must believe that what they think is right based on their own comprehensive doctrines, is right in general terms because they as individuals believe, in the first instance, that "government would be justified in adopting the measures they vote for" or, in the second instance, that "government would be justified adopting the measures they favour, and are prepared to indicate what they think would justify the adoption of such measures." These two requirements echo two classical formulations of the Kantian categorical imperative, namely: "Act only according to that maxim by which you can at the same time will that it would become a universal law"; and secondly, "Act in such a way that you always treat humanity, whether in your own person or in the person of any other, never simply as a means, but always at the same time as an end."[67] Citizens are obliged to think of others because voting or arguing for the adoption of a rule by government would affect all citizens. Citizens must also believe the measures they favour are justified as government action, which again would affect all citizens and, therefore, brings others into focus. And because others must be taken into consideration at all times, Weithman's principles are premised on the citizens seeing government as acting for the common, public good.[68] This in turn means that Weithman is concerned with justice at a 'political level' – i.e., justice when we act in common.

In Weithman's view, this will lead to something close to a liberal democratic model since: "A plausible common interest view for liberal democratic government will require respect

66 Weithman (2002) at 131–133.

67 On Kant, see Pasternak (2002) at 64 and at 57. See also Johnson (2004), accessible at: http://plato.stanford.edu/archives/spr2004/entries/kant-moral/

68 Weithman (2002) at 125.

for the rights and liberties traditionally associated with liberal democracy."[69] So, Weithman's framework is not the 'competition of interests' model of democracy because that requires only a concern for one's own interests. However, it is also different from the Rawlsian concern because it believes that we do not know enough "about the morality of political decision making in the face of deep disagreements about justice, including the morality of majority rule."[70] The mainstream liberal position seems to adjudge this as morally suspect and indeed threatening, but Weithman is not sure. This is why his position is open to possibilities of political discourse that other liberal positions would reject. As he says:

> these conditions make it important to distinguish those whose political views we do not like from those who violate their duty as citizens. There may be many citizens who, without violating their duty as citizens, use religious and other comprehensive views to argue for political outcomes with which we are in deep disagreement. In that case, we should argue, vote and organize coalitions to oppose them.[71]

Weithman's propositions seem to straddle the concern with finding a means to achieve 'political justice' in the Rawlsian sense, with a concern for a debate around moral values and the 'whole truth'. His propositions want to construct principles for political justice that will force us to encounter, in the public sphere as we may also privately, what may be a diverse array of whole truth claims and to test their moral worthiness. Michael Sandel has articulated a similar perspective:

> It is always possible that learning more about a moral or religious doctrine will make us like it less. But the respect of deliberation and engagement affords a more spacious public reason than liberalism allows. It is also a more suitable ideal for a pluralist society. To the extent that our moral and religious disagreements reflect the ultimate plurality of human goods, a deliberative mode of respect will better enable us to appreciate the distinctive goods our different lives express.[72]

Both Sandel and Weithman, thus, want politics to be a debate about truth and moral values, and want truth and moral values to be a part of political debate. Even though there is a concern with political justice as such, this is not to be separated from a concern with interrogating and debating claims about the whole truth. This moves fairly considerably from Rawls, whose theory was restricted, explicitly, to the level of 'political justice'. It is thus that Sandel uses language that distinguishes what he proposes from 'liberalism', since a liberalism of a type that would avoid debates about the whole truth or conceptions about the good life

69 Weithman (2002) at 125.
70 Weithman (2002) at 216.
71 Weithman (2002) at 216. What Weithman is not exactly clear about is where to draw this line – i.e., when does someone 'violate their duty as a citizen' and might the expression of some political views (which we should tolerate even if we disagree) amount to such a violation (which we should not tolerate). One is also lead to wonder if the dynamic of power and it needs to be taken into account here. Not all voices are necessarily equally empowered: the better-financed and better socially positioned, and even better-educated, may have more-powerful voices. This is discussed further in chapter 5.
72 Sandel (1994) at 1794. See also Michael Perry's statement that: "Indeed, because of the role that such religious arguments inevitably play in the political process, it is important that such arguments, no less than secular moral arguments, be presented in – so they can be tested in – public political debate" in Perry (1997) at 130, n22.

would clearly fall short of what Sandel is arguing for and, indeed, would be less that what Weithman would want. Weithman's theory is institutionally very close to Wolterstorff's consocial position in advocating the removal of (almost all) constraints on the way in which religious views may be expressed in public political debate but, in spirit, it shares a commitment with Habermas' position to enable religious views to challenge other life conceptions and a concomitant commitment that it is only through such an open process that a fuller sense of our diversity can be genuinely grasped and appreciated.[73]

Ladd's critique of liberal absolutism

John Ladd's discussion of politics and religion, and the conclusions he draws about the role of religion in the public sphere, brings this last point home more fully and with greater philosophical sophistication.[74] What Ladd points out is that there are a variety of sociopolitical positions we can identify that posit ultimate ends, which are absolutes in terms of the specific positions. Hence, we have a variety of absolutisms, included among which we can count naturalism, atheism and religious absolutisms, but also, secularism and liberalism. Since each absolutism projects its own ultimate ends, we might view each of them like a Rawlsian comprehensive doctrine. For example, secularism affirms the primacy of the political over the religious (at least in public life), a position that Ladd traces to Thomas Hobbes and Jean Bodin, and liberalism, he contends, gives primacy to process and rights, such as the right to property and liberty. While we could perhaps agree on what should be our governing absolutism, in fact we do not. That we do not is both the source and expresses the fact of our diversity, which of course was the starting point for the liberal theory we have here considered. However, the problem with absolutisms, Ladd argues, is that if we do not accept the premises of an absolutism, then there is no way to move forward because we cannot talk to each other, a difficulty that has been recognised by the theories we have discussed above.[75] The Rawlsian liberal institutional solution to this problem was to eliminate these absolutisms from public political debate precisely so that we would be able to talk to each other and deliberate in a meaningful way. Habermas in a more moderated way and especially Weithman, on the other hand, want to allow these absolutisms to interact and clash with each other more. Ladd's solution is different. Ladd contends that while we should not say that all ideas are of equal value, we should have a presumption that there might be some value in them and, therefore, that they should not be dismissed out of hand. This would apply to religious doctrines as well. We should see religions as "experiments in living" from which we might learn. This is similar to Waldron's assertion that moral absolutisms, with the ethics and theology that support them, should not be absolutely thrown out, but looked into carefully to "gain the deepest sense we can of what lies behind them".[76] In part, this post-metaphysical perspective also seems very similar to what Habermas is suggesting. Ladd is calling for a non-absolutist form of pluralism, in which positions are not equally valid *per se* but because they share an equal presumption of validity are all tolerated

73 On how religious tolerance is connected and facilitative of democratic practices ("Now, pluralism and the struggle for religious tolerance were not only driving forces behind the emergence of the democratic state, but continue stimulate its further evolution up to now.") and of cultural rights, see Habermas (2006c) at 199.

74 Ladd (1988) at 276–277.

75 Ladd (1988) at 277.

76 Waldron (2012) at 23.

publicly. In this way, religious ideas would become public and their value assessed through public discussion.

Gaus: public justification and expanding public reason

Gerald Gaus adds an important and complementary dimension of analysis here. Gaus and Kevin Vallier posit a Principle of Public Justification, according to which "each citizen must have conclusive reason to accept each law as binding". [77] This, they point out, rests on a 'justificatory liberalism' (a term they reference from Christopher Eberle),[78] which includes political liberalism. Since religious reasons are not shared, however, they would appear inappropriate for public justification. Gaus and Vallier note that citizens of faith that might otherwise be liberal will reject the position that when discussing and debating publicly they should not be able to rely on religions reasons. In contrast, they argue (seemingly as a matter of fact) that: "Justified political outcomes need not, and often will not, be the result of a refined activity of public reasoning, but of electoral and legislative institutions and procedures that generate outcomes that all members of the public accept . . .".[79] Additionally, they assert that "what is important is whether a reason – be it 'secular' or 'religious' – is within the bounds of reasonable pluralism and how it enters into the network of other such reasons."[80] They thus hold that a commitment to public justification provides no grounds for the exclusion of religions reasons from politics. In another piece, Gaus opines that moral theory and political philosophy have gone astray because: "Philosophers all-too-often assume that they have moral insight that sets them apart from – and over – their fellow moral agents. *They* see the reasons that there really are, *they* see the true moral properties, *they* understand what justice demands about how society must be organized."[81] These assumptions are morally elitist and are problematic as such. Rather, what is required in our democratic age is that we must take seriously that "people of good will in a diverse society have differing views of what constitutes an acceptable way of living together, and there is no priestly class who can dictate to the rest how we are to live together."[82] Presumably, in light of what Gaus has said about philosophers, the priestly class that he refers to includes any putative 'philosopher-kings'. Now, if we accept Gaus and Gaus and Vallier's points of view, we can see that these also push back at political liberalism and its limitations and open the possibility of other ways of considering the role of religion within a liberal framework.

Constructing a theory: justice as discourse

Each of the 'liberal' positions discussed here has struggled with the same basic challenge that Rawls expressed: how we can create "a stable and just society of free and equal citizens profoundly divided by reasonable religious, philosophical and moral doctrines?" They all share Rawls' desire to build a just society and, in the abstract, some sort of a stable social order. In so doing, they all embrace the normative commitment of liberal theory as a critical component of such a social order. But, as they demonstrate, neither their views

77 Gaus and Vallier (2009) at 51.
78 See Eberle (2002).
79 Gaus and Vallier (2009) at 71.
80 Gaus and Vallier (2009) at 71.
81 Gaus (2013) at 84 (emphasis in original).
82 Gaus (2013) at 84.

on the meaning of a 'just social order', of what 'stability' demands, or how either might be achieved, are entirely shared. Indeed, the liberal position sees our plurality of moral, philosophical and religious views as being deep and incommensurable, and indeed perhaps incompatible, when it comes to constructing some sort of political justice. At the same time, this outlook acknowledges that our deeply held beliefs are probably where we will look for our sense of the good life and will be the wellsprings of wisdom and principle upon which we draw to fashion our ideas about what we should do day to day in our relations with other citizens at the individual, private level, as well as with our governments, law and institutions of the state at the public level. The challenge, therefore, is to find a point of justice that is fair, in spite of disagreements about fairness itself.

Addressing this question takes us back to fundamentals. The logic of a democratic system means that all citizens should be allowed to participate in deliberating about our political policies and principles, including, in the case at hand, about what would make our politics fair. Clearly, we will need to ensure that in these deliberations everyone that wants to participate is allowed to do so. To achieve this end, we have to recognise that we may be more divided than the Rawlsian liberal position suggested, because we are divided even about what fairness – that touchstone of liberal virtues – means. We will, in short, have to embrace a greater and more raucous polyphony than liberalism may have imagined. At best, and at its best, our politics can allow us to dialogue in the hope that through this dialogue we can come to decisions about the appropriate principles of fairness and, of course, about the structure of our society. Justice thus conceived would lie in allowing all divergent opinions to be expressed, even those about what and how we may engage in discussions. It is thus a composite theory drawing elements from what has been discussed already. It takes the essential challenge that Rawls outlines as its animating impulse and embraces the normative commitment of liberal theory that is reflected in Rawls' framework. It seeks, however, to overcome the divide between 'liberal' and 'theological' positions that Audi and Wolterstorff stipulated by noting that all of the options they discuss differ not in their goal of achieving fairness based on a normative liberal theory, but about the best institutional form(s) by which this may be realised. It further takes seriously the critiques of Rawls' theory as being too restrictive and constraining on religious expression in public political debate to achieve its *own* stated ends. The critiques made of Rawls by Habermas and Weithman appear to be driving at this point and aiming to provide corrective principles (Habermas' translation requirement and Weithman's two propositions) that would both better realise the liberal goal while safeguarding against theological diktats. Gaus (and Vallier), in turn, pushes the envelope of public reason with respect to religion, arguing that Rawlsian constraints do not need to be applied.

Justice as discourse adopts these concerns and the basic thrust of the remedies proposed by proposing that religiously inspired language be given a wide space in public political debate, and allowed to be influential upon but never solely decisive of state policy or to be invoked as the justification of official state action. Moreover, it embraces the perspectives of 'critics of liberalism' like Sandel and Ladd who have questioned the neutral status of classical liberal theory by suggesting that liberal theory is value-laden in a way that betrays its aspiration to be a space in which different and competing values can equally and fairly interact and vie for public recognition. Justice as discourse would, firstly, seek to provide what Sandel called more capacious public space by allowing religious ideas to be expressed and thereby to challenge values as well as to shape policy. In so doing, it, secondly, accepts that we may achieve neither a stable consensus nor a type of political discourse that will be entirely universally comprehensible – or, as Ladd put it, that we may be confronted by incompatible absolutes.

While a stable consensus was Rawls' aspiration, we may be better served by accepting that our differences will persist in spite of discussion. We might say, then, that justice would lie in *discourse*, without any normative conception of fairness. A notion of justice as discourse would have as a key requirement that we agree to listen sincerely to the views of others, and that they agree to listen to us. Justice as discourse, however, still believes in the value of liberal theory in facilitating the expression of our diversity if we release it from its (classical) Rawlsian formulation.

With respect to Habermas, as we have seen, when Habermas specifically considers religion's public role, the broad and unrestrained perspective that appears to emerge from his description of the method of discourse ethics is restricted by his translation requirement and, therefore, there is a continued limitation on religion's public voice and place in the public sphere. Justice as discourse wants to push the logic of Habermas' argument further on this point. The translation requirement was Habermas' way of addressing the concern of incomprehensibility of religiously derived political reasons, a concern shared by Rawls. While sensitive to this concern, justice as discourse accepts that we may not, and probably will not, have reasons that are entirely intelligible to one another and this will make both our listening to others and our being heard much more difficult than in a system where we relied only on common reasons. This, however, is the price we may have to pay, and may gladly agree to pay, for a politics that is expansive enough to embrace a deeper notion of pluralism than has been plumbed by the standard liberal position, both in its (classical) Rawlsian formulation as well as in variations to this model that we have considered. This pluralism may be as socially inveterate as it is individually and communally inspiring. Certainly, though, it would include our various religious convictions as well as allowing them more space than Rawls' formulation would want to accept. Ideally, as Waldron states, citizens should offer their political statements, including such religious convictions, as contributions to discourse, where everyone else in the polity may consider and offer modifications to this statement and likewise contribute to the conversation.[83]

Justice as discourse also proposes an ethical perspective on liberal justice that comes from within liberal theory itself. At the heart of the theory is recognition not only of the fact of our diversity, but also a commitment to allowing this diversity to shape the decisions we make in common. Those decisions will include not only institutional forms we establish, but also the very life ambitions we set for our polities. As Ian Bartrum contends, non-public reasons should be part of political discourse as they promote "paradigm changes" that ultimately unable society to progress, much like how society has shifted its scientific understanding of a geocentric scientific phenomenon to that of heliocentricity.[84] An example where religious views had once shaped law for good, as presented by Joel Nichols and James McCarty III, was the collapsing of the state-supported apartheid system that was "in large part because of prominent theological leaders who drew upon [biblical arguments] and argued for specific actions of resistance".[85]

Inevitably, therefore, justice as discourse will lead to discussions about ultimate questions about the nature of justice. Rawls famously proposed a theory of 'justice as fairness'. What Habermas' discourse theory suggests, however, is that the very criteria of fairness

83 Waldron (2012) at 13.
84 Bartrum (2014) at 483. See also Movsesian (2011) at 5.
85 Nichols and McCarty III (2014) at 604; see also Movsesian (2011) at 7.

and, hence, of justice cannot (and probably should not) be proposed by philosophers.[86] Gaus' above-noted point that restricting the type of reasoning that is acceptable for public deliberation to what philosophers would find to be appropriate risks a philosophers' hubris is also germane here. The hubris would be that only philosophers have special moral insight, that only they see things as they really are and, thus, that only they can understand justice.[87] Rather, the great promise of liberal theory is that the content of justice will be defined from discursive political debate. There is, of course, a considerable risk in this, which is that we may not agree, and this in turn would compromise the stability of our political orders. However, if out of a concern for stability we must compromise the diversity that we can bring to the definition of justice, we will have violated the very ethic of liberal theory itself. In this respect, we can see liberal theory facilitating the expression of our diversity if we release it from its Rawlsian formulation.

Justice as discourse is strongly influenced by Habermas' theory of discourse ethics, which, not surprisingly, has a strong intellectual connection to his idea of post metaphysical thought, and his call to embrace polyphonous complexity. As Habermas says, "Discourse ethics . . . views the moral point of view as embodied in an intersubjective practice of argumentation which enjoins those involved to an idealizing *enlargement* of their interpretive practices."[88] The enlargement of interpretive practices imposes demands on all of us to be respectful of alternate positions. So, discourse ethics is a method to achieve the type of exposure to each other's ideas and calls for an 'ideal role taking'. Ultimately, Habermas perceives this as a procedural moral and legal theory, so much so that he says:

> I propose that philosophy limit itself to the clarification of the moral point of view and procedure of democratic legitimation, to the analysis of the conditions of rational discourse and negotiations. . . . It [philosophy on this Habermasian account] leaves substantial questions that must be answered here and now to the more or less enlightened engagement of participants, which does not mean that philosophers may not also participate in the public debate, though in the role of intellectuals, not of experts.[89]

If Habermas' ultimate end is procedural in the sense he has described, his methodology to achieve this end, that is to say the substantive content of discourse ethics, calls for a particular type of political engagement of all of us with each other:

> Under the pragmatic presuppositions of an inclusive and noncoercive rational discourse among free and equal participants, everyone is required to take the perspective of everyone else, and thus *project herself into the understandings and self world of all others*; from this interlocking of perspectives there emerges an ideally extended we-perspective from which all can test in common whether they wish to make a controversial norm the basis of their shared practice.[90]

86 This position is part of the larger debate about whether justice should be conceived of in procedural or substantive terms, Habermas' suggestion tending to the former.

87 In general terms, this reopening of public discourse to religious views is particularly crucial, as Zachary Calo asserts, given that "political and intellectual foundations . . . [are] increasingly imperilled", and require religious legal theory to contribute particularly to human rights law, but also to jurisprudence. See Calo (2014) at 504 and 519; and Movsesian (2011) at 5.

88 Habermas (1995) at 117 (emphasis in original).

89 Habermas (1995 at 131.

90 Habermas (1995) at 117 (emphasis added).

Justice as discourse versus some alternatives

Before concluding this chapter, it will be useful to explore justice as discourse further by examining it in comparison to alternative theories proposed by Veit Bader and Abdullahi An-Na'im. Bader and An-Na'im are significant here for different reasons. Bader's work posits a novel outlook on the place of religion in the state and in political discourse. An-Na'im, on the other hand, considers Muslim environments specifically. Justice as discourse must, therefore, engage with both theories.

Bader's 'priority for democracy'

Veit Bader has noted that church–state relationships are diverse "in states that all share the principles of liberal democracy".[91] Bader further notes the critiques of the "radical exclusion of religious reasons and arguments from public debate and politics in political liberalism."[92] As an alternative, he argues for a 'priority for democracy' which takes into account that "constitutional principles and public morality of liberal democracies . . . should be as freestanding as possible with regard to *competing secular and religious foundations* . . ."[93] Bader thus argues for a normative model based on what he calls nonconstitutional pluralism (NCP) which:

> combines constitutional disestablishment or nonestablishment with restricted legal pluralism (e.g. in family law), administrative institutional pluralism (*de jure* and *de facto* institutionalization of several organized religions), institutionalized political pluralism, and the religio-cultural pluralization of the nation.[94]

Continuing, Bader asserts that:

> NCP requires specific information rights for organized religions and corresponding information duties by state agencies regarding contested issues, participation in public fora and hearings, inclusion in advisory councils and corresponding consultation rights and duties to listen, and so on.[95]

Bader favours NCP, as opposed to the alternative of nonestablishment and private pluralism (NEPP), which "declares a strict legal separation of the state from all religions as well as a strict administrative and political separation".[96] It (NEPP) is opposed to the institutionalisation of religion that NCP posits on Bader's account. The model of the US approximates NEPP, while India, Belgium, Australia, Germany and the Netherlands post-1983 constitutional reforms approximate NCP.

What Bader's analysis and position, like some of the others we have mentioned earlier, usefully indicates to us is that liberal theory can accommodate institutional patterns that vary from Rawlsian requirements and, more interestingly for our purposes, that liberal theory can allow for a richer role for religious convictions in public debate than some of its early institutional formulations envisaged.

91 Bader (2003) at 268.
92 Bader (2003) at 265.
93 Bader (2003) at 266 (emphasis added). On priority for democracy, see also Bader (1999).
94 Bader (2003) at 271.
95 Bader (2003) at 271.
96 Bader (2003) at 271.

Justice as discourse would differ from Bader's theory in two respects: one institutional, the other conceptual. Institutionally, Bader's model appears to be dependent upon being able to locate institutional representation for religious communities and thus to develop 'institutionalised pluralism'. The heritage of Muslim contexts will, as we will see below, raise issues that challenge Bader's framework for precisely this reason because Islam is unlike Christianity in that there is no Church, and consequently, no institution "invested with the epistemological authority to affix the imprimatur of religious truth upon a statement and send it forth as such into society".[97]

How might an NCP model work without any institutionalised religious body to act as a representative? And how can it work with a tradition that has never known a sort of church structure and in which, on the contrary, religious authority has never rested unambiguously with a hierarchical clerical establishment but rather most commonly with diffuse theologian-jurist-scholars who have been respected for their learning, rather than their office *per se*. In contrast, justice as discourse depends on no such institutional system.

Conceptually, because of its requirement for institutionalised pluralism, Bader's model runs the risk of neglecting *inter*-community diversity. Justice as discourse recognises that having religious voices expressed through corporate representation is problematic because each religious community will, in fact, be composed of individuals with diverse personal outlooks. Corporate representation, however, would not be able to capture all of this diversity and in so doing could exclude the full range of opinions that religious believers could express and may end up hearing only the most powerful, and therefore most dominant, voices. Rather than accepting institutionalised pluralism, justice as discourse locates diversity at the individual level and is thus concerned with capturing this more fine-grained plurality and bringing it to bear on public political discourse.

An-Na'im's 'civic reason' / 'public reason'

Abdullahi An-Na'im has developed a theory for the relationship of *shari'a*, the state and politics, which he refers to as either public reason or civic reason. His proposals are as follows:

> First, the modern territorial state should neither seek to enforce Shari'a as positive law and public policy, nor claim to interpret its doctrine and general principles for Muslim citizens. Second, Shari'a principles can and should be a source of public policy and legislation, subject to constitutional and human rights of all citizens, men and women, Muslims and non-Muslims equally without discrimination. In other words, Shari'a principles are neither privileged or enforced as such nor necessarily rejected as a source of state law and policy simply because they are derived from the Shari'a.[98]

An-Na'im's proposals are based on the view that:

> the inherent subjectivity and diversity of Shari'a principles mean that whatever is enacted and enforced by the state is the political will of the ruling elite, not the normative system of Islam as such.[99]

97 Ahmed (2016) at 192.
98 An-Na'im (2008a) at 334–335.
99 An-Na'im (2008a) at 335.

Out of this concern he posits that:

> To avoid such difficulties, I am proposing that the rationale of all public policy and legislation always be based on what might be called 'public reason' whereby Muslims and other believers should be able to propose policy and legislative initiatives emanating from their religious beliefs, ***provided*** that can support them in a public, free and open debate with reasons that are accessible and convincing to the generality of citizens . . .[100]

In a slightly later work for which his essay was a precursor, he develops a concept of 'civic reason' in, he claims, distinction to 'public reason' as used by Rawls. He asserts that:

> I am in general agreement with Rawls' thinking, as clarified (sic) by Habermas, subject to an overriding concern about transplanting those ideas to Islamic societies at large . . . let me first recall my definition of civic reason as the requirement that the rationale and purpose of public policy or legislation be based on the sort of reasoning that most citizens can accept or reject and use to make counterproposals through public debate without reference to religious belief as such. This view can probably be supported by Rawls and Habermas.[101]

And later,

> For our purposes here, I believe it sufficient to affirm that the concept of civic reason should be rooted in civil society and marked by contestation among different actors seeking to influence policy through the agency of the state.[102]

Ultimately, though, An-Na'im is "emphasising an Islamic perspective to maintain the religious neutrality of the state despite the connectedness of Islam and politics".[103]

An-Na'im refreshes the idea of a civic consensus for Muslim contexts in a further essay,[104] in which he notes the problem of identifying an "Islamic" political perspective given the range of interpretations that may exist among Muslims.[105] Hence, the civic consensus is premised on finding a basis that is acceptable to all citizens, Muslim or not. However, this consensus does not need, à la Rawls, to rely upon an exclusion of religious reasons from public reasoning. An-Na'im wants a more inclusive politics but coupled with a religiously neutral state.

There is much that justice as discourse shares with An-Na'im's civic/public reason, but there are also differences. Notably, justice as discourse shares with Na'im a grounding in the political thinking of Rawls and Habermas and the view that religious principles should be allowed to be proposed as the basis for public policy or even as legislation, but should

100 An-Na'im (2008a) at 335 (emphasis in original).
101 An-Na'im (2008b) at 100.
102 An-Na'im (2008b) at 101.
103 An-Na'im (2008b) at 137.
104 An-Na'im (2015).
105 As he says: "On the other hand, there is a wide diversity of opinion among Muslim jurists on every conceivable issue and each Muslim has a choice among competing views, as his or her individual consciousness dictates. It may be true that the majority of Muslims prefer to conform to the practice of their local communities rather than exercise individual choice in practice. Still, for Muslims maintaining the right and duty to seek Sharia justification is integral to their right to religious self-determination" (An-Na'im (2015) at 246).

not be necessarily enforced or rejected as such. Relatedly, justice as discourse does not seek to limit religious discourses to a purely private domain. Moreover, as will be developed in subsequent chapters, justice as discourse also emerges out of a reading of the intellectual, political and legal history of Muslim contexts that emphasises the diversity and plurality of understandings of the *shari'a* and of religious principles more generally.

Where justice as discourse differs, however, is in grounding itself not just on the ideas of Rawls and Habermas, but in a larger and more diverse, tradition of liberal theory in which, though Rawls and Habermas are prominent participants, they are not the only voices. This means not simply that more theorists are considered (a rather banal point, perhaps), but rather that a more robust use and defence of the normative temper of liberal theory as such, and the usefulness of this theory for Muslim contexts is taken up by justice as discourse. This differs in degree, but also it seems in ultimate purpose, from Na'im's position that is grounded fundamentally in an argument derived from an "Islamic perspective". In addition, justice as discourse frees religious reasoning from the limitations that Rawls' (proviso) and Habermas' (translation requirement) impose upon it and which An-Na'im seems to accept when he talks about the need for 'accessible' reasons to be offered. Justice as discourse sees the process(es) of providing accessibility as potentially compromising the full expression of plurality – which was the great motivation for liberal theory. Furthermore, it accepts that some public reasoning that may be 'unintelligible' to some may well be a consequence of embracing our real diversity. However, this should be seen, not as desirable *per se*, but as an acceptable compromise in order to capture diversity.

Expanded public reason

As we have seen in considering Gaus and Vallier's views earlier, there are conceptions of a type of public reason – in their case the Principle of Public Justification – that embrace the use of religious reasons in public discussion. Indeed, Gaus and Vallier say, simply, "properly understood, a commitment to public justification provides no grounds for the exclusion of religious reasons from politics".[106] Fred D'Agostino's position that classical liberalism's constraint on the types of reasons that can properly be used for public discussion (and justification) highlights a failure of liberals to appreciate contested nature of these reasons lends implicit support to Gaus and Vallier's assertion, and to the point that we can only settle our contestations temporarily.[107]

Justice as discourse shares the embrace of religious reasons and the corollary view that the normative scope of public reason needs to be thought of in broader terms than Rawls suggested and even in more expansive terms than Habermas has proposed. Additionally, it accepts the need for on-going deliberations such that decisions for today will not necessarily be determinate or appropriate for tomorrow.

Where justice as discourse can be distinguished from Gaus and D'Agostino's position is in the emphasis it gives to certain notions. The first notion is the importance of discourse. Justice as discourse emphasises that our fundamental ideas of justice will be developed in context and in discursive space. In saying this, it asserts that although an ideal of justice may remain constant, the expressions will change. Justice is thus seen as something 'in becoming' out of discourse. Second, and relatedly, justice as discourse also emphasises the expressive function that allowing the expression of religions reasons can have. Cass Sunstein explains

106 Gaus and Vallier (2009) at 51. See also Gaus (2009).
107 See D'Agostino (1996).

this with respect to law. He says that law may have an expressive function in the following manner:

> Thus a second understanding of the expressive function of law does not concern itself with effects on norms. Instead, its grounding is connected with the individual interest in integrity . . . we might say that personal behavior is not concerned solely with producing states of affairs and that, if it were, we would have a hard time making sense of important aspects of our lives. There are also issues involving personal integrity, commitment, the narrative continuity of a life, and the individual and social meaning of personal conduct.[108]

Justice as discourse embraces the idea that the expression of religious reasons can have an important symbolic and expressive function in a manner akin to that that Sunstein has identified for law.[109] This view, therefore, amounts not just to a position that says that there are no good reasons for excluding religious reasons in public deliberations, but rather that there may be positively important symbolically ends served in allowing these expressions. In this respect, if standard approach liberalism finds that justice is better served in constraints that will reduce complexity by bracketing out certain types of reasoning better to facilitate mutual intelligibility, justice as discourse proposes a programme of additions rather than reductions. This can still fit within liberal theory, but it reorients the theory not to 'solve complexity' (and find stability in that way) but to embrace it and find stability into marshalling it into discourse. This is a liberalism robustly open to different types of thinking and reasoning – to pluralism. Finally, and building upon those two comments, justice as discourse may be said to step outside of the framework of public reason more explicitly that Gaus or D'Agostino appear to suggest, and to accept a public discourse that encompasses a more radical pluralism of acceptable pubic reasons.

Justice as discourse thus understood may share more ground with the bases of Rajeev Bhargava's idea 'principled distance' understanding which is derived from considering the case of India.[110] Drawing on Sandel's insight that "the requirement that religious reasons be excluded from liberal-democratic politics in offensive to religious persons",[111] Bhargava says that 'principled distance' "rejects the standard liberal idea that the principle of equal respect is best realised only when people come into the public domain by leaving religious reasoning behind".[112] Justice as discourse shares this insight but also Bhargava's other point that his principled distance recognises that while religion may not have special public significance, that does not mean it has (or should not have) any public significance.

Conclusion

We can still safely label justice as discourse a liberal theory inasmuch as its principles all stem from the liberal concern to address in the best way possible the challenge of diversity and

108 Sunstein (1996) at 2026–2027.

109 Indeed, Sunstein starts his essay by discussing actions more generally before moving to law. He says: "Actions are expressive; they carry meanings. This is true for nearly everything we do, from the most mundane to the most significant" (Sunstein (1996) at 2021).

110 Bhargava (2013).

111 Cited in Bhargava (2013) at 76.

112 Bhargava (2013) at 85.

the plurality of our moral, ethical and religious outlooks. Additionally, it shares the normative commitment of liberal theory that the full range of our diversity should be brought to bear on public decision-making. Where it differs from the 'mainstream' liberal perspectives represented by Habermas and, primarily, by Rawls is in seeking to push the boundaries of the liberal embrace of diversity further than each of these theorists, especially so in the space allowed for the expressions of political sentiments that may be inspired by religious outlooks or convictions. In so doing, while conscious of the concern about the potentially (and, in fact, very likely) divisive nature of religious ideas in public debate, justice as discourse undoes the restrictions that both Rawls and Habermas would impose on religious reasons. An expansive liberal theory on these principles will be, I will argue, well suited to all societies, but particularly to Muslim contexts in which religious commitments are strong, by providing enough space for the expression of these commitments on matters of public concern while at the same time safeguarding the capacity for a diverse range of moral views to be expressed.

Rawls and others have addressed the challenge of diversity with the concomitant issues of political stability and mutual comprehensibility by suggesting that we need a framework in which certain types of reasoning is limited when it comes to properly public deliberations and decision-making. We might say that these perspectives rest on a 'subtraction' metric, removing or restricting some types of arguments that may irreducibly divide us in order to obtain a (more) shared basis for reasoning in common. Justice as discourse, on the other hand, posits an addition perspective in which our diversity is better dealt with by being expressed. This is primarily because justice as discourse emphasises the discursive, political and deliberative process over settled conclusion about the content of justice. Justice thus becomes more closely conceived of as a verb, rather than as a noun.

Justice as discourse implies secularism of a particular type and requires us to theorise about the boundaries of this secular space in relation to the state, to civil society, to politics and to the law. In addition, it invites us to consider practical institutional options that give expression to its principles. The next chapter addresses these matters before this moving on to flesh out what it means to discuss 'Muslim contexts'.

2 Justice as discourse in application

We ended the previous chapter by introducing the notion of justice as discourse. Justice as discourse is really a modification of what Paul Weithman called the 'standard approach' liberalism,[1] particularly as this approach was represented in the contemporary period by Rawls' political liberalism, and was developed after considering several reactions to and critiques of Rawls' theory. As we have seen, liberal theory continues to evolve. It is grounded in a social and political history but it itself has a history out of which it develops: it is thus that Audi and Wolterstorff referred to a broader family of liberal positions, with Wolterstorff agreeing with Weithman that all of the positions within the family propose a restraint on the use of religious reasons in deciding and deliberating about political issues in public.[2] Justice as discourse is thus a label for a version of liberal theory. What distinguishes it from Rawls' theory and also from Habermas' reaction to Rawls, is that, like Weithman's positions, it allows a more expansive role for religious speech in public discourse. Sensitive to John Ladd's concern about liberal absolutism and to Jean Bethke Elshtain's worry of 'liberal monism', especially when it comes to religious speech, justice as discourse seeks to remove the fetters on the *expression* of religiously-derived arguments and reasons in public political debate. In so doing, however, it shares the concern of more classical liberal views with the *implementation*, in policy, of religious dictates. Nonetheless, and to be clear, justice as discourse embraces several principles shared with standard liberal theory. It is, thus, a conceptual wrapper around a certain type of broadly liberal theoretical conceptions, which seek to provide an expanded role for the religious positions and arguments in public political debate.

In this chapter, we will further explore justice as discourse. We will do this, firstly, by explicating certain principles that it shares with classical liberal theory. Secondly, we will examine what it means to implement justice as discourse as a set of political principles. Specifically, we will begin this second task by considering the sense of 'secularism' that is both implied and necessary in justice as discourse. We will then move on to discuss what role the theory conceives of for religious discourse vis-à-vis the executive and judicial authority, civil society, legislative provisions and the articulation of political arguments.

Justice as discourse and classical liberal theory

Diversity

Justice as discourse shares some key principles and concerns with classical formulations of liberal theory. The first is on the issue of diversity. Religious diversity within a defined

1 This is a phrase used in Weithman (2002).
2 Audi and Nicholas Wolterstorff (1997) at 75.

community is, of course, not a new phenomenon, and neither is it particular to just once civilisation. The approach that is taken to this diversity, however, has much evolved, especially in the past few hundred years and especially in Western Europe. During the sixteenth century, the so-called 'Wars of Religion' between Catholics and Protestants ravaged France. Under slogans like "*une foi, une loi, un roi*" ('one faith, one law, one king'), sectarian conflict raged until the Treaty of Nantes was concluded in 1598. To achieve the end of bringing about peace, it was felt necessary to decouple the social order from any confessional tradition – in effect to separate out religion and the state. This separation notion became a hallmark for a new, liberal model for the relationship of the state and religion. Indeed, as Stephen Holmes notes, "liberal beliefs about the proper relation among law, morality and religion first acquired distinct contours during the wars of religion that ravaged France between 1562 and 1598".[3] Thus, initially, the liberal attitude arose out of a concern for social peace. Over time, however, the liberal model evolved into a concern with protecting individual freedom of conscience. The mechanism to realise this end, however, was the same. Individual conscience could only be maintained, it was felt, by preventing the power of the state from imposing religious uniformity.[4] Thus, religious diversity was transformed from being viewed as an unwelcome aberration of non-conformists who ideally would be made to see the error of their ways and brought about to the true faith through either coercion or conversion, or, if not this ideal, then barely tolerated, to a feeling that freedom of religious belief (or lack of belief) is among the most important rights that society can grant to its citizens and that the energies of the state must weigh in not to bring non-conformists 'on side', but rather to protect them so that they may hold on to their beliefs. Slightly ironically, perhaps, the public protection of religious consciousness gave rise to the view of many thinkers that religion can only "co-exist within a liberal order when kept in a private dimension of social interaction".[5] Religion was thus privatised on the theory that in a pluralistic society religious sentiment could only appropriately be expressed in private settings so that state and public discourse would be insulated from any particular individual religious belief.

With the advent of the modern nation-state, generally linked to the changed pattern arising out of the Peace of Westphalia of 1648, an institutional distinction emerged between the state and its religious character. This is not to say that, at this point, church and state were separated or that there was any "disestablishment": the legal expression of that idea came later, especially in the constitution of the United States, and of course is still not present *de jure* in many parts of Europe (even if it exists in a *de facto* sense). Instead, what happened was a distinction between what we might call, to use the well-known Durkheimian distinction, the 'profane' and the 'sacred'. This, of course, is the delineation between the sacred, which is extraordinary and set apart from the routine course of daily life, and the profane, seen as ordinary and constituting the reality of everyday living. The state and political life became profane or this worldly, and in this sense separated from the other worldly and sacred world of religion. As a consequence, political life and the state were secularised in a particular way. Political association that would previously have been linked to a divine founding of society in some sort of sacred time (hence the "*une foi, une loi, un roi*") was now linked to a political process in social and profane time. Charles Taylor identifies these

3 Holmes (1998) at 5.

4 Though it comes much later in time, the words of Justice Black of the US Supreme Court reflect the fear: "colonial history . . . [has shown that] . . . zealous sectarians entrusted with governmental power to further their causes would sometimes torture, maim and kill those branded 'heretics', atheists and agnostics." *Cantwell* v. *Connecticut* (1940) 310 US 296 at 303, per Black, J.

5 Sadurski (1990) at 189.

conditions of our modern, post-Westphalian, political order. Discussing what he terms the 'modern social imaginary', Taylor notes that:

> Plainly, this imaginary is the end of a certain kind of presence of religion or the divine in public space. It is the end of when political authority . . . [is] inconceivable without reference to God or higher time.
>
> More precisely, the difference amounts to this. In the earlier phase, God or some kind of higher reality is an ontic necessity. . . . What emerges from the change is an understanding of social and political life entirely in secular time. . . . This is the picture of *le social fondé sur lui-même* (society as founded on itself) of which Backzo speaks.[6]

Contemporary classical liberal theory arose out of the social and political context just described and out of an acceptance that in the new profane time there will arise an irreducible diversity of views.

Justice as discourse shares this premise and the related concern for allowing, in the first instance, the full diversity of these views to enter into public political debate. However, it also takes seriously critiques that have argued the standard liberal position has been too restrictive to achieve its own end – namely to be open to the range of our views – by being too constraining of the expression of religious voices in public political debate. Thus, justice as discourse is willing to allow for a more-open and fulsome expression of religious views in public discussions. In this way, it seeks to be more expansive and pluralism enhancing by better capturing the diversity of views, religious views included, and allowing them to inform matters of public policy. Justice as discourse thus emphasises processes and methods of discourse. It was the risk that particular religious outlooks would be directive of public policy that was the great historical struggle which engendered liberal theory. This historical background likely also accounts for the special concern with religious voices influencing public policy, and it is in response to this that critiques have suggested that too much was done in this vein. In now taking the position that the standard version of liberal theory may be too restrictive, justice as discourse seeks to better capture the original liberal impulse, namely to bring to bear the full range of our diversity into public decision making.

Neutrality

The second shared concern, which is closely related to the issue of diversity, is with neutrality. Liberal theory insists on the state being neutral with respect to conceptions of the good and in respect of how, subject only to basic public order limits, individuals within the state pursue their personal ideas of the good. Neutrality is rightly seen as a precondition, and a facilitative condition, for diversity because any deep set or strongly existing commitments would limit the range of options that the state would consider. If the state is neutral as to what goods it should pursue, however, and what goods the individuals that it regulates may pursue, then a full range of options is available. Therefore, neutrality is ultimately an anti-perfectionist principle of restraint, preventing any restrictions or burdens to be imposed based on any particular values, and is fundamental to liberal theory.[7]

6 Taylor (2004) at 187–188.

7 Dimock (20002) at 191; George (1993) at 158–159. See also, Raz (1986): Joseph Raz highlights two types of anti-perfectionism, the first being that of neutrality as is discussed here, and the other, the 'exclusion of ideals'; however, as Raz also notes, proponents of the two types rarely distinguish neutrality from the exclusion of ideals.

The commitment to neutrality is thus necessary for the widest possible array of the diverse views that will be held by individuals to be given a chance to influence public decision-making. The neutral state would thus be open not only to how individuals seek to live their own lives, but also to what they may urge the state to pursue as its goals.

Justice as discourse embraces the value of neutrality in providing the platform for broad public input and debate about how we should act in common and through the agency of the state. In so doing, it suggests that it is not necessary and indeed even counterproductive to broad public debate to limit the expression of religious ideas or values in public political discourse. In this, it does not accept the argument that there must be limits on religious expression *per se*, because of the potential for this type of expression to be confrontational, provocative or confusing. This is similar to the thinking that seems to have inspired Justice Brennan in the US context to say:

> That public debate of religious ideas, like any other, may arouse emotions, may incite, may foment religious divisiveness and strife does not rob it of constitutional protection. . . . The mere fact that a purpose of the Establishment Clause [part of the First Amendment of the U.S. Constitution] is to reduce or eliminate religious divisiveness or strife, does not place religious discussions, associations or political participation in a status less preferred than rights of discussion, association and political participation generally. . . . The State's goal of preventing sectarian bickering and strife may not be accomplished by regulating religious speech and political association. The Establishment Clause does not licence government to treat religion and those who teach or practice it, simply by virtue of their status as such, as subversive of American ideals and therefore subject to unique disabilities. . . . In short, government may not as a goal promote 'safe thinking' with respect to religion and fence out from political participation those . . . who it regards as over involved in religion. Religionists no less than members of any other group enjoy the full measure of protection afforded speech, association, and political activity generally.[8]

Justice as discourse puts its faith in the contestation of public debate to test and challenge all ideas, including those that have a religious element, without these needing to be self-censored or limited in advance when engaging in public discussions.[9] As Justice Brennan goes on to say about the US system:

> The antidote which the Constitution provides against zealots who would inject sectarianism into the political process is to subject their ideas to refutation in the market-place of ideas and their platforms to rejection at the polls.[10]

Classical liberal theory has been criticised as being excessively worried about, and therefore excessively exclusionary of, religious expression in public discourse, notwithstanding its principled commitment towards public neutrality. As Rawls' states:

8 *McDaniel* v. *Paty et al* 435 US 618 (1977) at 640–41; per Brennan J. concurring in judgment.

9 As Rawls says: "But the ideal of public reason does hold for citizens when they engage in political advocacy in the public forum, and thus for members of political parties and for candidates in their campaigns and for other groups who support them" (Rawls (1993) at 215). For further discussion of the implications of this point, see Bonotti (2015).

10 *McDaniel* v. *Paty et al* 435 US 618 (1977) at 642.

> [Religious] and philosophical doctrines express views of the world and our life with one another, severally and collectively, as a whole. Our individual and associative points of view, intellectual affinities, and affective attachments, are *too diverse*, especially in a free society, *to enable those doctrines to serve as a basis of lasting and reasoned political agreement.*[11]

Rawls gets around the impossibility of actual agreement by introducing the requirement for *reasonableness*, such that overlapping consensus may still be achieved on a reasonable political conception of justice. Any disagreements would, thus, be a result of unreasonableness.[12]

However, justice as discourse presses the case for neutrality specifically at this point. Within the concept of neutrality is both impartiality and inclusiveness. Indeed, it is impartiality which is conceived of here as the basis for inclusiveness, since if the state was indeed partial to some set of principles it would, *ipso facto*, be inclined to exclude other principles. At the same time, justice as discourse is not insisting on the impartiality of reasons to make them into 'good' public reasons in the manner that Rawls might insist upon. So, justice as discourse is especially concerned with neutrality towards the public expression of religious language, accepting that this language quite clearly contains the capacity to be itself partial and politically divisive, and to arouse strong emotions and reactions. That potential alone is not, however, good reason for restricting such language or for limiting the principle of neutrality. Justice as discourse is thus willing to allow religious expression to compete for public acceptance within a market place of ideas defined by a broad and expansive politics.

Limits

In order to maintain neutrality and to allow for the diversity of expression, liberal theory has posited that limits must be placed on the public role of religion. We have heretofore been considering limits on the expression of religious values or arguments in public discussions and debates, which represent one aspect of the limits.

The other aspect of limitation, however, is the reliance on particular religious arguments as matters of policy. Here, liberal theory is clear that no religious argument should *per se* be able to dictate matters of public policy. That is to say, it would be unacceptable for a conclusion or position coming from any religious tradition or pronouncement to be determinative, without any further debate or discussion, of a political issue. Moreover, if after debate, if such a view were to hold sway, it is important that it would not be justified or rationalised on the basis of its religious pedigree. To do so would be, firstly, to compromise the political neutrality of the state and, secondly, to thereby sacrifice the diversity of potential views about and options for state action.

As Andrew March warns, religious arguments must be subject to the following considerations:

> (1) [T]he fundamental moral attitude towards others expressed in our public speech, (2) the democratic legitimacy of public decisions, (3) the justice of public decisions,

11 Rawls (1993) at 58 (emphasis added).

12 Rawls (1993) at 488: Rawls raises one aspect of unreasonableness to be in believing that God's kingdom on earth demands that all political institutions be based on one particular religion. *Contra* Waldron (1999) at 149–164, on his critique of Rawls' and assertion that pursuing agreement is futile – disagreements about justice may be just as pervasive as those of faith and comprehensive doctrines. See also Christiano (2000) at 513–543; Estlund (2000) at 111–128.

(4) social solidarity, and (5) the ability of a democratic society to respond to collective problems. Whether an argument issued in public has a "religious" or "comprehensive" character is insufficient for evaluating its impact on these important political goods.[13]

Justice as discourse shares this concern and the insistence that no religious opinion should be determinative of public policy because of the state's prior commitment to a religious outlook. Thus, justice as discourse would require that a fine distinction be made between allowing religious expression and those expressions being decisive of an issue of public policy. In other words, justice as discourse, like standard liberal theory, insists upon an independent political ethic. As Charles Taylor points out, the traditional independent political ethic of the West was an ethic that was independent from religion. However, this need not be the case. An independent political ethic does not need to mean that religion is less relevant to public life, but rather only prevents the state from backing religion. Taylor suggests that this, in fact, was the original meaning of the First Amendment to the US constitution with its dual emphasis on non-establishment on the one hand and free exercise on the other.[14] It is this delicate ground, balancing being (potentially) influenced by religion on the one hand, while also not backing a particular religion on the other, which justice as discourse seeks to occupy.

Whereas the standard position drew the line of balance at the level of the expression of religious arguments in public political debate, justice as discourse draws it around the implementation of policy justified by religious convictions. It demands that the state not commit itself to adopt the views of a particular religious tradition as matters of policy. Next, we will discuss more specifically where this line must be drawn with respect not just to the state but also to civil society, law and politic debates more generally.

Justice as discourse and the secular

Secularism

As mentioned, justice as discourse necessarily implies an element of secularism. To understand the nature of this secularism, we must look at the history of the concept of the secular and its cognates.

For this purpose, we must again turn to developments in Europe. The term secular itself is has its roots in the Latin *seacualris* but came to be derived in Middle English from the Old French *seculer*.[15] Its sense in this context related to the 'worldly' or 'this worldly' things which were temporal and 'in the world' or 'in society', as opposed to being in purely spiritual or 'other worldly'.[16] Thus, *secular* was a term used to describe members of religious orders that went out of the monastic life to work in society. Hence, the phenomenon, without any colour of the oxymoronic or ironic, of 'secular priests' out in the world working with and ministering to the people versus others who would remain in their cloisters. A form

13 March (2013) at 524–525.

14 Taylor (1998) at 35.

15 See Keddie (2003) at 14.

16 See Taylor (2007) at 265; Taylor (1998) at 31. Taylor (2007) at 265 (also (1995) at 270) describes the 'temporal' secular as opposed to the 'spiritual' secular. In this vein, Casanova has pointed out that the words for 'century' in both Spanish (*siglo*) and French (*siècle*) are derived from the Latin root from which 'secular' also emerges and this evidences how this root is connected to profane time. See also Casanova (1994) at 15ff.

of the secular was thus born out of a religious tradition. In a similar vein, José Casanova notes that there existed what he calls a 'double dualist' classification in pre-modern Europe. On the one hand, we had a distinction between this world and the other world. But the worldly and temporal 'this world' was itself split between the religious and purely worldly – viz., the 'secular'.[17] The idea of the secular today is built around this heritage, even though it has transformed it.

In time, the 'this worldly-ness' of the idea of the secular asserted itself more robustly and distinguished itself more profoundly from the 'religious'. Taylor marks the advent of modern, Western secularism as developing particularly out of the Wars of Religion mentioned above, at which time it was sought to create a public domain that was regulated by norms independent of confessional allegiances.[18] This is the sense of what Taylor finds to exist in the modern social imaginary. Grotius's words, cited by Taylor, explain this imaginary in which "even if God did not exist, these norms would be binding on us".[19] An idea of the secular was critical to this Grotian understanding because it expressed the concept of the distinction between the temporal or worldly from the spiritual and religiously-grounded.

In light of that, Taylor asserts that a facet of the newness of the (modern) public sphere is its 'radical secularity'.[20] In this paradigm, common, social action takes place within a framework that does not need to be established in some 'action-transcendent' dimension – whether this is based on God, a great chain or laws from time immemorial. This, Taylor contends, is what makes the modern public sphere radically secular and this is what is new about it. As we can see, this early or emerging sense of the secular has political ramifications inasmuch as it grounds political life on a different basis.

It was not until the nineteenth century that the concept of the secular became adopted, and adapted, by those freethinkers who would call themselves 'secularists'.[21] In England in 1851, the terms secularist and secularism, in these senses, were employed by the atheist George Holyoake, who was looking for respectable (and probably more socially palatable) alternatives to 'atheist' or 'unbeliever' or 'freethinker', all of which would have been socially as well as politically pejorative.[22] The secularists were espousing a *normative* doctrine of secularism, which advocated that beliefs and values should not play a role in the political affairs of the nation-state.[23] In doing this, they were advocating something that was beyond the notion of the secular that we have seen above. The nineteenth-century secularists were engaged in a more comprehensive re-working of the relationship between personal morality and state law than was seen before, and of the medieval conception of a social body of Christians.[24] Yet the elements of this re-orientation do seem to have been echoed within the earlier sense of the secular in two ways. First, as we have noted, in the aftermath of the Wars of Religion, there emerged an acceptance of confessional difference without persecution (or at least not such repressive persecution) as a way to secure some social peace. Second, once the political order was decoupled from the divine order (because it was now possible to have different divine orders co-existing within one political order) – and, in this sense, became

17 Casanova (1994) at 15.
18 Taylor (2007) at 214. See also Taylor (1998) at 32.
19 Taylor (1998) at 34.
20 Taylor (1995) at 267.
21 Asad (2003) at 23–24.
22 See Royle (1974).
23 Keddie (2003) at 14–15.
24 Asad (2003) at 24.

secular – it became easier to push the argument a bit further and urge that confessional matters, and indeed matters of conscience, should be excluded from society's political life altogether. Indeed, if the secular move that occurred above was necessary and successful in making the political order safe for different Christian confessional communities, the emergence of those with different convictions, such as George Holyoake's atheism, would naturally want the socio-political order made safe for their points of view as well. The solution was to take matters of religion out of politics, so as to protect those that had no religion.

Notwithstanding the links that these moves had with the past, this concept of the secular was clearly different from the one described above in which the secular was linked to an aspect of the work of the Christian Church. And this is precisely because this normative secularism was making a 'non-religious' argument, namely staking out a political position in favour of purging matters of religious conscience from public discourse.[25] Indeed, in this conception we get the emerging sense of how in the West today we counterpoise religion and the secular as opposites.

Secularism, as a normative 'ism', was able to argue not just that there be a neutral public space, but indeed that religious conviction must retreat from this space all together. As Talal Asad puts it: "From the point of view of secularism, religion has the option of confining itself to private belief and worship or of engaging in public talk that makes no demands on life. . . . Either is equally the condition of legitimacy."[26]

The secularism demanded by justice as discourse does not, however, make such a strong claim. While it participates in the 'radical secularity' of the modern age by not grounding social action in some 'great chain of being' metaphor but rather seeing it as an activity in profane time and while it does insist on a neutral, in the sense of an *a priori* impartial, public space, it does not take the normative step of saying that religion must make no demands of public life. Furthermore, it insists upon action taken in the name of the state being justified independently of any religious reasoning and, as such, the secularism it rests on "requires citizens be emancipated from state and ecclesiastical diktat; they should be free to believe or to worship according to their conscience and ethical judgments".[27]

Secularisation

Closely allied to the concept of secularism has been the social process of secularisation. Casanova argues that secularisation has as its core a functional differentiation between 'secular spheres' – primarily the state, economy and science – from the religious sphere, and the specialisation of religion into its own sphere tending to the private needs of individuals.[28] This means that these spheres have become de-coupled from the control of religion or theology – that they proceed independently – while, on the other hand, religion assumes the role of ministering to citizens' 'spiritual', 'other worldly' needs. This differentiation is for the sake of neutrality between the state and all religions, or for defending every individual's "freedom of conscience", or for allowing democratic participation for all citizens, whether they are religious or non-religious.[29]

25 William Connolly has savaged this sort of claim referring to it as a secular conceit to provide a single, authoritative basis for public reason. See Connolly (1999) at 5.
26 Asad (2003) at 199.
27 Keane (1998).
28 Casanova (1994) at 19.
29 Casanova (2009) at 1051.

According to Casanova, two sub-theses flowed from this process: one was that this process would bring the progressive shrinkage and decline of religion – the 'religion in decline' thesis; the second was that secularisation would bring the privatisation and marginalisation of religion in the modern world – the 'privatisation thesis'. Casanova argues that both of these sub-theses have been proved wrong. In fact, his central claim is that religious traditions are refusing to accept marginalised and privatised roles which secularism (and here it must mean a normative secularism) has decreed for them, and are challenging the claims of social spheres (like the market) to be exempt from "extraneous" normative considerations.[30]

While religion (viz. religious traditions and those of religious conviction) is in these senses pushing back at its marginalisation and privatisation, the results of the process of secularisation in the form of functional social differentiation are evident. It is the case that over time there has been a differentiation between religious and political institutions, though of course this has manifested itself differently in different societies. Nonetheless, along the important social vectors that Casanova has mentioned – the state, the economy and science – we can see that religion is no longer in control as it once was. Science, for example, is no longer determined by the strictures of theology such that it is difficult (albeit in the 'Creationism' discourses taking place in the US today, not entirely impossible) to imagine a Galileo-like situation occurring now. Similarly, the market today is not controlled by the fiat of religious authorities. As Sami Zubaida has noted:

> The Reformation, followed by the Scientific Revolution and the Enlightenment represented departures from [a] state of religious ambiance. To simplify matters, it was the processes of capitalism and the rise of the modern state which led to institutional differentiation and specialization, with various organisations and functions splitting off from religion, the churches and their authority. Philosophy, law, medicine, government, education and, more recently, family and sexuality, split off from religious authorities and cognitions.[31]

Non-Western secularisation

Secularisation is not limited to European democracies. Abdou Filali-Ansary notes that while Muslim societies have not experienced secularisation *qua* differentiation as an internal or autonomous move because of external influences which either started the secularisation process or disrupted it (a matter on which, he says, historians disagree):

> [S]ecularisation is already a reality in the Muslim world. No Muslim society today is governed solely with reference to religious law; religious traditions no longer possess absolute or near-absolute predominance (except perhaps in some remote rural areas); and newly emerging leadership classes are almost everywhere displacing or marginalizing the clerisy of theologico-legal experts who used to control meaning and organisation in these societies.[32]

Suffice it to say that although some of the historical processes have been different, a functional social differentiation by way of a separation between religious and socio-political institutions is evident in Muslim contexts as well, albeit with a different historical trajectory.

30 Casanova (1994) at 5.
31 Zubaida (2005) at 442.
32 Filali-Ansary (1996) at 78.

Bhargava also notes that Western conceptions of political secularism had not travelled well to other societies.[33] Bhargava uses India as the basis of comparison, asserting that while Western secularism requires the exclusion of religion "for the sake of individualistically conceived moral or ethical values",[34] such a model does not accommodate the needs of societies like India that have deep religious diversity. Because India had been "born in a deeply multi-religious society", it is not averse to religion in public discourse, and does not therefore separate religion and the state.[35]

In Bhargava's conception of secularism in India, the state maintains secularity by maintaining a principled distance from all religious institutions for the sake of equality,[36] which flexibly allows for the inclusion or exclusion of religious and the engagement or disengagement of the state.[37] This, in turns, demands a contextualised secularism that perpetually requires "fresh interpretations, contextual judgements, and attempts at reconciliation and compromise" that results in reasonable satisfaction on all sides.[38]

Justice as discourse

Justice as discourse rests on this particular sense of the secular. It is a this-worldly secular but one that does not seek to expunge religious convictions from any public role. Taylor notes the 'radical secularity', which of the modern public sphere is much more than 'not religious', and states that indeed we could still engage in religion even if we live within this radical secularity.[39] The secular thus does not necessarily exclude principles, ideas or policies that might be derived from religious convictions from public life, nor of course does it insist that they should be there. The secular, in fact, is agnostic both about the truth of religious convictions and about their public policy-influencing and law-influencing role. Jeffrey Stout reinforces this point when he notes that a secularised ethical discourse is not necessarily a commitment to secularism (as a normative position), because it entails neither the denial of theological assumptions nor the expulsion of theological expression from the public sphere. Believers might still see the political order as ultimately under divine judgement, though of course others may not. But, Stout asserts, this means only that theocracy is over, not that the Antichrist has taken over the political sphere.[40] Thus, it is inaccurate to see the secular as simply 'anti-religious'. What the secular does demand, however, is some guarantee of a continual this-worldly focus, and this will have political and, thereby, legal implications.

Waldron seeks to make clear the distinction between appealing to religion as *theoretical* rather than *practical* authority in secular public discourse. Appealing to religion as practical authority imposes religious duties and norms on society, striving towards a theocracy; but on the other hand, appealing to religion as theoretical authority qualifies expertise provided through religion. While the secular ought to deny religious interventions insofar as exerting it as practical authority, Waldron asserts that "there is nothing implicitly theocratic about drawing on theoretical authority" since religion can aid as an intellectual guide for resolving such moral and political issues.[41]

33 Bhargava (2011) at 11.
34 Bhargava (2011) at 12.
35 Bhargava (2011) at 15.
36 Bhargava (2011) at 16.
37 Bhargava (2011) at 17.
38 Bhargava (2011) at 19.
39 Taylor (2007) at 192. See also Taylor (1995) at 270, n15.
40 Stout (2004) at 93. Stout further notes that a religiously plural democratic culture no more shares atheistic commitments than it does religious ones.
41 Waldron (2012) at 8–9.

Therefore, a secular law and politics will have to be one that stands apart from (though not necessarily hostile to) any particular set of religious beliefs. This end seems clearly to require the following: (i) the state should be neutral towards the religious beliefs of its citizens and should treat citizens equally, regardless of their religious beliefs (or lack thereof); (ii) the state should protect freedom of religion and conscience; and (iii) governmental and public institutions should be autonomous from the direct control of any religious authority. These requirements may, however, be achieved in different ways, and indeed they are not incompatible with a certain embrace of religion, drawing upon religion as theoretical authority.

In his study of a 'struggle for Islamic democracy', Noah Feldman notes that, for example, the lack of formal separation between church and state in the UK, and the fact that most schools in Bavaria are Catholic, does not preclude our considering the UK or Germany to be meeting the tests of a secular, liberal democracy.[42] Feldman recognises that liberal democracy requires that governments should be neutral about what matters most to citizens, leaving these decisions up to individuals. As part and parcel of this, it is further necessary to respect the individual's right to worship and to provide religious liberty for citizens. Nonetheless, he notes:

> But so long as the government does not force anyone to adopt religious beliefs that he or she rejects, or perform religious actions that are anathema, it has not violated the basic right to religious liberty. Separation of church and state may be very helpful in maintaining religious liberty, as it is in the U.S., but it is not always necessary for it.[43]

Amartya Sen, who describes himself as an unreformed secularist, applies a similar line of thinking to state support and funding for 'religious' institutions. Sen points out that a separation of the state from a particular religious order, and thus the independence of the state from religious authority, does not mean that the state must steer clear from dealing with religion of religious communities altogether. Rather, what is required is simply that the must treat religious communities *symmetrically*.[44] If the state is to support religious communities, it must support them all in the same way, or it may support none of them in any way.[45]

A secular framework, therefore, does not have to mean a 'laïc' model à la France or (inspired by France) Turkey, in which a sharp division is made between public life and religious belief, and strong divisions are applied to keep religious belief away from the state, the law and political debate.[46] It is not incompatible with a formal, legal separation of church

42 Feldman (2003) at 60.

43 Feldman (2003) at 61. See also Connolly, who notes that to adhere to the separation of church and state is not necessarily to concur in those conceptions of public life bound up with secularism. Connolly (2000) at 5.

44 Sen (1998) 482 at 456–457.

45 In fairness to Sen, he seems also to be in favour of a politics in which religion plays no part as well, but he does say this is not a requirement of an independent state.

46 See, for example, Article 2 of the Turkish Constitution which makes secularism a constitutional principle by stating:

> The Republic of Turkey is a democratic, secular and social State governed by the rule of law; bearing in mind the concepts of public peace, national solidarity and justice; respecting human rights; loyal to the nationalism of Atatürk, and based on the fundamental tenets set forth in the Preamble.

Contemporary politics in Turkey may be changing this model, but Article 2 is, at present, still part of the constitution.

and state, though it does not compel it.[47] It does not prohibit state support for religious organisations or interests, so long as this is provided symmetrically, nor does it require it. This aligns with the observation that Taylor has made that today secularism may be misconceived. It is not, he contends, about the relationship of state and religion, but rather about the "(correct) response of the democratic state to diversity."[48]

Most importantly, such an understanding of the secular shows that it is possible and consistent to meet both the requirements of the secular as well as leaving open the possibility for those of religious beliefs to participate meaningfully in public discourse and the shaping of public policy and law. In this, it puts paid to the assertion that there cannot be, to borrow a phrase, 'the dance of the secular and the religious'.[49]

We can now state in summary the requirements that the version of liberal theory we are labelling 'justice as discourse' will demand. In order to allow the expression of the full range of diversity, justice as discourse, in distinction from and arising out of the critiques of the classical liberal theory, seeks to allow an enhanced role for the expression of religious arguments in the public political discourse. Doing so, however, raises the risk that some religious views will effectively overrule other religious views or views which have no religious grounding. To prevent the plurality limiting consequences of this possibility and to preserve individual freedom of conscience, justice as discourse insists on a neutral state. This, in turn, means that there must be appropriate limits on the public role of religion to preserve this neutrality. These limits are to be found not in needing to limit religious expression but in needing to limit how any such expressions are made into public policy. In taking this view, justice as discourse posits a more expansive space for religious values and ideas than does classical liberal theory. The need for limits, however, necessarily also requires a secular state – but it is secular in the way of being agnostic as to religious (and indeed non-religious) arguments, not hostile to them, an understanding that still allows a substantial role for religious views and arguments.[50]

The key now is to define where lines need to be drawn to preserve this important secular character, which is itself an expression of the neutrality that liberal theory insists upon, in order to guarantee that the full diversity of individual views may be expressed.

This exercise compels us to consider the application of justice as discourse within a political order. In so doing, we are able to elaborate what justice and discourse demands as a matter of implementation and institutional form (taking account of the requirements we have just been discussing) and thereby to enrich our understanding of the theoretical framework elaborated in the previous chapter.

Implementing justice as discourse: the axes of state, law, civil society and politics

Executive, bureaucratic and judicial authorities

We have already stated that justice as discourse requires the state to be neutral and, *ipso facto*, secular in the manner described above. What does this requirement mean in implementation?

47 We may discover that a formal separation is, however, not only convenient but also a better fit for denomination neutrality. This will be addressed in a subsequent section of this study.

48 Taylor (2011) at 36.

49 I borrow the phrase from Sajoo (2004).

50 See Lægaard (2008), which discusses Tariq Modood's idea of 'moderate secularism' that is related to the point made here. See also Modood (2008) available at: www.opendemocracy.net/article/faith_ideas/europe_islam/anti_sharia_storm

Theories of the state abound and conflict. Thus, as Bob Jessop has noted, the innocuous-looking question 'What is the state?' gives rise to conceptual chaos.[51] Perhaps the most prominent theory is that of Max Weber, who defined the state as follows:

> The primary formal characteristics of the modern state are as follows: it possesses an administrative and legal order subject to change by legislation, to which the organised activities of the administrative staff, which are also controlled by regulations, are oriented. This system of order claims binding authority, not only over members of the state, the citizens, most of whom have obtained membership by birth, but also to a very large extent over all action taking place in the area of its jurisdiction. It is thus a compulsory organization with a territorial basis. Furthermore, today, the use of force is regarded as legitimate only in so far as it is either permitted by the state or prescribed by it . . . the claim of the modern state to monopolize the use of force is as essential to it as its character of compulsory jurisdiction and continuous operation.[52]

Weber's definition is suggestive of a number of key characteristics of the state: a centralised and bureaucratically organised administrative and legal order; binding authority over what occurs in its area of jurisdiction; a territorial basis; and a monopoly on the (legitimate) use of force.[53] All understandings of the state, therefore, emphasise that the state exercises power. The essential Weberian insight is that this power is exercised through an organised, bureaucratic order and, thus, that it acts as binding (even if it not the sole source of social power).

Justice as discourse is concerned with no pre-set commitments, religious or otherwise, being adopted as determinative of matters of public policy. This limit would apply particularly to those acting for the state through its organised capacities, especially in executive or judicial roles. That is to say, that no minister, judge, civil servant or other official who has the capacity to set or influence public policy should be allowed to have her or his decision about

51 Jessop (2006) at 111.

52 Weber (1978) at 56. The Weberian definition has been challenged by a range of different conceptions of the state. While Marx and Friedrich Engels developed no coherent theory of state themselves, they portrayed the state as reflecting underlying economic structures and interests, conceiving of the state as an instrument of the ruling class and a repressive arm of the bourgeoisie (Hay (2006) at 60–62; see also Jessop (2006) at 116). This Marxist perspective has influenced other state theorists of a broadly Marxist orientation. Hence, Antonio Gramsci defines the state as 'political and civil society' and sees the state as hegemony armoured by coercion, and Nicholas Poulatzas views the state as a social relation biased by virtue of its structural and strategic selectivity (Jessop (2006) at 113.) Taking a slightly different tack, Foucauldian approaches have undermined the authority of the state by emphasising multiple sites of power – beyond just the state – with the state as the site of government rationality ("governmentality") but within a complex in which power is ubiquitous (Jessop, 2006 at 120). Feminist perspectives, which themselves range widely, also do not present one coherent state theory, but they challenge two important aspects of the Weberian framework. First, they challenge the understanding of the state as the only vehicle of permitted violence, noting in particular that violence perpetrated by men on women is often allowed to happen *de facto* if not *de jure*. Second, feminist analyses challenge and critique the type of public/private distinction made by traditional state theory. The private is conceptualised as the domestic or family sphere, as opposed to the public realm of the state and civil society (the latter, therefore, not as private). On this analysis, women's preponderant role in the private sphere is held functionally to exclude them from equal participation in public sphere (Jessop, 2006 at 121–122). Finally, we can consider the discourse analysis and strategic relational approaches to the state. Discourse analysis suggests that the state does not exist in and of itself, but rather is an illusory product of political imaginaries and narrative and rhetorical practices. The strategic-relational approach notes that state power is a contingent product of the changing balance of political forces within and beyond the state, conditioned by the institutional structures of the state (Jessop, 2006 at 123 and 124).

53 Gill (2003) at 2ff.

this policy set by any pre-existing religious commitments that they may have personally, nor should they be allowed to justify any public policy they adopt by reference only to their own (or any other) religious views. In the case of the political executive and civil service, their direct role in determining and implementing policy makes clear the limits that are being placed on them. Judges might appear a different category because they are at some remove from the political executive. The same restriction must apply to judges, however, because of their legal authority (which can commit the state) and their normative power. This is not to say that these officials may not consider perspectives or arguments coming from religious traditions when contemplating matters of public policy, but it does mean that the reason for adopting any specific policy cannot be justified exclusively on that policy being either required by, or supported solely on the basis of, a religious value. Officials exercising executive or judicial authority will, therefore, have to have other reasons – independent from any religious basis – to justify their decisions. Even if their decisions should result in similar policy prescriptions as (a particular) religious tradition or outlook would lead, their reasons may not be derived from the religious views. A judge could not, therefore, justify her decision in a case solely based on her personal religious views, nor on a reason coming from any religious tradition. She will have to find and use reasoning that does not have a religious basis, though she may cite, if she wishes, parallel religious values that would accord with her judgment. Similarly, no minister or civil servant could make a policy decision or pronouncement based on her personal religious views, or other religious views, and would have to be able to provide independent and freestanding reasons justifying her chosen policy. The strongest and sharpest line must thus be drawn between the state as represented by those exercising executive or judicial authority in its name and religious values.

Legislative provisions

Aside from the above-noted constraints on the way in which judges provide reasoning for their decisions, justice as discourse would also require that positive law legislative provisions do not invoke any religious grounds for the rules or requirements that they stipulate. This would mean two things: firstly, that no legislative provisions should reference, cite or otherwise invoke any religious doctrine as the basis for the provisions, and secondly, that no overarching or omnibus legislative provisions should be based on a religious grounding. Thus, for example, declaring the nature of the state to be associated with a particular religious outlook would not be acceptable since this would *prima facie* indicate that that state is not neutral and therefore not fully open to diverse religious as well as non-religious views of its citizens. Another strict and hard line must therefore be drawn around any explicitly religious basis for legislative provisions. As an example, a statutory provision that stated that divorces could be granted 'according to the provisions of Islamic law' and would, therefore, necessitate that judges find what these provisions are would fall afoul of justice as discourse. That said, justice as discourse is willing to allow religious values to influence the formulation of legal rules through more discursive and political processes so long as the justification for any legislative requirements is not made on the basis of religious doctrine or prescription.

Civil society: community organisations, NGOs

Invoking the concept of 'civil society' is also to introduce a term – like the term 'state' – whose definition is contested. José Harris suggests four models of 'civil society'.[54] Model 1

54 Harris (2006).

posits that civil society is virtually coterminous with government, law enforcement and the state. Model 2 views civil society as consisting of private property rights, commercial capitalism and the legal, institutional and cultural systems which support these. In this sense, civil society captures sites of economic and social power held in private hands rather than in the hands of the state as representing the public. On Model 3, 'civil society' consists of that set or range of voluntaristic no-profit-making civic and mutual help movements that coexist with but have a different ethos from either the state (Model 1) or the market (Model 2); this understanding locates civil society as akin to what Alexandre de Tocqueville called 'civil associations' in his *Democracy in America*. Finally, on Model 4, 'civil society' means universal standards of democracy, fair procedure, rule of law and human rights, conceived of as the basis of 'civilised society'. As Harris notes, the term 'civil society' has radically changed its meaning over the course of the two thousand years since the idea emerged in Ancient Rome, such that "[the term] remains curiously obtuse, malleable and [a] much contested idea, difficult to define categorically by reference to either *what it is* or *what it is not*".[55] Notwithstanding this conceptual challenge, contemporary discourses have by and large employed 'civil society' in the sense of Model 3, to designate those forms of social organisation that are not under direct governmental control and administration (though they may receive governmental funding).

Adopting this sense of 'civil society', justice as discourse would not constrain any non-governmental organisations, whether these be more informal community-based groups or large and more-formalised NGOs, from adhering to, asserting publicly or advocating politically from the basis of religious values. This would include lobbying of political representatives and the expression in publications or through other fora of positions and ideas that may be grounded in religious beliefs. This is near to saying that no constraining line must be drawn around civil society organisations, but this may not exactly be the case. In the provision of services or in rights to participate in activities, religious-orientated civil society organisations may exclude those who do not share their religious outlooks. While there would be no problem if, for example, non-adherents were excluded from a religious service, there may be cases where non-governmental, religious organisations take on functions that are supported or regulated by the state and in which, therefore, any religiously exclusionary behaviour could be problematic. Faith-based schools are perhaps the most obvious example. It is difficult to theorise in the abstract about what constraints may have to be imposed on civil society organisations in cases where they engage in activities in which the state has an interest, but in such circumstances it may be necessary to constrain religiously exclusionary behaviour, in the name of preserving the secular, in the sense of neutral, character of the state. For faith-based schools, this would probably mean a commitment to either fund all such schools in some equitable manner or not to fund any of them, and it may require admissions regulations if there is funding. Such a constraint, however, would be a much weaker and tentative line than would be imposed on the state's executive or judicial officials or on a religious basis for legislation. Moreover, the constraint would be minimal: it would only go so far as necessary to preserve the neutral and secular character of the state; any advocacy or other activity by the civil society groups would be unconstrained.

Political reasons

The most substantial difference between justice as discourse and Rawls' political liberalism comes in the role that religious outlooks may play in the broad zone of discursive politics and

55 Harris (2006) at 140 (emphasis in original).

general political debate. Political liberalism, even with Rawls' proviso, insists on constraining religious (and other) comprehensive doctrines in public political debate in order that all reasons in such debate are grounded in what Rawls called "proper political reasons",[56] namely reasons that are not given solely on the basis of comprehensive doctrines, including religion.

In common with the critiques of this position discussed in the preceding chapter, justice as discourse would remove the constraint of providing 'proper political reasons' and allow citizens individually as well as collectively to publicly express and advocate in religious terms and on the basis of religious reasoning. In this, justice as discourse also goes beyond even Habermas' alternative to Rawls, precisely because it removes the translation requirement Habermas would impose and allows religious reasons to be expressed in legislative deliberations.

The political arena is thus conceived of as a zone of public discourse but private opinion. That is to say, whether individually or in a collective, when citizens engage in political discourse at this level they would have to do so as private citizens, expressing private views – not the views of the state or government. This zone of politics would, however, include formal political parties and other political lobbying structures and may even see these organisations receive public funding or public support for their funding (in facilitative tax treatment, for example). To ensure equality, justice as discourse would insist that if any such support is given, it must be provided on a symmetrical basis to all organisations of the type – i.e., to all political parties (though there may be requirements that such parties should have a certain number of legislative seats or percentage of the vote, etc.). The receipt of public support, however, would not compromise the view that these organisations would be expressing private views. Thus, both Political Party A and Political Party B may get funding from the public treasury without this funding meaning that the views of either party are views of the state; each would understand themselves as expressing a private (though in the case of parties, not individual) set of political ideas. Justice as discourse would allow, though not compel, public support for political expression.

Within the zone of politics thus posited would also be included more informal political expression. The publication of pamphlets or newspapers, the holding of debates, the distribution of policy papers, the submission of 'letters to the editor', and other such political expressions. In all of these sorts of activities, justice as discourse would allow those with religious convictions to express these convictions as such and to advocate for public policy to reflect their particular concerns and to subject these views, as Justice Brennan said, to public scrutiny and to support at the ballot box. This is, therefore, the area where there would be no constraints but for the above-noted requirement that if public support from the state is provided for such organisations, it must be provided symmetrically.

Conclusion

Justice as discourse seeks to retain the strengths of the liberal outlook and, in particular, liberal theory's desire to allow for broad expression of different viewpoints. At the same time, it is also an attempt to develop a conceptual framework that will overcome some critiques that have been directed at classical liberal theory, particularly in the restrictions that this theory imposes on the expression of views in public political debate that are based upon or inspired by religious convictions. To this end, the goal of the framework is to develop a broader public space that is more receptive to a diversity of viewpoints, including, and *particularly*, those that may have religious groundings.

56 Rawls (1997) at 783ff.

In this chapter, we have noted that achieving this goal necessarily implies a public space that is secular but, in so being, not one that is hostile to religious sentiments. This raises a tension. How might arguments and opinions coming out of religious commitments play a legitimate role when we come to debate matters of public importance on the one hand, while we still maintain the particular, and necessary, element of secularity on the other? The answer proposed herein lies in articulating boundaries that will both allow diversity to be expressed as well as secure the necessary element of secularity.

We have further noted that these boundaries have to be drawn in relation to the sites of power and authority that could limit expressions of diversity. It is thus that the bureaucratic and institutional capacities of the state, as reflected in its executive, administrative and judicial officials, must be restrained from using their powers either to advance or to hamper any particular religious view(s). This means further that no reliance can be made on such views in the exercise of state offices, whether in an executive policy-making, or administrative or judicial reasoning capacity. Necessarily, these restrictions will have to be ensured by the courts. For this, courts will need to be empowered with guarantees of freedom of thought, conscience and belief, freedom of expression and freedom of association the defence of which would then enable them to constrain authority as and when necessary. Equally, such provisions should be the limit for securing the agnostic secular space that justice as discourse would demand. Any more robust assertions of secularism should be avoided as prejudicial to the expression of religious viewpoints and, hence, of the full gamut of political diversity.

Such a schema both recognises and embraces the fact that restricting the organised state does not mean that these institutions will be immune from the influence of religious convictions. As alternatives to the Weberian conception of the state have indicated, the formal structures of the state are not the only site of social power. Justice as discourse is, however, committed to allowing the state to be influenced by diverse views and by other sites of social power; to allow these ideas, even to seek to, as Talal Asad has put it, "reform the life ambition of the secular state itself".[57] Thus, outside of the institutions of the Weberian state, justice as discourse proposes that religious convictions should be given a wide zone to operate within the sphere of civil society and in relation to discursive politics undertaken in informal ways. Critically, this would be permissive of the expression of religious reasoning as a legitimate variety of political reasoning.

Finally, it is important to recognise that the requirements of justice as discourse in terms of implementation offer a set of political principles as boundaries or limits for the political order. Consistent with classical liberal theory, these would obviously be compatible with different types of the political institutions, i.e., uni- or bi-cameral legislatures; constitutional monarchies or republics; Common, Civil or other types of law regimes, etc. Thus, Rawls discussed his political liberalism as applying only to the level of 'constitutional essentials' (though he was less clear about what these were)[58] beyond which political liberalism did

57 Asad (2003) at 199.

58 It is interesting to speculate on why Rawls leaves 'constitutional essentials' somewhat vaguely defined. Perhaps he thought where this line was drawn would rightly be itself a matter of debate and contestation that courts should settle. As he says in footnote 7 of "The Idea of Public Reason Revisited" (Rawls (1997) at 767):

> Constitutional essentials concern questions about what political rights and liberties, say, may reasonably be included in a written constitution, when assuming the constitution may be interpreted by a supreme court, or some similar body.

This defines but in a rather loose way. Alternatively, maybe this is just an area of Rawls' theory that we have to accept as needing elaboration, though sadly, now, we cannot press Rawls to be clearer.

not really have anything to say. Justice as discourse applies more widely. Mainstream liberal regimes, whether of the Rawlsian variety or otherwise, can and do exist in a variety of institutional forms and thus we can think of, for example, the United States, the UK, France, Canada, etc., as all being 'liberal' even though they have different institutional forms. The same would apply for justice as discourse; it, too, can consistently exist with a variety of institutional arrangements.

The delicate balancing act between being influenced but not committed, being open but not beholden, that justice as discourse proposes rests on walking a fine line. However, the only way it seems possible to allow the widest and most expansive variety of political outlooks – including especially those that may arise from religious convictions – to speak to our political decisions and choices, is to establish a line that is strong enough to keep the coercive power latent in the state uncommitted to any political (and religious) outlook, while also porous enough to be challenged by such outlooks through other locations of discourse and of social power, whether these be located in elements of 'civil society' or the articulation of 'proper' political reasoning. Justice as discourse thus attempts to modify the requirements of classical liberal theory enough, but only just enough, to allow this theory to achieve the aim which it always set for itself: that is, to allow the widest possible range of conceptions of the good to be posited and to compete for societal acceptance.[59] It is the contention of justice as discourse that for this to be realised religious sentiments must be allowed to be expressed more freely than they are under the restrictions of classical liberal theory, and additionally that they should be allowed to express themselves on their own terms and in their own languages. Moreover, it will be argued later that this new balancing is especially appropriate for Muslim contexts where the relationship between religion, politics and law has been shaped by a particular dynamic and which are today in need of a way of drawing lines to embrace the interplay of these forces in a manner that is appropriate to the legacies of their histories.

59 Of course, a feminist, for example, might say that inherent or pre-existing allocations of power mean that free and fair competition can never happen. More generally, it might be argued that there will always be dominant groups in any society who will be able to use 'neutral' principles to maintain their dominance.

3 Muslim contexts I

History and heritage

It is better to trust in the Lord than to put confidence in princes.[1]

We have thus far considered the role of religion in public political discussions in terms of normative political theory and the issue of the relationship of the 'secular' and the 'religious' and their political implications, which was developed out of 'Western' contexts and was indeed applicable to them. Given that this work is addressed to environments where Islam is a majority religious tradition – what I call 'Muslim contexts' – at certain points in the discussion reference was also made to the particularities of these contexts or to implications that may be distinctive to these environments. We are now at a point where it is important to unpack more fully the special characteristics and structures of Muslim contexts. Of course, this chapter (indeed, no chapter) can never hope to cover everything that one could gather under the heading of 'Muslim contexts' in a comprehensive way. What this chapter does want to address, however, is that particular part of the heritage of, and thought coming from, Muslim contexts that is relevant to the issues with which we are concerned, namely issues of political and legal order and structure. Another general aim of this chapter is to reinforce the relevance of the issues discussed earlier to Muslim contexts by demonstrating their significance both to concerns of the past and present of these contexts. Lastly, but by no means least, the final general aim of this chapter is to provide the basis for 'connecting the dots' between the above-noted general issues that this study is concerned with and the unique context in which, and for which, it seeks to address them. This chapter and the next draw upon studies done by historians and present from these an interpretive account of what the relevant history of Muslim contexts tells us about the interactions of power, religion and the law. In this way, this chapter will make it possible to marry the generic discussion to a specific milieu and thereby construct an analytical as well as normative framework – a task that will also be addressed in the following chapter.

Accordingly, this chapter will begin by examining the idea of 'Muslim contexts'. We will explore both what unites these contexts as well as the diversity that exists within them. Second, we will consider how in the history of Muslim societies religion, politics and law have been related both in theory and in practice. From this we will see that while not always accepted in theory, in actual practice, religious and political authority have occupied different places for most of the history of Muslim contexts. This means that Muslim contexts have indeed experienced secularisation in the sense of the functional social differentiation

1 Holy Bible (King James version), Psalm 118:10.

discussed earlier and that this has had, and continues to have, substantial political and legal implications, especially with the emergence of the nation-state. Moreover, in what will follow this chapter, we will see that there is substantial support within contemporary Muslim contexts for democratic structures which still leave open a place for religious sentiments. This chapter thus makes the independent, though perhaps somewhat implicit, claim that much of the liberal theory and liberal framework we have seen previously has relevance to the Muslim milieu we will discuss herein.

Why use the term 'Muslim contexts'?

I use the expression *Muslim contexts* both deliberately and advisedly, with each part of the expression seeking to elicit a particular meaning. The latter part of the term is perhaps easier to understand. The societies in which Muslims live exhibit a great deal of diversity. That this should be so is hardly surprising. Countries of Muslim majority are first of all spread over an enormously large area, stretching from, essentially, Morocco, across North and West Africa to Central and West Asia, into South Asia and down and east across the vast expanse of the Indonesia archipelago. In addition, of course, there are significant Muslim minority populations in India, China, and, of more recent settlement, in Western Europe and North America. The geography of Muslim presence alone is, therefore, enormous. Add to this geography more than 1400 years of a rich history[2] and total numbers consisting of about one billion people, approximately one-sixth of the world's population, and the range of experiences and conditions that inform and shape Muslims is tremendous. Indeed, that Muslim societies should be a monolith considering these factors would be a shock. As Carl Ernst says:

> Muslims are the majority population in more than fifty countries that vary widely in language, ethnic composition, natural resources and level of technology, and they form significant minorities in many other countries. Why, then, should it be so natural for non-Muslims to assume that all Muslims are and act the same, regardless of the conditions in which they live? Is it conceivable that all Muslims are identical, and that they have no location in time and space?[3]

Indeed, Norman Calder addresses a similar point:

> There are probably hundreds of Muslim creeds . . . written out by different scholars. The significant creeds are those that emerge within a discursive tradition through an informal, consensual acknowledge of value that is quite different from the formal procedures of the Roman Catholic hierarchy.[4]

Neither is the plurality of the Muslim world new. It has existed since centuries as Islam spread to different parts of the world where it encountered different cultures and traditions.[5] For example, as Clifford Geertz notes in his study of Morocco and Indonesia:

2 The Muslim calendar dates from the *hijra*, that is, Muhammad's pilgrimage from the city of Medina to Mecca, which took place in 622 of the Common Era (CE).

3 Ernst (2003) at 12.

4 Norman Calder (2010) at 161.

5 Wael Hallaq has noted, for example, the 'ubiquitous plurality' of early Muslim legal thinking up to the tenth century CE, albeit a plurality that became somewhat more circumscribed, but not eliminated, in later history. See Hallaq (2001) at 61.

> to say that Morocco and Indonesia are both Islamic societies, in the sense that everyone in them (well over nine-tenths of the population in either case) professes to be a Muslim, is as much to point to their differences as it is to locate their similarities. Religious faith, even when it is fed from a common source, is as much a particularizing force as a generalizing one . . .[6]

What Geertz and Ernst help us to realise is that Muslim contexts are characterised both by different interpretations of faith as well as by different influences coming from the local situation.[7]

If the fact of diversity is not new,[8] what is more recent is the (greater) recognition of this plurality. As Riaz Hasan has noted globalisation – presumably through the means of vastly improved modes of communication and travel – is showing Muslims the diversity in Islam and allowing them to experience the reality of different Islamic cultures.[9] We can thus see that there is not a singular 'Islamic' response or answer or position, but rather that it is better to speak of the responses (answers, positions) of Muslims. And of course, we are not dealing in all Muslim contexts with just Muslims. Muslim contexts encounter both intra- as well as inter-religious diversity.[10] Indeed, on this point, it is important to remember that Islam, because it emerged historically after Judaism and Christianity, self-consciously sees itself as part of a message that explicitly *includes* its Abrahamic cousins.[11] The Qur'anic text has numerous references both to the biblical prophets as well as their messages, and confirms these as coming from the same source; hence the concept of the *ahl al-kitab* (Peoples of the Book).

In the face of this diversity there are, of course, two options: one is to try to ignore it or eliminate it, the other is to embrace it and, perhaps, draw strength from it. While the latter is

6 Geertz (1971) at 13–14.

7 In the perpetual debate between Islam and modernity, Kristine Kalanges points out the relationship between *shari'a* and modern constitutionalism and that between Islam and democracy. She proceeds to note that the diversity of views on issues such as human rights represented indicates the weakness of monolithic accounts of the debate over Islam and democracy and is compounded by "differences in religious, ethnic and national identities of Muslims, and by complex political and economic histories of Muslim states, as well as the need to differentiate between electoral democracy (for example) and genuine constitutional liberalism" (Kalanges [2014] at 278). Also see, Kalanges (2012).

8 The sheer, profound diversity of Islamic thought is underscored by Gerhard Bowering when he notes that "Pan-Islamism has remained a distant dream, secularism severed the bonds of a long and venerable Islamic heritage while fundamentalist movements forced Islam into a puritanical straightjacket and militancy brought murder and destruction". In this regard, "Islam has not created a comprehensive system of political thought able to integrate the disparate elements informing its current stage of development". Emerging currents in political Islam are attempting to articulate ideologies and organise movements that aspire to inner purity, ethical strength, personal freedom and collective dignity. Burdened with political and cultural fragmentation and labeled by the West as a violent religion, "Islam thirsts for a new paradigm of political thought that will enable it to construct its future as a peaceful order in a pluralistic world" (Gerhard (2015) at 23).

9 Hasan (2002) at 243.

10 Kalanges herself reiterates the general notion that there no singular, monolithic definition of experience of the treatment of *shari'a* and modernity. She notes that while the secularization thesis seems to have some traction in Europe, elsewhere '"it was generated counter-secularization movements and a greater role for religious institutions in public policies and culture". This is especially pronounced in Muslim societies, where the relationship of Islam and modernity has been contested (Kalanges [2014]).

11 The Qur'an makes several references to earlier scriptures and to earlier prophets, including Jesus (Isa), David (Daud), Moses (Musa), Noah (Nuh) and Abraham (Ibrahim), and says that it confirms these scriptures. The Qur'an further says that it is the final revelation in this line. See Qur'an 3:03; 3.48, 3:50, 4:163, 5:44, 5:46, 5:110, 61:06.

not easy to do, the first seems to be an obscurantist exercise in futility. Thus, it is important to talk about context*s* (in the plural) versus a context, thereby keeping in mind the locations in time and space and the diversity that this will, inevitably, engender.

This diversity is additionally significant because it belies any attempts, whether by academics, journalist or other observers of Muslims, or indeed of Muslims themselves, to speak as if what they observe or what they say represents the view of 'Islam'. Thus, Ernst further notes that:

> Although it is common to hear people say, for example, "Christianity says that . . ." or "according to Islam . . .," the only thing that can be observed is that individual people who call themselves Christians or Muslims have particular positions and practices that they observe and defend. No one, however, has ever has ever seen Christianity or Islam do anything. They are abstractions, not actors comparable to human beings.[12]

Of course, in certain cases, there are religious authorities and bodies that can speak for certain communities. Christianity may not be able to say "x" or "y", but the Roman Catholic Church, for example, can. In the case of Islam, however, Ernst's observation is even more poignant because there has never been a church structure or a clerical organisation or hierarchy with the same authority as in the case of the Christian churches, or in certain other religious traditions. Indeed, while there may not be the position of 'Christianity', there have been and continue to be the positions of the recognised, corporate, Christian churches. The same, however, cannot be said of an 'Islamic' position, since there have never been institutions which have been able to speak with the same level of authority in the name of the faith. The 'clerics' of Islam, various styled as imams, maulvis, shaykhs, mullahs, etc. – with perhaps the only notable exception being the Imam in Shia Islam – have been recognised as clerics in this sense by others in the community. Occasionally, as we will see in more detail below, governments have sought to validate and appoint people to clerical office, but this has not really given these people normative clerical authority (even if it gave them administrative authority). Thus, to the first term of the phrase, I use the word 'Muslim', rather than 'Islamic' to avoid the sense of speaking in a religiously normative way, and to emphasise that the contexts that I am speaking about are contexts composed of the views of Muslims rather than of 'Islam', as if it were some entity that can be understood outside of the expressions of Muslims.[13]

12 Ernst (2003) at 51. See also in the same spirit Panjwani (2005).

13 It is in this sense that I have some discomfort with titles such as that of Hamid Hadji Haidar's *Liberalism and Islam: practical reconciliation between the liberal state and Shiite Muslims* (Haidar, 2008). My concern arises from how one defines the parameters of 'Islam' or even the views of 'Shiite Muslims'. In his text, Haidar has to confront this point and states the following:

> It should be noted that by Shiite Islam this book refers to the theory that justifies the Islamic Republic of Iran in its ideal form. There are, however, many basic principles and values that are characteristic to all Twelver [i.e., the majority Shiite community] Shiite Muslims throughout the world. Yet, in controversial and sensitive cases, this book constructs its arguments largely on views and ideas developed by Imam [i.e., Ayatollah] Khomeni (1902–1989). . . . In addition, in many cases a reference will be made to the views and ideas developed by Muhammad Hussein Tabatabai (1903–1981).

Haidar's work thus appears as an evaluation of the practical reconciliation of liberalism (he uses JS Mill and John Rawls as his liberal theorists) and the theory of the Islamic Republic of Iran as expressed by Khomeni and, secondarily, Tabatabi. This is both more focused and more limited in scope than the title of his work at first reading suggests and his conclusions must be understood in this more specific frame.

The diversity just described is even more significant because it means that there will, of course, be multiple positions, interpretations and understandings that Muslims will hold on what Islam demands and what they would wish to see occur in the societies in which they live. In short, that there will be the 'irreducible fact of pluralism' both within and across Muslim contexts that is constant and enduring.

What is the same, and what is different, about Muslim contexts?

One might be tempted to ask if Muslim contexts can be, and are, so diverse, then what if anything makes them different from other contexts of either a religious or non-religious type? Moreover, if Muslim contexts are so varied and thus can mean an enormously wide range of opinions and perspectives do they actually mean anything? Indeed, does it make sense to use the idea of 'Muslim contexts' or is this term a mere chimera?

Discussing Muslim contexts is not disingenuous because there are important elements that make these contexts distinctly Muslim (though, it bears repeating, not necessarily 'Islamic'). Most fundamentally, within Muslim contexts two sources are taken seriously and considered basic. One is the text of the Qur'anic revelation; the second is the person, example and traditions of Muhammad b. Abdullah, i.e., the Prophet Muhammad (d. 632 CE). The salience of both of these sources is perhaps obvious, but no less significant for being so. The Qur'anic text is considered the most significant and sacred scriptural source within Muslim contexts. It is the basic, foundational reference for a Muslim outlook. Similarly, the example, teaching, actions and model of Muhammad are looked to both as a moral exemplar and source of guidance as well as, often, a paradigm for emulation.

This is not to say that Muslims in all their contexts (both in a contemporary sense and over the years) have always understood either the Qur'anic text and message or the example and teachings of Muhammad in the same way. They certainly have not. What makes their contexts distinctly Muslim is not an unanimity of interpretation but rather a consensus on the significance of, and reference to, these two basic sources, notwithstanding the myriad views that they may generate. In short, these foundational sources are taken seriously and addressed with a certain gravity as basic to the community of Muslims, and this is what unifies and binds together these contexts and distinguishes them from non-Muslim contexts. Outside of Muslim contexts, the Qur'anic text and the Prophetic example, while they may be studied, respected and even venerated, are not going to be basic, foundational sources for one's world view or 'whole truth'.

To illustrate this point, we can draw an analogy from literary criticism. In his groundbreaking work *The Great Code: the Bible and literature*, the eminent Canadian scholar Northrop Frye argued convincingly that the Bible was a sort of leitmotif that ran through the history of Western literature.[14] Though an oversimplification of Frye's argument, the essential point (or at least *an* essential point) that Frye was making was that one cannot fully appreciate the corpus of Western literature without understanding the enormous reference, explicit and implicit, that it makes to the Bible. In other words, the Bible is the 'great code' to this enormous literary heritage. We might say, then, that Muslim contexts are those in which the Qur'anic text and the Prophetic example operate as a type of 'great code'; and non-Muslim contexts will operate on different 'great codes'. This coding idea means, of course, that Muslim contexts are not geographically defined *per se*; rather, they are defined

14 Frye (1982).

by the existence and operation of the Muslim code. This may occur in countries of Muslim majority populations but it could also occur among Muslims where they are in a minority; what is important is the 'coding'.

From these essential sources, however, has grown a much larger edifice of thought and reflection. This whole complex of Muslim societies and cultures might be characterised as a working out, in multiple locations of time and space, of the meanings of the essential sources. Just as the Bible would have informed the corpus of Western literature in so many ways, so too the essential sources of Muslim identity have informed another corpus of literature. But, of course, the influence has been not just on literature but also on science, philosophy, history, law, art, architecture, etc.; in short, the whole range of human experience and activities. This heritage is also imbedded within and is a part of the character of Muslim contexts, and it is distinctive because it evokes a different range of references than do other contexts. Thus, for example, instead of thinking of St Thomas Aquinas as a preeminent figure in theology and law as may be the case in contexts informed by Christianity, in Muslim contexts one might think of al-Ghazzali (d. 1111 CE). So, Muslim contexts have a whole range of references that will be different, though not necessarily always so or exclusively so, from non-Muslim contexts. Just as the essential sources of Muslim contexts, *qua* a 'code', are not geographically constrained, neither is the broader heritage of thought and references. These, too, will be found, *mutatis mutandis*, in Muslim communities in different parts of the world and at different times.

All of this is to establish that there is something to the idea of Muslim contexts. There are essential, foundational sources – a sort of great code – that are both pre-eminent and basic, and then there is the whole civilisation (some may prefer to say *civilisations*) that has developed out of a dialogue over time and in different locations with the code. As Mohammad Ashgar Khan notes when talking about the Muslim world encompassing about one-sixth of the world's population and stretching from Morocco to Indonesia, there is, for want of a better term, "an 'Islamic factor' prevalent in these countries. . . . There is a thread of affinity which runs across national boundaries . . ."[15] However, this does not compromise that within the civilisation(s) there has been and continues to be great diversity of interpretation, perspective and practical manifestations (in institutions, etc.) and, thus, that there must be an appreciation of the plurality of Muslim contexts.

In consequence, by addressing Muslim contexts I mean to address all those for whom the 'code' I have just described is foundational. This would include countries of Muslim majority but also minority Muslim populations, whether of large numbers both absolutely and as a percentage of their national populations, for example, in India, or of relatively small numbers (in both senses) as they may be in Australia. Necessarily, however, what is said here will have different application in these different situations and, thus, I focus on majority settings. In these environments, I hope to show how justice as discourse is useful where there is a predominantly Muslim code. Indeed, it is in these settings that I hope this work will make the greatest impact. In this sense, I hope to make a contribution to a challenge identified by Hassan Hanafi, who argues that:

> The major risk for the future is that Muslim societies will be offered only fundamentalist/secularist alternatives. Unless Muslim advocates of a middle course resume the serious task of developing and implementing pluralistic and representative conceptions of state

15 Khan (1995) at 1.

> and society from within the Islamic tradition, Islam will offer no conception of civil society.[16]

What Hanafi seems to suggest is that there is a polarisation of options for Muslim societies where religion is either supposed to be entirely defining ('fundamentalist') or must be entirely excluded ('secularist', though of the laic variety), and hence the need for other options. By positing the framework I do, I hope to make a contribution to developing a 'middle course', both by challenging the polarisation that Hanafi appears to assume, and then developing within this framework a pluralistic and representative conceptions of state and society, a part of which includes the role of civil society, consistent with an interpretive account of Muslim heritage. This task requires taking seriously the needs of Muslim societies, important aspects of which I seek to elucidate later in this chapter.

It is also important to address the relevance of 'Muslimness' as a category. As Ernst notes, Muslims are affected by all the major factors of life that influence all of us: economic class, access to political power, ethnicity, gender, nationality, location, language and history, and thus "To assume that Muslims, and Muslims alone, are driven to act *exclusively* by religion, apart from any other factors that shape our lives, is more than absurd. It dehumanises Muslims . . ."[17] A similar situation affects any general category, let us say 'women' for example. Are there issues that affect women in general or does a 'feminist outlook' become an untenable premise? For that matter, can there be a 'Black' outlook or a 'British' outlook? We cannot deny the variation that runs throughout a category of Muslims (or of women or of the British) and the various other factors that might stimulate the outlooks and actions of the peoples in this (these) category(ies). Neither, however, should we, on the other hand, deny that there might be some significance to the fact of Muslimness (etc.). Muslims clearly are separated and divided by geography, language, economic situation and even aspects of history and yet those who call themselves Muslims accept, I would suggest, some basic elements – namely, as I have formulated it, the Qur'anic text and Prophetic example, the elements of my Muslim 'code'.

Benedict Anderson has developed the idea of an 'imagined community' – community that is not based on direct, face-to-face interaction but rather on an imagined, and one might say projected, affinity and communion.[18] Anderson's imagined communities are linked to the nation and to the development of national print-languages, but the concept of a community stemming from some source and generating from that a communion among its members is useful. Indeed, the long-standing idea that emerged among Muslims of the *ummah* (community) being a broad community of faith encompassing all Muslims and having a sort of transcendent character, which unites Muslims in bonds of fraternity (and sorority) within a defined geographical area, but also trans-nationally, has been, and continues to be, a locus of identity for Muslims and seems very much to be the type of imagined community that Anderson envisages. As he says:

> the nation is always conceived as a deep, horizontal comradeship. Ultimately it is this fraternity that makes it possible, over the past two centuries, for so many millions of people, not so much to kill, as willingly to die for such limited imaginings.[19]

16 Hanafi (2002) at 74. Akeel Bilgrami has termed this polarized situation a "clash within civilisations" (adapting Samuel Huntington's now famous "clash of civilisations" phrase) (Bilgrami (2003)).

17 Ernst (2003) at 28 (emphasis added).

18 Anderson (1991) at 6.

19 Anderson (1991) at 7.

The same may be said for the *ummah*. That the *ummah* is not the same because its members all think the same, speak the same languages, enact the same rituals or come to the same views on what their religio-legal rules require, etc., and that on any one of these or other matters there might not be a unifying core, should not make us despair of the category.

Grappling with the sameness of difference and the imprecision of some categories which still seem to make sense, Ludwig Wittgenstein, using the example of games, develops the idea of 'family resemblance'.[20] In Wittgenstein's analysis, in a category like 'games' or 'numbers' there may not be one thing that all games or all numbers have in common and yet there is resemblance, similar to the "various resemblances between members of a family: build, features, colour of eyes, gait, temperament, etc. [that] overlap and criss-cross in the same way".[21] Hence, there may be no *one* thing that all in a family may have in common and yet there can still be a 'family resemblance' that unites them. Our inability to give a definition based on a single common thing – e.g., all games do this, all numbers are like this, everyone in the family shares this trait, or all Muslims do/think/believe 'x' – does not mean we might not discern family resemblances. "We do not know the boundaries because none have been drawn" and we should instead think that "the strength of the thread does not reside in the fact that some one fibre runs through its whole length, but in the overlapping of many fibres".[22]

The code suggested above generates an imagined community of the *ummah*, which unites Muslims not in an exact sameness or even one expression of exact sameness, but only as parts of a similar family with subtle and complex resemblances. And this, in turn, means that they can all relate at some level to the working out of this code in the history of their co-religionists and, thus, participate in a certain common – albeit diverse – legacy. This is not, however, a legacy of a linear history. Among some of the groups that will be discussed below, the Fatimids and the Abbasids existed at the same time, the Umayyads in Spain outlived the Umayyads in Damascus, and the Ottomans both existed at the same time and outlived the Qajars in Persia and the Mughals in India. Thus, while we must recognise the inter-sectionality of Muslims and the complications of the legacy, we need not make the fact of their being Muslims irrelevant; we need not either destroy or deny the code.

Navigating liberal ideas and theories past colonialism

At the outset, an issue that warrants an address is whether liberal ideas and theory are incompatible with Muslim contexts in the first place. This question has become increasingly prominent in legal thinking partly because it has always been important as to whether a broadly liberal framework of law (and society) can speak to Muslim contexts, but it is also extremely important now, in light of the rise of the post-secularist narrative.[23] The main crux of the criticism is this: that liberal ideas and theory have permeated Muslim contexts through the alienating experiences of colonialism and have, thus, become intrinsically interwoven with colonial hegemony and suppression. This potential alienating feature poses difficulties in

20 Wittgenstein (2001).

21 Wittgenstein (2001) at para 67.

22 Wittgenstein (2001) at paras 69 and 67.

23 It is interesting to note Mahmood's observations that in dissertations on the compatibility of liberalism with Islam, Islam always seems to bear the burden of proving its compatibility with liberalism, whereas the question has almost never been posed in the reversed manner; "we do no ask for example, what it would mean to take the resources of the Islamic tradition and question many of the liberal political categories and principles for the contradictions and problems they embody?" (Saba Mahmood, "Questioning Liberalism, Too" online: *Boston Review* at https://bostonreview.net/archives/BR28.2/mahmood.html).

taking anything with the heritage of colonial power to transplant it to a modern context and plays on certain post-colonial ideas of intellectual subservience. While it will be readily acknowledged that some of these theories have origins in the 'West', this criticism is perhaps overstated, for what it overlooks is the historically symbiotic relationship between what may now be termed 'Eastern' and 'Western' civilizations in the sharing of knowledge and the mixing of cultures, traditions and practices. This fact is not readily extinguishable. Indeed, there was often transboundary communications between these places, and the history of geography and *sharedness* seems to militate against the idea of culturally hermetically sealed elements.

Consider Bowering's observations that historically, Islam has exerted tremendous influence following its conquests of the Middle East, North Africa, the Iberian Peninsula; the Iranian Islands, Central Asia and the Indus Valley. In the process of which, Islam quickly "inherited the legacy of ancient Egyptian philosophy and science, assimilated the subtleties of Persian statecraft, incorporated the reasoning of Jewish law and the methods of Christian theology, absorbed cultural patterns of Zoroastrian dualism and Manichean speculation and acquired wisdom from Mahayana Buddhism and Indian philosophy and science".[24] He goes on to underscore that since the end of Late Antiquity and through most of the millennium of the early and late Middle Ages, the Islamic world was "the leading culture on the globe", excelling in realms of philosophy and the natural sciences, logic and metaphysics, astronomy, optics, alchemy, geography, medicine and architecture.[25] One also has to consider the potential artificialness of bifurcating 'East' and 'West' through drawing too a strict dichotomy.[26] To view the relationship of 'East' and 'West' as the interface of hermetically sealed ideological units disregards the geographical and historical flourishings that have occurred as a result of the constant transmission of ideas and is thereby misconceived.[27] That the relationship between the 'East' and 'West' has been a dynamic one is apparent and ought not to pose insurmountable difficulties for liberal theory to be understood in Muslim contexts. Indeed, when one considers that secular law and Islam occupy a common space inasmuch as they both seek to wrestle with questions that citizens would be concerned with, it becomes increasingly clear that there are aspects of Muslim heritage that may be seen as compatible with liberalism.[28,29]

24 Bowering (2015) at 2. Bowering goes further on to observe that during the ascendancy of the Abbasid Empire, "the practice of philosophy, medicine and the sciences within the Islamic empire was at a level of sophistication unmatched by any other civilisation". Indeed, it managed to secure pride of place in such diverse fields as architecture, philosophy, maritime navigation and trade, and commerce by land and sea and saw the founding of the world's first universities (at 2).

25 Bowering (2015) at 12.

26 See for example, Teemu Ruskola, 'Where Is Asia? When Is Asia? Theorizing Comparative and International Law' at https://lawreview.law.ucdavis.edu/issues/44/3/Concept%20of%20Asia%20in%20International%20Law/Ruskola.pdf (last assessed 12 March 2017)

27 Also note, for example, the influences that permeate what may be colloquially deemed as religious states in the context of Muslim countries is oftentimes a simplistic term. In this regard, Hussein Ali Agrama attempts to answer the question of whether Egypt is a secular or a religious state given that the state itself exhibits peculiar ambiguities: its constitution names the Islamic *shari'a* as the principal source of law, yet its legal system is largely derived from European, mostly French-based, law (Agrama [2010] at 497).

28 See also Jamal (2010) for a historical and macro-perspective showing that there exist elements of liberalism and pluralism within Islam. Fadel, on the other hand, opts for a more micro-level analysis, situating threads of liberalism interwoven into the greater tapestry of Islam's individual doctrines. (Fadel (2008)).

29 It is also worth noting Abdullahi An-Na'im's own contention that Muslim contexts do not conflict with political liberalism, on the basis that law and religion fundamentally exist on separate planes; they are thus "complementary, not competing" (An Na'im, 2013).

The politico-legal legacy

Critical to this study is a discussion of the political and legal heritage of Muslim contexts. We can begin by looking at the inter-relationship between political and religious authority, and thereafter at legal authority. It is often pointed out that Islam has never known a 'church' in the Christian sense of an organised, hierarchical and authoritative body. Indeed, since its early years, after the period of the so-called *"Rashidun"* or "Rightly Guided" caliphs (the last of whom, Ali b. Abi Talib, died in 661 CE), a *de facto* split between political and religious authority has prevailed. Casanova acknowledges and asserts that in its early days Islam was both a religious as well as a political community, with Muhammad having the roles of both political and religious leader.[30] Nonetheless, he argues that since the time of Muhammad there has been differentiation between political and religious roles within Muslim societies, and hence a type of secularisation. But all of this needs to be unpacked and explained through a brief overview of salient elements and episodes of the political and legal history of Muslim civilisations.

Muhammad, the prophet, the leader and the lawgiver

We begin with Muhammad himself who, according to tradition, received his first revelation in 610 CE while he was in the city of Mecca, which was his home. As he began to share his revelation, from about 613 CE onwards, and to receive more, a group of followers gathered around him. Muhammad's message, however, challenged the structures and religious traditions of his Meccan society, and the authority of the Meccan tribes, and as his influence and following grew, so did the annoyance he caused to the powers of the time.[31] The situation became tense and ultimately very precarious for Muhammad, so that eventually he was left with no choice but to seek refuge elsewhere. He and a small group of his followers left Mecca to migrate north to the city of Medina in 622 CE. This migration, known as the *hijra*, marks the beginning of the Muslim calendar which dates events from the *hijra*, designates as 'AH' (after *hijra*). In Medina, Muhammad and his community of Muslims met with much greater success. He was, in short, able to establish a community of followers as a political as well as spiritual entity. Here, however, Muhammad also encountered Jewish communities who, not unlike the Meccan tribes, were at least dubious of his message. Having some political authority, Muhammad was able to establish a relationship between his community and the Jews – though a compact known famously as the 'Constitution of Medina' – though over time, the power of the Jewish clans in Medina was reduced. This agreement laid the groundwork for the emergence of Muhammad's followers as a political community, as his followers were to constitute an *ummah* (community) among the clans of Medina. Eventually, the idea of the *ummah* expanded to embrace a fellowship of all Muslims, and this is still the word used for the community of Muslims today.

Muhammad's position was thus one of both religious and political authority and later emerged also as a legal authority. The revelation Muhammad received, which Muslims believe is now collected in the Qur'an, articulated a vision of right conduct and the best way to live and gave guidance to those who would follow it. The idea of the *shari'a* (a term that is actually not used very frequently in the Qur'anic text itself) was thus an attempt to articulate this vision. Hence, the term *shari'a* may be seen as an abbreviated form of the phrase

30 Casanova (1994) at 48ff.
31 Lapidus (2002) at 21.

ash-shari'a al-islamiyya (or the Islamic way or path – *shari'a,* in fact, coming from the same lexical root as the contemporary Arabic word for road or street). This pathway needed to be explained and expounded and, during his lifetime, Muhammad was the authority to do so.[32]

The extent to which Muhammad intended to establish a polity as part of his mission is much debated. Anthony Black suggests that what Muhammad did was spiritual and political, and that part of Muhammad's point was that earlier theism had failed to come to terms with the problem of power. At the heart of Muhammad's project, then, was the transfer of power from empire to prophet, and from tribe and state to religious community.[33] Wael Hallaq, however, suggests that prior to his arrival in Medina, Muhammad probably did not have in mind the establishment of a new polity, let alone a new legal order, being concerned up until that time with "faith, morality and the purity of mundane existence".[34] Once in Medina, however, circumstances forced themselves on Muhammad and he became the head not just of spiritual community but also a political one. Regardless of whether the political establishment was intended in an *a priori* way or not, the move to Medina consolidated a political role for Muhammad. The nature of the political community, however, was different from the existing tribal or clan-based political groupings that predominated in Arabia at the time. The *ummah* was to be a community of faith-based submission to God and his prophet. As the Qur'an says (Qur'an 48:10): "Those who swear fealty to you [Muhammad] swear fealty by that act unto God. The hand of God is over their hands." On the other hand, a community defined by its religious character was something that was not unknown in the Abrahamic tradition in which Islam would be situated. The Jewish clans in Medina were an example and, equally, the idea of religious communities was mentioned in the Qur'an. *Sura* (chapter) 5:48 of the Qur'an states:

> We have revealed unto you a Book [the Qur'an] with the Truth, confirming whatever scripture was before it . . . for We have made for each of you [i.e., Muslims, Christians and Jews] a law (*shari'a*) and a normative way to follow (*minhaj*). If God had willed, He would have made you one community.

The arbiter of the law for the Muslims was Muhammad, who "solved legal problems as and when they arose, by interpreting the relevant Qur'anic revelations".[35] As Werner Menski notes, "He [Muhammad] was the leader the judge and spiritual guide of the emerging community," adding further that, "The multiplicity of the Prophet's functions shows that he was primarily engaged in applying God's Laws, inevitably involving human discretion."[36]

The various roles that Muhammad fulfilled for the nascent Muslim community were all linked to, and indeed forged by, the unique authority with which he was vested. Because the revelation came through his voice, Muhammad was the ultimate (physical) source for its explication. Because this revelation contained certain rules, and a sense of a divine path or law (the *shari'a*), Muhammad was invested with the legal authority in the articulating this path and applying these rules. Indeed, as has been noted, in this role, Muhammad's activities "created a large body of rulings, regulations, decisions and statements".[37] Finally, because the

32 See Welchman (2002) at 62 and also Brown (1997) at 363.
33 Black (2001) at 10.
34 Hallaq (2005) at 20.
35 Coulson (1968) at 54–79.
36 Menski (2006) at 295.
37 Menski (2006) at 296.

new community (the ***ummah***)[38] was one that was organised around a religious faith, rather than on ethnic or other lines, it fell to Muhammad as the expositor of this faith to also lead the community politically, and of course this role would have entailed legal consequences, as well. Through the unique vehicle and circumstances of Muhammad's prophetic authority there was, therefore, a powerful coincidence of religious, legal and political roles, all of which were exercised, *par excellence*, by the person of the Prophet. As Hugh Kennedy notes:

> But behind all his pronouncements was the knowledge that Muhammad was the chosen of Allah and that there would be divine punishment, horrible and unrelenting for those who disobeyed his command, while those who followed his ways would be sure of everlasting bliss. His practices and decisions, known as Sunna, were to be the future guidelines in the Muslim community.[39]

It might go almost without saying that Muhammad's authority and the above-noted roles he fulfilled by virtue of that authority were unique, not just in the common sense of the term, but really as 'one-of-a-kind' in the context of his times because of the special mission (or activity) in which he was engaged. Thus, Muhammad was, and is, unique in the Islamic tradition in the way Moses and Jesus are in Judaism and Christianity, respectively. The leadership that Muhammad exercised, therefore, represents, on the one hand, an ideal, because it was infused with unparalleled insight into the divine plan arising from the communion that the Prophet enjoyed with God. On the other hand, this exemplar was also unrealisable after Muhammad's death because it became an article of Muslim faith that the particular nature of the communion was not going to be enjoyed by anybody else thereafter. It is thus that Muhammad is known as the 'seal of the prophets' by Muslims, with the Qur'an as the final revelation.

The conflict between the ideal model of the Prophet and the unique authority he exercised that seamlessly covered political, religious, and legal matters (to which we can add for greater accuracy, moral as well) and the incapacity – almost by definition – for this model to be replicated by those who would follow him, would be a tension that runs through much of Muslim politico-legal developments and the heritage that these have bequeathed to contemporary Muslim contexts, and it is to the next stages in the development of this heritage that we can now turn.

After the prophet: power, law and religion

Succession to Muhammad:[40] *the early caliphs and the emergence of the Sunni and Shia traditions*

Muhammad's death in 632 CE initiated a sort of crisis in the early Muslim community. At stake was the nature of leadership that would succeed him. Studies of this early period are legion, such that covering this time in scholarly depth would require at least an independent

38 On the concept of the *ummah,* see the discussion above and also Black (2001) at 13. Black describes Islam as being defined by submission to God and outlining the relationship between God and humans. The very concept of Islam, then, he argues, catches the fusion between religion and government, sacred and secular (at 13).

39 Kennedy (1986) at 47.

40 I borrow this heading from the title of a very comprehensive study of the situation immediately following Muhammad's death by Wilferd Madelung: *The Succession to Muhammad* (Madelung, 2004).

study in and of itself. For purposes of the legal and political heritage that we will require, however, there is a set of prominent points that we may review.

First and foremost, there emerged from the question of succession two major models of leadership. The majoritarian model, which we now know as the Sunni tradition, chose Abu Bakr as the first caliph to succeed Muhammad. While the role of the caliphs changed over time, to simplify matters what we can note is that the caliphs gained their authority either from having been chosen by the community of Muslims, in the case of the first four caliphs, or, later, by being part of a dynastic line. The first four caliphs – Abu Bakr, Umar, Uthman and Ali b. Abi Talib – are collectively regarded as the 'Rightly Guided' caliphs. All four were intimate companions of the Prophet and were raised to the caliphate by being selected by the community. This, along with their close relationship with Muhammad, gave them particular esteem in the eyes of the community even though they led in very turbulent times, and, in fact, the last three of these early caliphs all met their death by assassination. Given that they could not simply 'take over' from Muhammad because of the uniqueness of his position, the precise nature of caliphal authority was something that was worked out in the community. The caliphs were the heads of the Muslim community and they exercised primarily political and also a type of legal authority, but the receiving of revelation had ended. Hence, except in the sense of the other major model, namely the Shia model which is described next, the caliphs were not invested with anything like the same measure of religious authority as Muhammad because they were not seen to be in direct communion with the divine. In short, they were his successors but of a qualitatively different kind.[41] If this was the case with the early caliphs, it applies even more so after the rightly guided caliphs. What is important to note, however, is that even these first four highly revered individuals were not unchallengeable in the way that Muhammad was.

Ali b. Abi Talib was Muhammad's cousin and son-in-law, having married Muhammad's daughter, Fatima. He was also from the same clan (or house or family group) as Muhammad, the 'Banu Hashim' (i.e., Clan of Hashim). Ali's father and Muhammad's uncle, Abu Talib, had been the head of the Banu Hashim and had raised Muhammad, whose own father had died before Muhammad was born. On Muhammad's death, a section of the community believed that Ali was the rightful successor to Muhammad and, indeed, that Muhammad himself had declared this succession very shortly before his death. Those of this opinion constitute what we now refer to as the Shia (or Shi'i) tradition. While almost certainly not fully formed as a doctrine at the outset, the Shia tradition held that the rightful successor to the Prophet should come from the prophetic family, known as the *ahl al-bayt* (or 'People of the House'), starting with Ali and following in hereditary succession through the progeny of Ali and Fatima. As mentioned above, Ali was also the fourth of the selected 'rightly guided' caliphs, but was regarded by the Shia as the first *rightful* successor. The Shia further maintain that Ali and his successors were endowed with special, divinely-sanctioned authority greater and over and above that of Ali just being a close companion and relative of Muhammad and, moreover, that this authority is transmitted to Ali's descendants. Thus, the Shia use the term *Imam* to designate their leaders and the concept of the office of the Imamat as the institution of leadership. While the Shia also maintain that the Qur'an was the final revelation, they invest the Imams with the capacity to interpret the Qur'anic text authoritatively and, furthermore, see the Imams as acting and living – and where the opportunity would present itself of ruling – infallibly.

41 For a fuller discussion of this topic, see Haider (2014).

After the rightly guided: early dynasties

With the death of Ali b. Abi Talib in 661 CE, the political contours of the Muslim community changed significantly. Ali was succeeded as caliph by Muawiya (b. Abu Sufayn), who was able to assert his authority as caliph from his base in Syria. Muawiya reigned as caliph from 661–680 CE but more importantly was able to change the form of succession to establish the first familial dynasty, known as the Umayyads, which lasted from 661 to 750 CE. The dynasty gets this name because Muawiya came from the 'House of Umayya' ('Banu Umayya'), one of the significant family/kinship groupings in Arabia at the time. The establishment of a dynasty, with lineal succession, marked a fundamental change in the nature of the political leadership and of the authority with which it was associated. The rightly guided caliphs were among the closest companions of Muhammad, expected therefore better to understand and to express the prophetic legacy. The Umayyads, however, were established by their military and political might and succeeded by their bloodline. Thus:

> The caliphal state now stood as a more mundane imperial power, no longer based directly on Islam. Rather it was supported internally as well as externally by a particular complex of military and physical power which was partially supported in turn by the Islamic faith.[42]

In short, the logic of 'monarchy' was established and this rested on a very different type of authority to that which Muhammad, *par excellence*, and the rightly guided caliphs thereafter represented.[43] Naturally, this had political and religio-legal implications.

As the political governors, the Umayyads made rulings on a host of legal matters, including those that the Qur'anic text or Prophetic traditions (*Sunna* as collected in reports called *hadith*) may have spoken to, and, of course, they would not have been able simply to disregard these sources even if they wanted to do so. On the other hand, the Umayyads succeeded to an office that, because it had been occupied by boon companions of Muhammad who had also made several legal rulings in their time, was invested with a great deal of religio-political and religio-legal authority. Indeed, the early caliphs seemed to have used the title of *khalifat Allah* ('Deputy of God'), rather than the later *khilafat rasul Allah* (Deputy of the Messenger of God).[44] This deputy status, however, rested in a dynastic line not in closeness or companionship with Muhammad. So, we have a double legacy combining the establishment of a dynastic system with a monarchical logic, on the one hand, and the inheritance of a religious and legal authority, on the other.

There is some scholarly controversy about the upshot of this double legacy. Sami Zubaida asserts that "It would seem that in the first century of Islam, the Umayyad and first Abbasid [the Abbasids were the dynasty that followed the Umayyads] caliphs were endowed with supreme religious authority, including in matters of interpreting and elaborating, and even promulgating *shari'a* rules."[45] Anthony Black, however, while accepting that the Umayyad

42 Hodgson (1974) at 218.

43 This is not to say that all scholarship agrees that the Umayyads were not making claims that were actually religious for their authority. Patricia Crone and Martin Hinds (Crone and Hinds, 1986), argue that the Umayyads saw themselves as rightful successors because of their familial relationship to the third caliph, Uthman (who was of the same clan), and thus rightful successors to the Prophet. As we will see, however, the result of the system initiated by the Umayyads would lead to a different conclusion.

44 See Crone and Hinds (1986) at 43.

45 Zubaida (2003) at 74.

caliphs laid down rules in many different areas, asserts that the idea that the caliph could contribute to the actual development of the *shari'a* found little support outside court circles.[46] These different opinions are significant for an understanding of the time, but even Zubaida's assertion is a harbinger of an important change. This change, now nascent, was a differentiation, or better decoupling, of political and legal authority. Black's claim suggests that even in the time of the Umayyads this was already taking place; Zubaida, on the other hand, would seemingly place this development later in history after the Umayyads and the early period of the Abbasids. Both analyses, however, point in the same direction. In fairness, Black's claim is stronger as he argues that many Muslims including proto-Sunni religious experts (i.e., the *'ulama*; to be discussed next) saw the Umayyads as deviating from the correct norms of Islam and lacking norm-defining legal legitimacy as a result. The rule of the next dynasty, the Abbasids (750–1258 CE), would see further developments to the caliphal role and, ultimately though not necessarily intentionally, to a greater separation between religio-legal and political authority. Of course, however, these changes would not follow a straight path.

The Abbasid capital was Baghdad, instead of the Umayyad Damascus, and by this time Muslim territorial conquests had moved beyond the Arabian Peninsula and was encountering the ancient culture(s) of Persia. Early in the Abbasid period, Ibn Muqaffa (720–c.756 CE), a Persian who had served as a secretary under both the Umayyads and the Abbasids wrote his *Message* (*Risala fi'l-sahaba*) addressed to the caliph al-Mansur (r. 754–775 CE). In this work, Ibn Muqaffa promulgates ideas of the patrimonial system of ancient Iranian government and seeks to apply them to the caliphate. The patrimonial conception put the state as within patrimony and benefice of the ruler. As noted by Black, as part of this conception, Ibn Muqaffa's theory wanted to give the ruler power over the law by taking the law into his own hands.[47] Ibn Muqaffa, however, seems not to have won the argument, at least not dispositively, and at least not in the sense that in later years (Ibn Muqaffa was executed by the caliph in c.756 CE) others would try to reassert claims of the same type; a clear indication that Ibn Muqaffa's ideas did not succeed in establishing the supremacy of the caliph over the law when they were first proposed. Indeed, in an opposing vein, Abu Yusuf, the chief judge (*qadi*) in the time of the caliph Harun al-Rashid (r. 781–890 CE) in his *Book of Taxes* (*Kitab al-kharaj*) while addressing the caliph reverentially, emphasises the caliph's strict accountability to God by adherence to 'God's law'. This might be seen to be a very respectable position for a judge to take but, of course, it also articulates a position diametrically opposite to Ibn Muqaffa's formulation. The caliph al-Mamun (r. 813–833 CE), one of the more significant Abbasid caliphs, attempted in his time to develop the high ideal of imperial dominion and make the 'deputy' independent of the religious leaders, and in this he was supported by the scholar al-Jahiz (c. 776–868/9 CE). The theoretical arguments for the supremacy of the caliph *qua* deputy would, of course, have had to be backed up by effective, actual political power. For the later Abbasids, however, this would never be realised. By the time of one of al-Mamun's successor, al-Mutawakkil (r. 847–861 CE), Turkish slave soldiers had come to dominate over the caliph in terms of real power, and the various provinces had become effectively independent under new, local, dynasties headed by *amirs* or *sultans*.

Marshall Hodgson, in fact, characterises the 'High Caliphate' as the years 692 CE to 945 CE, during which time the caliphal state was a well-established empire. After 945 CE,

46 Black (2001) at 19.
47 Black (2001) at 22.

the caliphal state was sometimes only a figurehead.[48] The Abbasid caliphate continued, however until 1258 CE when Baghdad fell to the Mongols, but by this stage the caliph was really only a local power that retained a symbolic authority. Black concludes that the emerging Sunni consensus on the role of the caliph was, thus, "damagingly unclear".[49]

This lack of clarity, however, was not only because of the political weakness of the Abbassid caliphs, or, to put it differently, the political weakness of the caliphs was not only the result of rival political leaders. Something else was also developing, the germs of which have been alluded to earlier and which we must now examine.

The development of the law: the schools, the **fiqh** *and* **usul al-fiqh**

> Certain fields of thought and practice came to be dominated by piety-minded representatives of the Islamic hope for a godly personal and social order – a hope inherited from the Jewish and Christian priests and monks and rabbis and their flocks. . . . Among both Sunni and Shi'i Muslims, a host of pious men and women who came to be called the '*ulama*, the 'learned', worked out what we may call 'Shariah-minded' programme for private and public living centred on the Shariah law. They exercised a wide sway, but not exclusive control, in Muslim speculative and theological thought. They exercised an effective – but never decisive – pressure in the realms of public order and government and controlled the theoretical development of Muslim law.[50]

We have in the period from about the eight to tenth centuries CE the emergence of the great classical tradition of 'Islamic law' stemming out of the orientations of the so-called piety minded. Why did this body of people and the classical legal tradition of which they would be the expositors develop? As Roy Mottahedeh has noted, "It was by no means inevitable that law should have become so central to higher learning among most Muslims in the pre-modern period."[51] However, there is no denying that it did become so central, and in many respects remains so today. There may be several reasons for this, of which we may consider the following. First, of course, time was passing from the actual presence of Muhammad and the immediate impact of his authority. Second, and relatedly, with this passage of time were also coming new issues, particularly as the area under Muslim hegemony was expanding. Third, was the fact that the type of authority Muhammad enjoyed, enhanced and confirmed by his receiving revelation, was not to be found again, even among the immediate and close and senior companions from which the Rashidun caliphs were drawn, and certainly not, increasingly, thereafter. Fourth, the rule of the Umayyads and later Abbasids was seen as at variance to 'Islam' (which really was only perfectly represented by Muhammad's authority and ideal example) at least in the eyes of the piety minded for whom the Abbasids represented "at best a compromise with their pious ideals for Muslim society".[52] Finally, but by no means least, was the character of the new religious system that had emerged. The new community was a religious community, after all, and it had as its linchpin the command of God expressed first through the medium of the Prophet and thereafter through the revealed Book. For Muslims, then, the event of the Qur'anic revelation elevated the basic social need

48 Hodgson (1974) at 233.
49 Black (2001) at 30.
50 Hodgson (1974) at 238. On the last point see also Kelsay (2002) at 10.
51 As-Sadr (2003) at 1.
52 Hodgson (1974) at 280.

for law into something more substantial. Indeed, while it is generally accepted that of the approximately six thousand verses of the Qur'an, no more than five to six hundred at most have what one might call legal content *per se*, the Qur'anic ethos envisions humanity striving to live in accordance with God's rules and directions and in God's way or path. Thus, there are references to the boundaries or limits (*hadd*, pl. *hudud*) that Muslims should not transgress, and to following God's path or way (*shari'a*), an idea also captured in the oft-invoked prayer to remain on the right or correct (and in this sense divinely sanctioned) path (*al-sirat al-mustaqim*). This has led to a conceptualisation of the realm of law in Muslim contexts that is more extensive than it is generally thought of in, say, the contemporary West. To some extent, the legal tradition aspires to characterise all acts in God's eyes.[53] The ethos of the Qur'anic text, then, spurred on those who would articulate this conceptualisation, especially so once Muhammad was gone and there was a different character to the political leadership. The piety-minded '*ulama* may thus be seen as having taken on the responsibility for understanding and articulating God's will as part of a moral hermeneutic.

Early legal formulation drew both upon pre-Islamic legal practice where this was not seen as incompatible with the Islamic (and particularly Qur'anic ethos) as well as local custom. As Annelies Moors has noted: "As long as they were not contrary to Islamic principles, existing provisions were incorporated into the Islamic legal system, providing space for considerable variability in legal practice."[54] Prophetic practice and traditions were also important but, in the first century, as Muhammad's authority was seen as anchored in the Qur'an and he as a spokesperson and interpreter of God's word, rather than as law-maker in and of himself. Additionally, though as we shall see this was to change, the rulings of the early, and especially, Rashidun caliphs, were also drawn upon to construct the legal norms. This meant that the caliphs "were not independent agents of legislation, but integrally dependent on prior exemplary conduct and precedent, only one source of which happened to be decisions of previous caliphs".[55]

The agents of the legal formulations were the piety minded who arose at first as a pious opposition[56] to the Umayyads and, as such, operated largely outside of the pre-modern Muslim state structure. While the caliphal regimes appointed, as state officials, judges (*qadis*) who heard individual cases and while the accumulated decisions of the *qadis* did over time start to give some shape to Islamic legal practice, the real agents for this development were not the state judges but the independent scholars/jurists (who collectively came to be known as the '*ulama*).[57] Some of the '*ulama* were, in fact, appointed as judges, but many kept their distance from government and thereby gained prestige in the eyes of the people.[58]

The further and detailed history of the development of the classical tradition of Islamic law is well documented in scholarship[59] and does not, therefore, need to be retold with any

53 Thus, Muslim legal traditions know a five-part characterization of acts as forbidden, discouraged, permissible, recommended and mandatory.

54 Moors (1999) at 144.

55 Hallaq (2005) at 45.

56 The phrase 'pious opposition' comes from Noel Coulson's *A History of Islamic Law* (Coulson (1964)).

57 Weiss (1998), ch. 1.

58 Mottahedeh, "Introduction" in as-Sadr (2003) at 8.

59 In addition to Hallaq's, *Origins and Evolution of Islamic Law* and Coulson's *A History of Islamic Law* cited earlier, other well-known and seminal histories in English include Joseph Schacht's *An Introduction to Islamic Law* (Schacht, 1964) and *Origins of Muhammadan Jurisprudence* (Schacht, 1965), Knut Vikor's *Between God and the Sultan* (Vikor, 2005) and Hallaq's *Shari'a: Theory, Practice and Transformations* (Hallaq, 2009).

great elaboration. What we need to draw out from this history, however, are a few prominent points that have relevance for the analysis and argument being developed here.

The first point is that out of the scholarly efforts of the piety-minded *'ulama* there developed a body of legal material called the *fiqh*. Literally meaning 'discernment', the word *fiqh* describes a body of written material that represents an attempt to give practical expression to what the *shari'a* means. That is to say that, the *fiqh* was an attempted exposition in the here and now of the divine path expressed in the *shari'a* that only God knows perfectly. This establishes a fundamental distinction between the *shari'a* and the *fiqh*, both of which are often (and somewhat confusingly) translated simply as 'Islamic law' in English. One, *shari'a*, is Islamic law in the sense of the ideal path or way that God wishes; the other, *fiqh*, is Islamic law in the sense of the very earthly, human-constructed attempt to understand and practically express the ideal. The *fiqh* was the main work product of the *'ulama*.

Second, since the *'ulama* were basically private scholars mainly operating outside of the realm of political authority, one of the fundamental features of the legal tradition was that the *fiqh* developed in conditions of some considerable diversity and reflected this diversity in its substantive content. This was especially so in the early period of the eighth to tenth centuries CE. No doubt, part of this diversity was engendered by the very fact that the *'ulama* (or, initially, the proto-*'ulama*) emerged organically and were grouped only informally. Moreover, while they were able effectively to shrink the caliphs' authority to promulgate legal rulings, this power stemmed not from the organisation of the *'ulama* but rather from the authoritative basis and mantle that they were able to assume. It is important to note here that like other legal orders, Muslim legal traditions are concerned with social, including commercial, relations – matters which are grouped together under the heading of *mu'amalat*. Muslim legal traditions, however, also encompasses matters of religious practice and worship (*ibadat*), which are generally regarded as personal concerns outside the purview of 'law' in the other non-religious legal orders and, in particular, Western legal systems.[60] This makes these traditions more comprehensive and more wide ranging than contemporary Western legal systems, because the norms, inspired and derived from the faith, cover many more areas of human experience than in other systems. Colin Imber summarises these points with the following observation:

> the shari'a does not correspond to a modern understanding of law. In the first place, many of the legal rules which the jurists enunciate are neither enforceable nor intended to be so. . . . Second, . . . many of its [the shari'a's] provisions concern religious ritual, regulating man's relationship with God rather than man's relationship with man. In the sense that it regulates both worldly and religious matters, the shari'a is an all-encompassing and all-embracing law but, in the sense that many if its provisions have no application in practice, much of it is not, in the modern sense, law at all.[61]

Hence, following God's path and respecting God's boundaries means obeying 'law' in a much broader and potentially totalising way than in other traditions. However, we must also understand that, as Imber remarks, not all of the ritual aspects of *shari'a* would have been expected to be enforced and thus, depending on one's definition, may or may not be seen as 'law'. A corollary of the wide-ranging nature of *shari'a* norms, however, is that the

60 Of course, other religiously based legal orders, like Jewish law, include discussions of *ibadat*-type matters – e.g., ritual purity.

61 Imber (1997) at 30.

legally-minded pious scholars were able to occupy a greater area of social life and authority than could court-bound judges, and thus establish their influence in a more comprehensive way within Muslim tradition. Practically, this was accomplished by the legal opinions (*fatwas*, pl. *fatawa*) that the jurists would issue in response to questions about, essentially, how the *shari'a* was to be understood by believers, including on matters that would not ordinarily be addressed by courts.[62] It also evidences a gap between judges and jurists that was to endure.

The first conglomerations of the *'ulama* were geographically centred. Relying on a mixture of pre-existing localised custom of their area, basically centred on a particular city, and an interpretative consensus of the jurists in the locale, they developed regional legal communities. As time passed and the legal scholars developed more and more of a presence, in the Sunni world these regional schools became associated with, and named, after important individual scholars. Thus, by the tenth century, the four major eponymous schools in the Sunni tradition which still dominate today had emerged, namely, the Hanafi (after Abu Hanifa), the Hanbali (after Ahmad ibn Hanbal) the Maliki (after Malik b. Annas) and the Shafii (after Muhammad Idris al-Shafii). To these need to be added major schools in the Shia tradition, of which the most significant today are the Jafari (or 'Twelver' or Ithna-ashari) school, the largest of the Shia schools, the Ismaili and the Zaydi. In addition, there are the Ibadis, a numerically small group that sits outside the Sunni/Shia division. Within most of the schools (*madhab*, pl. *madhahib*) there are subdivisions between different communities of interpretation that for reasons of geography, history or theology have crafted a separate tradition.[63]

An understanding of the emergence of the different schools of Islamic law helps us understand that the tradition of classical Islamic law is probably best understood in the plural: it is not a 'Tradition', but rather a complex set of traditions. Moreover, all of the schools have been defined to a greater or lesser extent, though in almost all cases very predominantly, by the work of scholars. In most cases this has been the overwhelming way in which the school has been articulated, even in the Shia traditions.[64] Historically, then, we might see the body of the *fiqh* as the collection of various localized attempts, produced in diverse local contexts, to give expression to the normative ideals of the *shari'a*, a process made vastly more rich and complex with the spread of Islam over large geographical areas.

The emergence of schools of *fiqh* was followed by the emergence of another important part of the framework of 'Islamic law', namely the discipline of *usul al-fiqh* (lit. the roots of the *fiqh*), usually rendered as 'Islamic jurisprudence' or 'Principles of Islamic jurisprudence'. The *usul al-fiqh* was an attempt to systematise the sources and processes by which the *fiqh* was to be discerned. Within the Sunni traditions of Islam, the 'roots' of the *fiqh* came to held to be four: the Qur'an, the Sunna (sayings and exemplary conduct of Muhammad as

62 *Fatawa* are thus not unlike the *responsa* in the tradition of Rabbinical law.

63 As varied as this account of the different schools of law may appear, it is important to note that there were several other schools that existed in history but which have now died out, particularly in the Sunni tradition. Furthermore, each of the schools represents itself a larger or smaller range of opinions; thus, there may be majority and minority opinions within the Hanafi School, for example.

64 Here the contemporary Nizari Ismaili tradition is somewhat different. Whereas for the other Shia groups the Imam is not physically present but is rather held to be in occultation (*ghayba*) pending a future return, or in seclusion, the Imam of the Nizari Ismailis (the current Aga Khan) is physically present. Given the Imam's singular religio-legal role, it is the Ismaili Imam that is the key source of law for this community, and the Imam in this sense is much more than a scholar/jurist. (See further on this on this my article, Jamal, 2001).

captured especially in written *hadith* reports), *qiyas* (reasoning by analogy) and, finally, *ijma* (or consensus, notionally of the community but effectively of the jurist/theologians). Not surprisingly, *usul al-fiqh* developed first in the Sunni traditions because these traditions knew no authority like that of the Shia Imam to which they could turn for authoritative guidance. With the occultation of the *Ithna-shari*/Twelver Shia Imam, however, the Shia too developed an *usul al-fiqh*. This differed from the Sunni *usul al-fiqh* in one of the roots: Shia *usul al-fiqh* rejects *qiyas* in favour of *aql* (reason(ing)) and its *ijma* is the *ijma* of the Shia scholars. In addition, as well as the *Sunna* of the Prophet Muhammad, the Shia tradition gives importance to the *sunna* of the Shia Imams. The emergence of the discipline of *usul al-fiqh* thus represents a further level of scholarly sophistication and textual refinement to the working out of the law. Along with the *fiqh*, this means, as Norman Calder notes, that:

> The third century [after Hijra, viz. 9th to 10th centuries CE] sees a movement from jurisprudence which is a predominantly oral and socially diffuse informal process towards a jurisprudence which is a complex literary discipline, *the prerogative of a highly trained and socially distinct elite*. That movement . . . was no doubt a natural process but was also affected by school competition and government policy.[65]

I have emphasised part of Calder's words to bring home the point that the emergent '*ulama* developed an alternative source of normative authority to the political leadership and, as they developed, that the '*ulama* constituted a different social group as well. As the '*ulama* developed more and as their written production expanded, they were able to articulate the 'pious opposition' more strongly, more clearly and, crucially, more independently. As Crone and Hinds note, the reliance on the Book and the Reports (that is to say on the Qur'an and *sunna/hadith* as the primary sources or normativity) effectively "deprived the Caliph any say, *qua* Caliph, in the definition of Islamic norms".[66] The norms of the faith and the norms of 'Justice', the latter linked now to the divine and having a sense of the 'sacred', were thus set up independently from the state authority, which was 'profane'. This distinction marked out an important difference between state law and the *shari'a*.

It has been important to spend some time discussing the development of the proto- and emergent '*ulama* and of the discipline of *fiqh* because of the enduring legacy of these developments. Thus far, we have emphasised the challenge leading to the distinction between political authority on the one hand and religious (becoming religio-legal) authority on the other that the emergence of the '*ulama* and their work product and methodology (the *fiqh* and *usul al-fiqh*, respectively) engendered. But this was not, and is not, the only important consequence of these developments.

Notwithstanding that the '*ulama* may have emerged out of a shared sense of piety and indeed pious opposition to caliphal rule, and eventually agreed on basically the same methodology for their work – i.e. settled on the 'roots of the law' – they were not homogeneous. In part, this heterogeneity may have arisen because of the fact that the schools of law were influenced by the locales and local practices ('*amal*) out of which they emerged.[67] The

65 Calder (1993) at 164 (emphasis added).

66 Crone and Hinds (1986) at 58.

67 On this see, for example, Dutton (2002) for a study of the development of the Maliki School. Dutton makes the point that *sunna* in its pre-classical sense did not mean just the *sunna* of Muhammad as identified in *hadith*, but rather that it included the local practice ('*amal*) of Medina, which is where Malik was based, which itself was further elaborated by a process of consideration and definition (*ijtihad*) of these

upshot of this is that there was no authoritative consensus on what the *shari'a* meant and demanded. Theoretically, it may not be surprising to note that efforts to understand the divine will would lead to differing interpretations and understandings. Practically, however, the emergence of the different schools of law, in which the four Sunni schools and the Jafari (Shi'i) school generally co-exist in a condition of mutual respect and mutual toleration means that, for centuries, there has in effect been no unanimity on what the *shari'a* is in an absolute sense. Islamic law, or perhaps better Muslim legal traditions, thus, do not speak with one voice. From this, it follows that the sense of 'Islamic law' being understandable as if it was like, say, the Income Tax Act – that is to say expressed in a single, authoritative, comprehensive compilation of positive (and positivist?) law is not accurate in at least two senses: firstly, because this sort of conceptualisation blurs the difference between the ideal and the practical expression of the ideal, and, secondly, because of the diversity of the practical expressions. Instead, we have a much more plural and open-textured tradition(s). As Hallaq pithily states: "Notwithstanding all efforts to minimise plurality, [the] Sharia's *fiqh* was incontrovertibly pluralistic: this is simply one of its most essential features."[68] The emergence work of the '*ulama* and the development of the different schools of law, therefore, not only marked a differentiation between political and religio-legal authority but also evidence the fact that normativity in Muslim contexts has been expressed diversely for centuries.

The period around, and following, the establishment of the schools of law, was not, of course, the final chapter in settling the interaction between political, legal and religious authority for Muslim societies. Indeed, these processes continue to be worked out today. Additionally, however, we cannot see the story as told thus far as fully settling the issue of the developed heritage. What we have seen, however, to some extent establishes a watershed principle from which, in a fundamental way, there would be no retreat, as Black notes:

> The political decline of the Deputyship produced a *partial* spilt between religious and political power, between religio-moral-legal authority and political-military power. The former became the domain of the Learned [read: '*ulama*], the latter of the Sultan.[69]

The religio-moral-legal-authority here is the authority of the *shari'a qua* sacred law. On the political and military side, however, a type of 'administrative law' (or, perhaps better, the law necessary for administration), called the *siyasa shari'a* (roughly, 'political *shari'a*) was vested. The *siyasa shari'a*, however, as the 'law' of the political rulers and functionaries lacked the same normative weight or significance of the *shari'a* elaborated by the '*ulama*. In order to understand this process better, it is to selected relevant parts of the subsequent political history to which we must now turn.

Power, law and religion: the ongoing dynamic

As mentioned earlier, one early attempt to regain a united authority for the caliph came with al-Mamum (Abbasid Caliph, r. 813–833 CE). Al-Mamum sought to reconstruct a high caliphal ideal and to align the *shari'a* and the court. His method of doing so was to support

---

practices by later authorities. Hence, the Qur'an, *sunna* and *ijtihad* together were together the '*amal* of Medina and is it from this complex that the school emerged (at 3).

68 Hallaq (2005–2006) at 160.

69 Black (2001) at 38 (emphasis in original).

a strain theological of thought referred to as the Mutazila (or Mutazilite), which emphasised the use of reason and advanced the theological claim that the Qur'an was created in time. The Mutazilites were opposed by the Asharite school that asserted that the Qur'an was eternal and uncreated. Within this theological tussle, of course, lay an important political principle. Asharite thought was conformist and rejected rational speculation in favour of a textualist approach. The assertion of the uncreatedness of the Qur'an fits into this outlook because it meant that the Qur'an was a source that could neither be derogated from, nor interpreted through rational consideration, but was something simply to be followed, basically literally. On the Mutazilite, view, however, as something created the Qur'an was rather like human intellect (also created) and could be interpreted with the aid of rational consideration. In this Mutazilite process the Caliph could play a part in the interpretation but this was not available to him on the Asharite understanding. On the Asharite view, reliance had to be placed only on the sacred text itself and the reports (*hadith*), and these governed and imposed themselves on the caliph, not the other way around. Of course, these sources were also the province of the '*ulama* and so the Asharite position solidified the interpretative and normative authority of the '*ulama*. Al-Mamum's attempt to champion the Mutazilite view did not succeed, but that it was attempted at all does show that the theological position and the terms of settlement between caliphal authority and that of the '*ulama* were still open to consideration and debate in his time. As we saw, however, by the time of the Caliph al-Mutawakkil (r. 847–861 CE), the claim for primacy of the caliph over the '*ulama* was effectively a spent force and it would remain so definitively.

The one significant alternative arrangement of political and religious authority, to which we have already referred, was the Shia tradition. The establishment of the Shia Ismaili Fatimid empire in North Africa and then Egypt in the tenth century represented the manifestation in practice of the distinctly Shia conception of the relationship of political and legal authority. The leader of the empire was the Fatimid Caliph-Imam: *qua* caliph he was the head of state and holder of the caliphal political authority; *qua* Imam, however, he was also the ultimate religious authority. Thus, in one figure was combined the absolute ruler to whom allegiance was owed in both a worldly as well as religious sense. The Fatimid Imam thus manifested not just Shia theory but the type of combined authority that had not been seen, in practice, since the time of Muhammad. The Fatimids, however, ruled over an empire in which their Ismaili co-religionists were a minority, with Sunni Muslims in the majority even in the Fatimid capital of Cairo. Moreover, they ruled with a policy of general religious toleration towards other Muslim communities as well as towards Christian and Jewish communities, who were generally treated well and some of whom occupied senior positions of state.

While the Fatimid state thus represented a radically different relationship between religious and political authority (and a political rival) to the Abbasid regime, it was an alternative that occupied only a small slice of Muslim history. The Fatimids were in power in Egypt from 969–1194 CE, after which they were replaced by a new, Sunni, regime. After this time, the Ismailis became, as they have remained to this day, mainly a politically quietist sect. As a result, the Fatimid system has not represented a departure from the general trend in the relationship between religious and political authority within the heritage of Islam generally because it was a relatively short-lived alternative. Moreover, subsequent Shia polities (e.g. the Safavids and Qajars who were based in Iran) followed the Twelver tradition but did so after the occultation of the twelfth Imam and, hence, did not have the same figure of the Imam in and around whom to fuse religio-legal and political authority. The Safavid and Qajar political rulers (called 'shah') thus had to operate with religious authority residing in their '*ulama*.

Of course, the unique Fatimid structure did not represent the only innovation in the arrangements between religious and political authority, which remained in constant development, and it is useful to turn to some examples of this.

The rule of the Saljuqs (sometimes 'Saljuks') coincided with the latter part of the Abbasid period. The Saljuqs, who arose from Turkic slave soldiers, eventually achieved military and political domination, relegating the Abbasid caliph to a politically subsidiary position, albeit one which still held symbolic importance. Thus, the caliphate continued but with effective political power now being exercised by a Saljuq 'sultan.' This structure of caliph *and* sultan of course raised the issue of religious and political power once again. In short, even more so than the weakened caliphs, the sultans needed a way of situating their role within the developing normative hermeneutic being articulated by the *ʿulama*. Given the role of the *ʿulama* now and the continuation of the caliphate, it is perhaps not surprising that theories about the complementary nature of political and religious authority arose in this time. The Persian historian Bayhaqi (944–1077 CE), for example asserted that:

> The Lord most high has given one power to the prophets and another power to the kings, and he has made it incumbent on the people that they should submit themselves to the two powers.[70]

In similar vein, the great intellectual al-Ghazzali (d. 1111 CE) claimed that "God has singled out two groups of men and given them preference over others, one prophets; the other kings . . ."[71] As Black points out, "This was virtually the dualist position of many European advocates of the autonomy of royal secular power."[72]

Two points need to be made here. First, in advocating formulations that would accord with the *realpolitik* of the day, these theoretical perspectives evidenced that "Whereas in Europe the issues of religious and worldly power was an occasion for church-state conflict, over the centuries in Islam it was sheathed within rhetoric and mutual accommodation."[73] Second, this accommodation was following the basic lines we have seen earlier, namely that there was a separation of political and religious authority – the former may have been in the hands of the sultans now (and, to a lesser extent, the caliph), but the latter was the province of the *ʿulama*.

Another example to look at comes several centuries later with the Ottomans (c. 1290–1922 CE). The Ottoman sultan sought to maintain and promote *din ve devlet* – religion and empire (or dynasty). Within the Ottoman structure, the *ʿulama* were for the first time given a formal structure and system of ranks as part of the state hierarchy in a system tied to education and qualifications. The *qadis* in this structure administered both the religious law (*shariʿa/fiqh*) as well as the state legislation (*qanun* or *kanun*; deriving from the *siyasa shariʿa* authority). Indeed, the office of the *shaykhuislam* (or chief *shaykh* or head of the *ʿulama*) was a high office of state theoretically equivalent to that of the *vizier*[74] (basically an unelected prime minister). The Ottomans developed fairly detailed ranks and groupings of the *ʿulama*, and important acts of government had to be sanctioned by a *fatwa* from the *ʿulama*. We see in the Ottoman model thus both a regularisation of the *ʿulama* by the

70 In Lewis (1988) at 134.
71 In Lambton (1980) at 105.
72 Black (2001) at 94.
73 Black (2001) at 95.
74 Zubaida (2003) at 60–63.

state but still the persistence of the distinction between religious and political authority in the continued status of the *'ulama*. Here, perhaps more clearly than in the other examples we have considered, however, we also see a *functional* separation, albeit within a unified administrative structure, of religious and political authority.

A final example to consider is that of the Safavids mentioned above. A Twelver Shia dynasty, the Safavids ruled in Persia from 1501–1722 CE. Being Shia, and thereby inheriting the special role accorded to the Shia Imam the Safavids religio-political system may have been a departure from some of the systems we have seen above. By the time of the Safavids, however, the Twelver Imam was not physically present and thus the Safavid ruler (who took the ancient Persian title of 'Shah') did not have to contend with a figure that was in this position, and neither was he himself in this position, like the Fatimid Caliph-Imam. Nonetheless, the symbolism of the Shia tradition with the ideal of unified religious and political authority in the Imam was part of the Safavid context, and the Safavid Shah thus combined political authority with a greater measure of religious authority than any leader since the Fatimids. In the absence of direct access to the Imam, the Twelver Shia tradition had to develop its own *'ulama*, who became the effective holders of religious authority in a similar way to the Sunni *'ulama*. The Safavid Shah Ismail allowed the scholar al-Karaki (c.1466–1534 CE) to develop a theory of the *mujtahid* (that is to say a scholar who was able to engage in *ijtihad* or independent development/thinking about the law) that elevated the *mujtahid* to the status of a deputy of the Hidden Imam. This, of course, made the *mujtahid* the representative of the highest notional authority in the Twelver Shiism. Interestingly, it also affirmed a division and distinction between religious and political authority even in Shia context and even within a system of the Shah being more closely associated with sacred authority.

Conclusion and lessons from the heritage

We have now been able to look at selected episodes that tell us about the relationship between religious and political authority in Muslim history. In this, we have paid particular importance to the early years, the so-called formative and classical periods of Islam, because it was in these periods that certain fundamental ideas that resonated in the later centuries of Muslim experience were developed. It was in the early periods that the Muslim community had to confront at least two basic issues that would shape its outlook on the interaction of political and religious authority. The first was the nature of succession to Muhammad, specifically what role future leaders could have and how much of the mandate of Muhammad they would assume. As I have suggested above, Muhammad represented a type of leadership that was ideal and unrealisable because of the truly unique authority with which he was vested. Indeed, to reiterate, it was an article of faith that Muhammad was the 'seal (or final) of the prophets' and, therefore, it was not possible that a successor could step fully into his shoes. Second, the early Muslim community(ies) had to deal with the regulatory and legal needs of a rapidly expanding empire and naturally, as the community was now a religiously-defined community, it was the moral hermeneutic of their religion that would be a source for the norms and laws.

These issues set up a tension between religious and political legitimacy, and religious and political authority, that had to be resolved. The method of this resolution resulted in an overall sense in a differentiation between religious and political authority. The *'ulama* as jurist-scholars emerged as the custodians of religious authority and, in large measure, of the normative articulation of Islam. On the other hand, political authority continued to be recognised and allowed its own territory. But this method was practical rather than theoretical resolution. As Carl Brown notes:

> Rulers learned that they could usually get the acquiescence of their subjects provided they did not try to impose orthodoxy. Subjects learned that they could deviate in their religious belief and practice provided that they did not openly challenge government. Certain ulama could resist the blandishments of government office, others could accept, and all could accommodate in a system where no one – not even the caliph – presumed to speak ex cathedra (to use the Catholic term) on religious dogma. . . . The early Muslim community developed in a way that facilitated compartmentalization, isolation, and, thus, *non-resolution of potentially explosive issues involving religion and politics. . . . Muslims found it easier to rock along with a certain indeterminacy.*[75]

This 'rocking along' in turn meant several things. It meant a sort of secularisation of the political regime in the sense of a functional social differentiation, or de-coupling, of this (really, *these*) regimes from religious authority in a practical sense, notwithstanding the theoretical non-resolution of this issue. Contemporary historians have remarked on this trend. Mottahedeh, for example, asserts that the Islamic tradition has all the rich diversity of fifteen centuries of history within which real combinations of spiritual and political leadership in Muslim history have been rare and are usually fraught with compromise[76] and Ira Lapidus notes that "Despite the common statement . . . that the institutions of state and religion are unified . . . most Muslim societies did not conform to this ideal, but were built around separate institutions of state and religion."[77] Eqbal Ahmed agrees with this assessment, holding that the absence of such a fusion – of religion and political power – is a historically experienced and recognized reality, which shaped tradition of statecraft and the history of Muslim peoples.[78] And Nikki Keddie baldly states, "The supposed near identity of religion and politics in Islam is more a pious myth than reality for most of Islamic history."[79]

The means of this separation and differentiation – the distinction between the caliph/amir/sultan and the '*ulama* – also took place in a particular form. There is no establishment of a hierarchical Church to stand apart or outside of Government and the '*ulama* are not consecrated clergy and have no sacerdotal function. Thus, as Ahmed asserts, religious authority has been more plural and diffuse because there has not been one body with the epistemological authority to regulate and definite truth in a univocal way; as Wadad al-Qadi observes, "the entire community bore the burden of interpreting the revelatory-prophetic legacy".[80]

As we have noted, at times in the past, political authority has sought to impose this control, but this has been ultimately unsuccessful, something to which the above assertions attest. It meant also, as we have also seen, that there was not one 'Islamic' model to the relationship between political and religious authority but rather there were different Muslim responses to these issues. In short, Muslim contexts have indeed experienced a flow of history, and this should not be forgotten in considering their current situations.

75 Brown (2000) at 53 (emphasis added).
76 Mottahedeh (1995) at 115 and 126.
77 Lapidus (1996) at 25.
78 Ahmed (1995) at 19.
79 Keddie (1994) at 463.
80 Ahmed (2016) at 192. See also Calder (2000) at 68.

Within these evolutions, however, an undeniable part of the heritage has been the "continued importance of the early Muslim community as a political model", such that "The model of the early community remains an unsullied norm, but in the terminology of modern political science the maxims derived from the idealized model are not readily operationalised."[81] Moreover, however, even in theoretical terms as part of a normative articulation, there has not been one answer since, by the eleventh century, it was clear that a certain amount of legal diversity, as reflected in the more or less mutually tolerating schools of law arising from different interpretations of the religious message, was here to stay,[82] a factor that both reflects a certain commonality in the normative exposition of Islam but also the undeniable plurality of these expressions.

The legacy of the political and legal heritage Muslim contexts has thus seen a *de facto* distinction between religio-legal authority on the one hand and political authority on the other. This distinction was not widely accepted as a theoretical ideal[83] since the example Muhammad and the early community when political leadership was fully (or nearly fully) in harmony with religious authority and normativity continued, and continues, to be the exemplar, even if an unrealisable one. This factor in turn has engendered the continual negotiation of relations between religious, legal and political authorities as part of the heritage of Muslim contexts. The effective differentiation of these in a non-hierarchical and diffuse structures of religious authority, and the plurality this has engendered, has been a theme of the heritage, though one often not generally recognised by either Muslims or non-Muslims.

81 Brown (2000) at 49 and 50.
82 Mottahedeh, "Introduction" in as-Sadr (2003) at 15.
83 Mottahedeh, "Introduction" in as-Sadr (2003) at 27.

4 Muslim contexts II

Contemporary contexts

The preceding chapter reviewed salient themes in the politico-legal heritage of Muslim contexts. It pointed out the centuries-old differentiation that has been present – in fact, even if not settled in theory – between political authority and religio-legal authority. To make the discussion of Muslim contexts more complete, however, and to address the needs of these contexts today, to this historical survey one needs to add a contemporary dimension. This dimension will not simply be a continuation of the historical story, though there will be an element of this, but rather will also advance theoretical arguments about how this heritage may be understood today.

It is appropriate that the historical chronology covered in the previous chapter ended basically with the Ottoman Empire (1299–1922 CE). From the latter years of the Ottomans (historians often describe the decline of the Ottomans as starting from about 1699 CE), several significant changes had come about to the structure of political life for most of the world's Muslim populations. These seismic alterations to the pre-modern pattern of the rule of empires that had been the norm for Muslim contexts heretofore included, significantly, (i) the formal end of the caliphate in 1922 under the new, modern, Turkish state; (ii) the encounter with and experience of colonialism; and, related to the above, (iii) the establishment of the modern nation-state as the principal form of political organisation under which Muslims would live.

Before we turn to how these changes affected the ways in which the heritage(s) of Muslims were sometimes re-articulated, let us recall an important feature of the contemporary landscape, one that affects both Muslim and non-Muslim contexts but which is no less significant to us for this broader influence. As we noted, Casanova and others identify a contemporary trend towards the deprivatisation of religion globally, as religious voices seek to be heard on issues of public concern. Within this trend, the role of religion is an issue of particular salience in Muslim contexts where, perhaps more poignantly than in other environments, the voices of deprivatisation are speaking up and speaking louder. Keeping this in mind, we can unpack somewhat the significance of the three changes we have just noted.

As we saw, by the end of what Hodgson has called the 'High Caliphal period', the practical political power of the caliph was limited by the rise of other leadership in the sultans, amirs, etc., in whom actual political and military power resided. Notwithstanding this diminution in effective power, the office of the caliphate was still rich in symbolic authority. Moreover, the caliphate also represented, in a *mutatis mutandis* sort of way, the continuation of an institutional structure and type of authority that went back to the earliest days of Islam and to some extent drew on the example of the leadership of Muhammad himself. Indeed, it is these deep historical roots as well as the connections to the Prophet and to the continuation of his special authority (albeit imperfectly) that imbued the caliphate with its notional import, even long after its practical significance had faded. While in terms of political institutions and of governance the end of the caliphate was not as important because alternative offices were managing political rule, with the abolition of the caliphate, as feeble as it was practically, a great deal of rich 'Islamic' symbolism and potential repository for 'Islamic' identity was lost. This might in part explain why the re-establishment of the caliphate is such a *cause celebre* for certain contemporary Islamist groups. In their reckoning, with the revival of the caliphate would come a revival of Islam precisely because the caliph would be the symbol of Islam; his glory would be Islam's glory – a potent metaphor for the Islamists.

The abolition of the caliphate left open an important question: if the caliphate as a locus for 'Islam' was now lost, what would (and could) replace it? Was there another institution that could 'take up the cause', and what would this be? At the risk of belabouring the point, let us also keep in mind that the caliphate was practically almost inert – not dissimilar to a constitutional monarchy – only symbolically rich. Would any replacement be the same? In short, the removal of the caliph begged the question and allowed alternative institutional structures, including the modern nation state, to potentially claim the 'mantle of the Prophet'.[1]

The second great convulsion following on from (about) the end of the Ottomans was the domination of many Muslim societies by Western powers. As Mohammed Arkoun notes:

> What we call 'modernity' made a brutal eruption in to the 'living space of Islam' with the intrusion of colonialism as a historical fact. . . . Colonial endeavours of 19th century Europe sought justification in what was called a civilising mission. It was a matter of raising 'backward' peoples to the level of a 'universal' culture and civilisation.[2]

Emran Qureshi refers to this phenomenon as "globalisation of Western cultures in Muslim societies", and notes that much of 19th and 20th century 'Islamic' (I would prefer the term 'Muslim' here)[3] intellectual thought was conditioned by the encounter of Muslims with the colonizing West and that, in this regard, "there is a contestation of Islamic traditions taking place within the Muslim world".[4] On the one hand, Qureshi finds "Liberal Islamic thinkers [who] believed that the West's strengths needed to be emulated or indigenised: whether in reference to the struggle for gender-equality, human rights, or constitutionalism, as democracy was called in the early part of the twentieth century." On the other hand is the "Islamist/fundamentalist [who has] felt that Western influences needed to be expelled along with the colonizers".[5] The dust has not settled on this debate. The experience of

1 I borrow this phrase from the title of Mottahedeh's work, *The Mantle of the Prophet: Religion and Politics in Iran* (Mottahedeh, 2000).

2 Arkoun (1995) at 453.

3 This follows the discussion at the beginning of the chapter above about the conflation of a civilisational heritage on the one hand and a specifically, normative religious meaning on the other and Laila Ahmed's observation that:

> It is unusual to refer to the Western world as the 'Christian world' or the 'world of Christendom' unless one intends to highlight its religious heritage, whereas with respect to Islam and the Middle East there is no equivalent nonethnic, nonreligious term in common English usage, and the terms *Islamic* and *Islam* (as in the 'world of Islam') are those commonly used to refer to regions whose civilizational heritage is Islamic as well as, specifically, to the religion of Islam.

See Ahmed (1992) at 7.

4 Qureshi (2006) at 13.

5 Qureshi (2006) at 13–14.

colonialism both introduced Western liberal notions of democratic institutions and forms to Muslim contexts (as well as others) as well as altered the institutional structures of the pre-modern Muslim polity. In addition, the deprivatisation of religion has emerged in the Muslim world with vibrancy, especially in recent decades. Robert Heffner in his study of Islam in Indonesia has noted that global politics at the end of the twentieth century were marked by two major forces: "the diffusion of democratic ideas to disparate peoples and cultures around the world" and the "forceful reappearance of ethnic and religious issues in public affairs".[6] In addition, sadly, though perhaps partly as a result of the above, Qureshi also notes that "Today, polarizing Occidentalist and Orientalist caricatures and stereotypes have become ascendant within both the Islamic and Western worlds [which] attempt to explain behaviour through 'traits' that can be ascribed to a negative reading of the Other's religion or national culture."[7]

Finally, not just in the Muslim world but more generally, by the end of the Ottomans, our third convulsion was evident as the sun was setting on the age of empire and the modern, bureaucratic state was becoming the basic institution of political organisation. By the end of World War I, not only was the Ottoman Empire over but so too were the old Russian and Austro-Hungarian Empires. Of course, colonialism would still persist for some decades, and parts of the 'Muslim world' were placed under League of Nations mandates in the aftermath of World War I, resulting in the dismemberment of the Ottoman Empire so the transition from empire(s) to nation state was a gradual, iterative, process. Through the mandates and other interventions, the older organic and internal empires that had ruled in the Muslim world were largely displaced – either in favour of European (mainly British and French) empires or newly minted Muslim dynasties, like the Saudi or Jordanian monarchies. Nonetheless, the establishment of the modern state, even if still with ruling monarchies in places like Jordan, Saudi Arabia, Morocco and the Gulf states, meant a change of structure. The empires and dynasties of old were over.

The upshot of all of all of these shifts was to usher in a new political landscape for Muslim societies. While the same normative sources of reference may still be significant, the legal and political milieu of Muslim contexts had (has) to find a way to adapt to the new landscape. It is in this light, that Amyn Sajoo calls Muslim societies 'transitional' in needing to rearticulate their values in both a post-colonial context and one in which theoretical structures that had been developed in pre-modern social orders have now to face the reality of new structures, such as the modern state.[8]

At this point, it is necessary to be both clear and honest about the ground being tread here. This work, in fact, might be located within efforts to respond to the state of transition, to "write the next chapter in [the] story" of Islam acknowledging that "What is taking place now in the Muslim world is an internal conflict between Muslims, not an external battle

6 Heffner (2000) at 1.

7 Qureshi (2006) at 13. The UN, for example, heard a report on how to ease the increasing polarisation of Muslim and Western societies. See http://news.bbc.co.uk/1/hi/world/europe/6142308.stm. Ernst Gellner, for example, suggests that Islam imposes 'essential' constraints upon those committed to it. See his *Conditions of Liberty* (Gellner, 1994 at 211) and also his claims for the 'social pervasiveness' of Islam in his *Muslim Societies* (Gellner, 1981 at 2).

8 See Sajoo (2004). This is perhaps why there are a number titles coming mainly from Muslim authors that have a sense of taking steps towards something, rather than having reached an end or conclusion, e.g. Abdullahi an-Na'im's *Towards an Islamic Reformation* (An-Na'im (1996); *An Islamic Reformation?* (Bowers and Kurzman, 2004), the question mark at the end of their title (*An Islamic Reformation?*) suggesting the same thing, or Sajoo's own subtitle *Emerging Vistas* (Sajoo, 2004).

between Islam and the West. The West is merely a bystander . . ."[9] As part of this, John Bowen notes:

> So far, however, major theorists of pluralism in Europe and North America – John Rawls, Will Kymlicka, John Gray, Bhiku Parekh – have not had much to say about political and legal arrangements in Muslim-majority societies, or the normative debates among Muslims living in Europe or North America.[10]

This work aims precisely to cover some of this ground.

To proceed, we will look at a series of issues that the changes to the political landscape have raised for Muslim contexts and discuss responses that have been – and those that yet might be.

Reworking the law: replacement, codifications and *etatization*

While the encounter between Islam and the West raised different and sometimes diametrically opposed reactions, one interesting aspect is what it did to the religio-legal legacy that was discussed previously. The colonial state often took the organic tradition of Islamic laws resting in the hands of the '*ulama* and either supplanted it with the imposition of colonial law (as in Algeria and Indonesia) or sought to codify it into state law.[11] It was this latter pattern that occurred by direct colonial rule in, for example, British India, Malaysia and North Africa (Morocco and Tunisia), where various statues and codes were enacted.[12] Laws of personal status were often the only exceptions, but even these were regulated.

The Ottomans also attempted codification, though not under benign conditions. Whereas the terms of trade between the Muslim and Christian worlds were of relative equality, or even Muslim superiority, shifts in the balance of power eventually resulted in significant legal changes in the nineteenth century. The first of such attempts were the Capitulations, which were agreements conferring protection and rights to foreign merchants, and which gradually introduced European laws in Ottoman territories for European citizens.[13] While the Capitulations initially reflected an equal power balance,[14] shifts in the balance of power to the West changed their effect, climaxing in the Capitulations to France in 1569, whereby French consuls were conferred exclusive jurisdiction over French citizens.[15]

Thus, by the nineteenth century, there was some familiarity with European laws. As the Capitulations became irksome, and in seeking to modernise the Ottomans – by this time the so-called 'sick man of Europe' –turned to adoption of legal structures modelled on European codes. A substantial part of the codification process, therefore, was launched in the last

9 Aslan (2005) at 248. Of course, this makes essentially the same point as the claims of Akeel Bilgrami's 'clash within civilisations' argument and is related to Hassan Hanafi's assertion that new alternatives have to be developed for and by Muslims, which were mentioned in the previous chapter.

10 Bowen (2005) at 2.

11 Coulson (1964) at 154ff.

12 See in Pakistan, *The Muslim Family Law Ordinance (1961)*, a successor to the colonial era legislation. For Malaysia, see the *Muhammadan Marriage Ordinance, 1880*, and various state Islamic Family Law Enactments and Administration of Islamic Family Law Enactments. In Morocco, see the *Code of Personal Status (1956)* and subsequent amendments. For Tunisia, see the *Code of Personal Status, 1956* as amended.

13 Foster (2014) at 221.

14 Van den Boogert (2004) at 623; Ahmad (2000) at 2.

15 Augusti (2011) at 285; Eldemn (2006) at 290.

decades of the Ottomans with their Tanzimat reforms (1839–1876 CE), which introduced many codifications in several areas of law including, via the *Mejelle*, of (mainly Hanafi) personal law. Ottoman codifications, which naturally influenced many areas under the suzerainty of the sultan, reflected a substantial influence of the French Commercial and Penal Codes and post-Ottoman Turkey's reforms later reflected the influence of Italian law in the Criminal Code (1926), Germanic law in the Code of Civil Procedure (1928) and the Swiss Civil Code (in a 1927 replacement of the Ottoman *Mejelle* under the Republic of Turkey). Through these various means of direct replacement of the traditional laws, codifications undertaken by the colonial rulers and the influence of European laws through the legacy of the Ottoman codes, a profound change took place, which, in effect saw the political authorities of the state assert their power to define the terms of *shari'a*. Anver Emon summarises the effects of these codifications across Muslim societies:

> Both colonial administrators and Muslim national assemblies preserved Islamic law in codified form while modernising other legal areas such as commercial law. This reduction in jurisdiction and application arguably placated Islamists who felt threatened by modernisation and considered the preservation of traditional Islamic family law as necessary to maintain Islamic identity in the face of encroaching modernity. This phenomenon is widespread across the Muslim world, where colonial powers exerted force. The effect this had on the Shari'a, and in particular, Muslim understanding of Shari'a, was profound. The colonial treatment of Islamic law, whether in terms of redefining it or reducing its scope rendered the Shari'a reified and static in application and conceptual coherence.[16]

It is thus that, as Javaid Rehman asserts, "Islamic laws were adulterated by the disturbances of colonialis."[17] In short, the encounter with colonial/imperial rule, and the re-working of the traditional structures of Islamic law through this rule and codifications, raised the issue of, firstly, how to respond while still under colonial rule and, secondly, what to do with the traditional structures. Not surprisingly, there have been myriad ideas and responses.

As the modern state developed, it sought to change the traditional pattern of relations between political power on the one hand and religio-legal power on the other, by re-forming and regulating the *shari'a* as an instrument of the state and its administration. Sami Zubaida refers to this process as the *'etatization'* of the law (meaning here the *shari'a*), which was begun by the Ottomans in the nineteenth century.[18] For example, Zubaida notes that the "*Mecelle* [*Mejelle*] was written in accordance with a French methodology and format [of Civil law], but draws it substance and its initial axioms from the *shari'a*: the 'form' is European; the 'content' Muslim."[19] Berkes elaborates the significance of this 'legis-lising' of the *shari'a* (in other words, *etatization*):

> Although by no means a legislative act of parliament, the enactment of the Mecelle was the first instance of legislation within the field of Seriat [*shari'a*] exclusively by the sovereign and his government in their temporal capacity. Although no one could

16 Emon (2006) at 349.
17 Rehman (2005) at 24.
18 Zubaida (2003) at 121ff; particularly at 156.
19 Zubaida (2003) at 133–134.

> find any religiously legitimate grounds for declaring the Mecelle unacceptable from the viewpoint of the Seriat, there was no precedent for it in tradition.[20]

A similar pattern can be seen to have occurred later in Pakistan. In the current 1973 Constitution of Pakistan, Pakistan's official name is the 'Islamic Republic of Pakistan' (Part I, Article 1), Islam is the official religion of the state and, "the Injunctions of Islam as laid down in the Holy Qur'an and Sunnah shall be the supreme law and source of guidance for legislation to be administered through laws enacted by the Parliament and Provincial Assemblies, and for policy making by the Government" (Part I, Article 2); and the president of Pakistan must be a Muslim (Part III, Article 41).[21] Similarly, Art. 4 of the Constitution of the Islamic Republic of Iran, states:

> All civil, penal financial, economic, administrative, cultural, military, political, and other laws and regulations must be based on Islamic criteria. This principle applies absolutely and generally to all articles of the Constitution as well as to all other laws and regulations, *and the fuqaha of the Guardian Council are judges in this matter.*[22]

The *etatization* pattern has thus meant the encroachment of temporal, governmental, power into establishing and also defining the role and place of Islam and its traditional law in the state.

It is useful here to clarify the differences between this structure and the traditional structure. The pre-modern empire relied upon, was guided and checked by, was subject to and enforced the legal rules developed by the *'ulama*. But, as Khalid Masud explains, critically, even though *shari'a* rulings may have been enforceable by the state, they were not state law.[23] This is because determining the content of the law, except for those areas which the *shari'a* did not address or in the 'secular' law areas of administrative rules (the *siyasa shari'a*), was not something which was in the fiat of the state but instead in the hands of the *'ulama*. Indeed, as Masud further notes, Muslim moral traditions (including the *fiqh* as one type of moral tradition) evolved independent of state support and, although expecting the state to enforce the laws to ensure social regulation, these traditions did not allow the state to arbitrate between ethical differences (e.g., between the opinions of the jurists). Authority rested within the traditions and the scholars.[24] Khaled Abou el-Fadl adds to this that traditional Islamic epistemology tolerated and even celebrated divergent opinions and schools of law but that, today, in some countries of Muslim majority, the state has grown to be extremely powerful and "meddlesome" and it is centralised in ways that were inconceivable two centuries ago. For example, the modern states will these days often seek to control the clergy and the previously private religious endowments (*awqaf*; sing. *waqf*; which are trust-like charitable vehicles that could be established under classical *fiqh* rules). The problem and challenge today, Abou el-Fadl suggests, is that Islamic civilisation has collapsed under these new structures, and traditional institutions have been dismantled so that now new structures need to be erected.[25]

20 Berkes (1964) at 171.
21 See www.pakistanconstitutionlaw.com for the text of the Constitution of Pakistan.
22 See www.iranonline.com/iran/iran-info/Government/constitution-1.html (emphasis added).
23 Masud (2002) at 139.
24 Masud (2002) at 141.
25 Abou el-Fadl (2002) at 6–7.

John Kelsay, on the other hand, articulates a 'complementary thesis' in the traditional structure: according to Kelsay, both religious and political institutions may play complementary roles in the pursuit of human happiness. Hence, in the framework of 'classical Islam',[26] religion and politics were complementary, but independent, sets of institutions. Issues of Islamic legitimacy and moral authority rested with the *'ulama* but the government had at times the trappings of religion in, for example, the caliph leading prayers or preaching from the pulpit (or more commonly of having sermons preached from the pulpit in the name of the caliph), but neither moral power nor Islamic legitimacy.[27] Rather, the role of the political leadership was profane: to secure the peace of society.[28] Complementarity is not, therefore, to suggest identity,[29] though Kelsay does suggest it has meant some sort of established status for Islam albeit not one that should foreclose reform within Islam. Finally, Kelsay posits that contemporary Islamic political thought continues to seek out complementarity between religious and political authority, and in this complementarity created (and presumably continues to offer) a number of possibilities for a relationship between religious authorities and the state, without suggesting that there can be no boundaries between religion and the state.[30]

It is in this context that Hallaq has made the point that calling the *shari'a* 'Islamic law' interprets and manages into something other than what it was in the past.[31] The *shari'a* in its classical form was a discursive practice and cultural phenomenon and it is only under the influence of modernity that it has been entexted as 'Islamic law'. And, of course, a textualised *shari'a* particularly suits the needs of a modern nation-state structure. The pre-modern *shari'a* confronted power with its own truth but, returning to Masud's point, was not co-terminus with state law. Additionally, the *fiqh* was neither a totalizing statement of the law (inasmuch as there were other legal materials, like the *siyasa shari'a*), nor did it seek to control society. It was not an expression of the will of the state. The textualisation of the *shari'a*, however, through the *fiqh* (*qua* texts) has resulted, Hallaq argues, from the encounter of the *shari'a* and the state. While incompatible in the past because operating in different, albeit complementary, spheres, the modern state confronted the *shari'a* as a purely legislative entity and through the means of codification strove for its uniformity. A codified *fiqh* has thus been made part of the machinery of the bureaucratic state but this process has destroyed the moral and social hermeneutic of the *fiqh*, which, standing outside of the state, was its pre-modern condition.[32] The early vehicles for this codification and entexting given by Hallaq are examples we have already touched upon: the Ottomans operating under the shadow of European strength, and the Capitulations and British India. Hallaq makes the point, now obvious from his analysis, that Islamist movements that rest(ed) on

26 Although the phrase 'Classical Islam' is often used by scholars and commentators on Islam to denote, essentially, the pre-modern period of the caliphate(s), and while it is difficult to find an alternative nomenclature, the very use of the term 'classical' suggests that after this period there has been some decline, corruption or contamination of Islam. These implicit connotations, of course, feed into the ideological claims made by some Islamists, etc., for a return to Islam 'proper', based on 'classical', structures. For want of a better term, I will continue to use the term 'classical' though I mean it only to demarcate historical periods. I remain well aware of the implications of this type of language, though I also reject the normative authority of these implications.

27 Kelsay (2002) at 9.

28 Kelsay (2002) at 10 and 30.

29 Kelsay (2002) at 12.

30 Kelsay (2002) at 14.

31 Hallaq (2005–2006) at 152.

32 Hallaq (2005–2006) at 171.

a political-legal project of reestablishing the *shariʿa* have no sense of the actual historical *shariʿa* but mean an entexted, modern '*fiqh*-as-state-law' sense of the term that is at variance with its original nature. This is a politics that would have been alien to the pre-modern *shariʿa*.[33] He notes:

> What is notable about such espousals [of a received, modernized *shariʿa*] is that despite their many variants, they seem to possess a perception of a pre-modern Shariʿa that makes serious claim to objective knowledge. A particular practice determined by the *fiqh* is posited to have already existed . . . [but] such uses are estranged for the reality of the past – whatever that reality is – precisely to the same extent as modernity has ensured the conversion of the past into an ideological tool.[34]

In taking control of establishing the norms of Islamic law that may be enforced, the modern state has succeeded where the Caliphs al-Mamun and al-Mustasim failed: to put governmental authority in charge of the *shariʿa* and, inasmuch as the *shariʿa* is a normative expression of Islam, of the faith more generally. It is vitally important to remember, however, that this is a very modern phenomenon and that it has radically altered the 'classical' relationship that had prevailed previously. Indeed, it does more than that for it fundamentally wrong-steps the pattern and framework of 'classical Islam' and its history. *Etatization*, therefore, is not rescuing the *shariʿa*, but, as Hallaq explains, it is a morphing of the *shariʿa*'s nature. Thus, he states:

> But the *fiqh* was never 'the law' in its full range, in its realization within a social environment, nor does it ever constitute a totalising statement of the *law in practice*. . . . Attributing to *fiqh* roles of control and management is a distinctly modern misconception, a back-projection of our notions of law as a state vehicle for social engineering. . . . The integration and final transformation of *fiqh* into a code-like genre is wholly attributable to the success of modernity. . . . Yet the transformation into this new reality not only represented a metamorphosis but also announced the demise of the Shariʿa and its *fiqh* as Muslims knew them and *lived* them until two centuries ago.[35]

This, of course, raises the question of how then one might deal with the relationship of *shariʿa* and the state given the nature of the *shariʿa* and the fact that it did not involve coercive state power. It is to this that we can now turn in looking at the nexus between *din*, *dunya* and *dawla*.

The nexus of *Din*, *Dunya* and *Dawla*: religion, politics and the state – divided?

One of the supposedly major fault lines that might separate Muslim from liberal and secular frameworks is the idea that Islam does not know, and indeed cannot countenance, any division between 'church' and 'state', or between a faith (*din*) and the world (*dunya*).[36] Indeed,

33 Hallaq (2005–2006) at 154.
34 Hallaq (2005–2006) at 154–155.
35 Hallaq (2005–2006) at 167–168 and 171 (emphasis in original).
36 For example, in his work *The Law of Peoples*, John Rawls hypothesised a fictional state called Kazanistan. Kazanistan is a religiously committed state where the predominant religion is Islam. Specifically, in Rawls' Kazanistan: (i) there is no institutional separation between 'church' and state; (ii) Islam is the favoured

in a speech given in Canada, His Highness the Aga Khan, Imam (spiritual leader) of the world's Shia Ismaili Muslims (a minority branch within the minority Shia Muslim tradition), notes:

> Islam is all encompassing in the direction which it gives to Man's life. It is perhaps this very concept that the West, more familiar with the Augustinian Christian principle which separates the spiritual and material, finds difficult fully to understand and appreciate.[37]

As a result, it is oft asserted that Islam never developed a position of retreating from engagement with the worldly and, thus, with politics. For example, there is no monastic tradition in Islam where devotees can seek to live apart and in isolation, and can do so being fully in accordance with the tenets of their religion. The biblical maxim to 'Render therefore unto Caesar the things which are Caesar's; and unto God the things that are God's'[38] may have facilitated this possibility of a fully committed Christian being able to absent him or herself from the worldly affairs but, certainly, no such terse statement of principle appears in the scripture or other 'Islamic' textual sources. Some of this may, of course, have been due to the political circumstances at the advent of Islam. Unlike early Christianity, which faced both ideological opposition as well as severely constrained arenas for political activism, the early Muslim community was able very quickly and remarkably successfully to establish an empire by conquest. The state and the faith, then, were, if not exactly coterminous, certainly linked. Of course, the pre-modern Muslim polities were not religiously uncommitted. Islam in some form was the religious tradition of officialdom – though not necessarily in the sense of established by state law – binding both ruler(s) and ruled, though how it was expressed and how it was 'enforced' varied considerably over time and place. And this was the case even though other minority religious communities continued to exist under Muslim rule, albeit under particular conditions often as protected, but not equal, subjects of the ruler.[39]

---

religion; and (iii) only Muslims can hold upper positions of political authority and influence. Given that one of the touchstones of a liberal system is that the state will have no preset conception of the good, leaving this matter within the domain of either individual citizens or of associations, with the state remaining uncommitted, the conditions outlined above clearly seem to make Kazanistan a non-liberal place. Indeed, Rawls pays particular attention to condition (iii), noting that, 'This exclusion [i.e. condition (iii)] marks a fundamental difference between Kazanistan and a liberal democratic regime, where all offices and positions are, in principle, open to each citizen'. Thus, Rawls refers to the Kazanistanis as a decent, but non-liberal people for whom liberals can have respect and with whom they can reasonably interact (Rawls, 1999 at 75–76).

37 Speech given by His Highness the Aga Khan at the Foundation Ceremony of the Ismaili Jamatkhana and Centre, Burnaby, B.C., Canada, 26 July 1982 (Aga Khan, 1982); accessible at: http://ismaili.net/speech/s820726.html

38 *Holy Bible*, Matthew 22:21.

39 For the 'People of the Book' and others, this was the status of *dhimmis*. See on this Cahen (1960). *Dhimma* was a term used to designate the sort of 'indefinitely renewed contract through which the Muslim community accords hospitality and protection to members of other revealed religions on condition of their acknowledging the domination of Islam'. Those under this status were called *dhimmis*. The protected status was originally accorded to Jews and Christians (the Qur'anic 'People of the Book'), but later encompassed also Zoroastrians and other more minor faith communities.

Still, as we have noted, Islam has not known a canonical church structure as developed in Christianity, which could be 'established' *per se*. But some suggest that in this link between the spiritual and the material Islam does not separate 'church' and 'state' in theory, even if in practice there was no church and religious and political authority were separated. Thus, it is asserted that Islam has linked *din* and the *dunya* in a way that cannot accommodate diversity. The *din* and *dunya* nexus, however, m 58ay be read differently. It is true, as Sajoo points out, that a merging of the sacred and the secular became a 'leitmotif of Muslim civilisational experience';[40] however, as he goes on to assert, this does not mean that religion must be linked to the modern *dawla* (state):

> The world's 1.2 billion Muslims are diverse in their cultures and understandings of Islam. But they share a *weltanschauung* in which *din* and *dunya* (but not the modern *dawla*) are merged, so that both secular and sacred resonate in the public domain. Far from precluding the institutional separation of Mosque and State, this perspective takes no ideological position in this regard: the *umma* can thrive in a plurality of political arrangements. In other words, the occidental liberal conception of civil society is not inimical to Muslim traditions simply because it is wedded to secular space. . . . However, a radical secularity that banishes social ethics from the public sphere is patently inimical to Muslim society.[41]

Analysing the matter slightly differently, Abdulaziz Sachedina, considering the situation of Iraq as a case study, says flatly: 'Secularism with its insistence on the separation of "church" and "state" . . . is not responsive to a culture that demands keeping religion at the core of the emerging national culture. To put it differently, the "disestablishment" of Islam will not work'.[42] He does go on to note, however, that the Sharia 'provides a paradigm of civil religion by separating the jurisdictions in its laws. This principle allows religion to manage God's relationship to humanity without interference from any human institutions, including the mosque and the seminary'.[43]

Continuing, he asserts:

> This separation of jurisdictions is the closest the Sharia can come to secularism adopted in Western constitutions. It allows for functional secularity that can generate civic equality and mutual responsibilities at the human–human level of relationship, while maintaining the particularity and independence of the religious tradition from state administration.[44]

Sachedina's conclusion is that, as a result, 'Islamic heritage must guide rather than govern a modern nation-state'. This he sees as a challenge to religious communities and the way in which they might institutionalise a culture of inclusiveness.

Din and *dunya* link the spiritual and the material; the link asserts a place for a religiously inspired ethics in public life, and for religion in the 'world'. Both Sajoo and Sachedina,

40 Sajoo (2004) at 2.
41 Sajoo (2004) at 45.
42 Sachedina (2006) at 19.
43 Sachedina (2006) at 20.
44 Sachedina (2006) at 21.

though disagreeing in some parts perhaps, suggest that the *din/dunya* link can be separated from state administration (*dawla*) by pointing out the conceptual differences between a linkage between *din* and *dunya* on the one hand, and *din* and *dawla* on the other. These perspectives suggest a secularism of functional differentiation based on a separation of jurisdictions so long as faith can continue to be related to the needs of the world and not just the needs of individuals privately, and in this way guide rather than govern the state. As we have seen, in the experiences of Muslim history this has been the role that has developed. As Hallaq notes, the *shari'a*, though of course through its exponents among the *'ulama*, has confronted power with its own truth.[45] Moreover, an affinity between faith and the world has not meant that a single set of understandings of Islam has been dispositive, nor that a state could appropriate the mantle of religious authority and enforcement. Religious authority has been diffuse and multi-vocal and it has been within the province of the jurist-theologian-scholars, and expressly not political authorities. Thus, there has been a distinction between the 'sacred law' expressed by the *'ulama* (i.e. 'Islamic law') and the profane law of administration that was imposed by the political authorities.

An historical example will help here. In the preceding chapter, reference was made to the Shia Ismaili Fatimids who ruled from Egypt from the ninth to eleventh centuries CE, establishing an alternative, and rival, state and caliphate to the Baghdad-based Sunni Abbasids. As Shia Ismailis, the Fatimid religion–political structure rested, of course, on that particular form of authority of the Shia Imam, which, in brief recap, sees the Imam as the legitimate and *divinely inspired* successor to the Prophet and as a near 'caesro-papist' leader occupying at one and the same time the roles of imam and caliph. We noted above that the Fatimid political structure did not have a particularly great influence in Muslim history generally because of the relatively short duration of Fatimid reign in the context of Muslim history overall, and, even more, because of the different theological basis of the Fatimid system (*qua* a Shia system) as compared to the majoritarian Sunni traditions. Even during the Fatimid period, however, that is to say where, in a sense much more so than in the Sunni tradition, religious and political authority was united, legal diversity persisted. The Fatimids did develop a (Ismaili, obviously) legal code whose major text the *D'a'im al-Islam* (Pillars of Islam) was authored by the great Fatimid jurist the Qadi al-Nu'man, and this was the law of the Fatimid state. But it was not the only law to which one could appeal. The other different (Sunni) legal schools were still recognised, with their strength derived from the authority of their own jurist-scholars, who continued to hold positions of *qadis* for their various communities.[46] Moreover, high officials of state in the Fatimid period were not drawn exclusively from Ismaili adherents, or even, from just among Muslims. Ismaili, other Muslim, Jewish and Christian individuals rose to high public office, including to the highest office of *vizier*, which was occupied at times by both Jewish and Christian individuals. The Fatimid example is thus relevant here to make the point that even with the unity of political (calpihal) and religious (imamat) authority in one individual, the absolute unification of *din* and *dawla* did not take place, and that things were rather more plural. Once again, therefore, it seems that it is modern arguments to limit this plurality and to impose absolute uniformity through political institutions that are inconsistent with Muslim heritage.[47]

45 Hallaq (2005–2006) at 155.

46 On Ismaili history and thought, see Daftary (1989); and on the system of governance, see Vatikiosis (1957).

47 To be fair, not all modern structures deny the existence of at least juridical plurality. For example, Article 12 of the Iranian Constitution states (www.iranonline.com/iran/iran-info/Government/constitution-1.html):

So, the nexus of *din* and *dunya* seems separable, both in theory as well as in historical practice, from *dawla*: theoretically, because it may be read to engender a social ethic or a civil religion with a political secularity; practically, because religious authority and normativity has largely proceeded from outside of, and in opposition to, the state. This raises both an important theoretical vista as well as a practical challenge for the adoption of political values based on liberal outlooks with citizen participation *qua* citizens rather than qua Muslim, Jew, Christian, etc. We can engage with this by examining attitudes towards democracy among Muslim publics. Democracy is the appropriate vehicle to test the issue because, while there may practically be different versions of liberal-democratic states (in terms of different constitutional forms), democracy even at its most simple understanding is based on the participation of citizens in public decision-making. Democracy, thus, entails wide participation and must be in this respect liberal to accommodate that wide participation. That is to say that while there may be sham democracies that really have decision making made by a few, though with the pretence of democratic forms that are imperfectly or corruptly applied, a proper functioning democracy where citizen participation actually counts must not decide in advance what the state's conception of the good should be, but rather allow this to come from the citizens. In this sense, it would be liberal. Moreover, citizens who are in favour of democracy will likewise understand that they are in favour of their fellow citizens' participation in public decision-making and that it will not just be up to them (or those that they like or support) to make political decisions. Democracy and liberal theory are, thus, close allies, so by examining the receptivity to one we may gain insight into the receptivity of the other.

Contemporary opinions in Muslim populations

Empirical studies seem to reflect a welcoming of democratic ideas among contemporary Muslims. In their detailed study based on empirical evidence from the *World Values Survey*, Pippa Norris and Ronald Ingelhart draw the following conclusions:

1 There were no significant differences between publics living in the West and in Muslim religious cultures in approval of how democracy works in practice, in support for democratic ideals and in approval for strong leadership.
2 Muslim publics did display greater support for a strong societal role by religious authorities than do Western publics.[48]

Hence, they continue that "any claim of 'clash of a civilisations', especially of fundamentally different *political* values held by Western and Islamic societies, represents and

> The official religion of Iran is Islam and the Twelver Ja'fari school [in usual al-Din and fiqh], and this principle will remain eternally immutable. Other Islamic schools, including the Hanafi, Shafi'i, Maliki, Hanbali, and Zaydi, are to be accorded full respect, and their followers are free to act in accordance with their own jurisprudence in performing their religious rites. These schools enjoy official status in matters pertaining to religious education, affairs of personal status (marriage, divorce, inheritance, and wills) and related litigation in courts of law. In regions of the country where Muslims following any one of these schools of fiqh constitute the majority, local regulations, within the bounds of the jurisdiction of local councils, are to be in accordance with the respective school of fiqh, without infringing upon the rights of the followers of other schools.

What is different, however, is the placement of state authority above and beyond that of the juridical traditions, which is manifest even in the permitting, by the state, of some juridical plurality.

48 Norris and Inglehart (2004) at 146–47 and 154.

oversimplification of the evidence" and that "Support for democracy is surprisingly widespread among Islamic publics, even among those who live in authoritarian societies. The most basic cultural fault line between the West and Islam does not concern democracy . . ."[49] Values Surveys as reported by Mansoor Moadell, which looked at attitudes in Muslim majority settings of Egypt, Iran, Jordan, Morocco, Saudi Arabia and Turkey and compared these to the US, suggest similarly robust rates of support for democracy.[50] Among those expressing an opinion about democracy (i.e., excluding 'don't knows'), the percentage who agreed with the statement that "democracy is the best form of government" ranged from a low of 69% in Iran to a high of 99% in Egypt.[51] Interestingly, however, the Values Survey reveals somewhat mixed results when it comes to how democracy might work practically with 69% of respondents saying that it was important (23%) or very important (46%) that 'government implements laws according to the people's wishes' but 88% agreeing as important (15%) or very important (73%) that 'a good government implements only the *shariʿa*'.[52] While seemingly pulling in different directions, what the expression of these opinions illustrates in part is that an appeal to the normative values of Islam as expressed in the *shariʿa* remains important among the populations in these Muslim majority settings.[53] Justice as discourse is particularly useful here because it would allow for such religious sentiments, and indeed for the potential contradictions between the support for democracy on the one hand the *shariʿa* on the other, to be expressed.[54]

What other studies do suggest, however, consistent with Norris and Inglehart's second conclusion about the support for a societal role for religious authorities, is the importance of religion to the social conscience of Muslim peoples. An ICM poll conducted for the BBC reported that 97% of Indonesians surveyed, 98% of Nigerians and 92% of Lebanese said that they have always believed in God.[55] Similarly, other data from the 'Values Survey' showed

49 Norris and Inglehart (2004) at 154–55 (emphasis in original) and Inglehart (2017) at 20.

50 Moadell (2004); accessible at www.psc.isr.umich.edu/research/tmp/moaddel_capitol-hill-may04.pdf. See also Inglehart (2017) at 15 citing the 2010–2014 *World Values Survey*, showing that the populations of almost every country in the world – whether Muslim, Christian, Hindu, Buddhist or Confucian – see democracy as the best form of government. Overwhelming majorities of the population of both the Arab-speaking Islamic countries and other Islamic countries rated a democratic system as either "very good" or "good". A solid majority of the public in both Western and Muslim countries gives democracy high marks as the most efficient form of government, with 68% disagreeing that "democracies are indecisive" and "democracies aren't good at maintaining order" (all other cultural regions and countries, except East Asia and Japan, being far more critical). And equal numbers of respondents on both sides of the civilizational divide (61%) firmly reject authoritarian governance, expressing disapproval of "strong leaders who need not bother with parliament and elections".

51 Turkey, 88%, Jordan, 90%, Morocco 96%, Saudi Arabia 71%.

52 Although it bears mention that of the studies that focus more on the type or depth of Islamic beliefs, surprisingly most find no relationship between orthodoxy or Islamism and democratic support, as Jamal and Tessler (2008) and Meyer, Rizzo and Ali (2007) assert. In this regard, Moaddel is an exception.

53 Also note that intra-diverse views. See the survey results at www.pewglobal.org/2016/04/27/the-divide-over-islam-and-national-laws-in-the-muslim-world/, showing that the Muslim world is sharply divided on what the relationship should be between the tenets of Islam and the laws of governments. Across ten countries with significant Muslim populations surveyed by Pew Research Center in 2015, there is a striking difference in the extent to which people think the Quran should influence their nation's laws.

54 Spierings (2014) at 431 points out that in most cases, negative relationships with Islam are explained by the culturalist argument about Islam's conservativeness. Surprisingly or noteworthy, (unexpected) positive relations between Islam and democratic support are generally not explained by the alternative interpretations of Islam as discussed earlier, but in terms of instrumentalism, whereby democracy is way to power for Islamist.

55 See survey results at: http://news.bbc.co.uk/1/shared/spl/hi/pop_ups/04/world_what_the_world_thinks_of_god/html/1.stm. The Programme 'What the World Thinks of God' aired on BBC 2 on

high levels of respondents in these countries of Muslim majority considering themselves to be religious persons, and considering themselves to be above all else Muslims.[56] Rates of religious practice (participation in religious services once or more a week) ranged from 27% in Iran as a low to 44% in Jordan as a high.[57] This is significant given that Muslims are the fastest-growing major religious group in the world.[58] Finally, a survey done as part of the Pew Global attitudes research reveals high degrees of feeling that 'Religion is Very Important' in several countries of Muslim majority.[59] This survey notes, "More than nine-in-ten respondents in the predominantly Muslim nations of Indonesia, Pakistan, Mali and Senegal rate religion as personally very important [though] in Turkey and Uzbekistan people are more divided over religion's importance" (65% in Turkey said it was very important, while only 35% in Uzbekistan said the same).[60] The report further notes that "secularism is particularly prevalent in Europe" and that "wealthier nations tend to place less importance on religion – with the exception of the United States". Thus, "In Africa, no fewer than eight-in-ten in any country see religion as very important personally." Even where poll support seems mixed, some qualitative assessment suggests that religious feeling cannot be eradicated even by state imposition of a strict secular framework, as has been attempted in Ataturkist Turkey. As M Hakan Yavuz notes, "Although Turkey is a national and secular state, religion lies at the core of its political landscape and identity", such that "The underlying Islamic vernacular of Turkish society will continue to play an important role in the future evolution of Turkey's *intrinsic* character."[61]

Another Pew report provides what seems a good conclusion to all of this data:

> Muslims surveyed in the Pew Global Attitudes Survey favour a prominent – in many cases expanded – role for Islam and religious leaders in the political life of their countries. Yet that opinion does not diminish support for a system of governance that ensures the same system of civil liberties and political rights enjoyed by democracies.

Thursday, 26 February 2004 at 2100 GMT and on the BBC World Service on Sunday, 29 February 2004 at 1306 and 1806 GMT. Interestingly, in the same poll, 79% of Americans said that have always believed in God, 78% said they had studied religious texts and 71% said they would die for their beliefs (or God).

56 The figures for those considering themselves to be religious persons were 62% in Saudi Arabia, 82% in Iran, 94% in Morocco, 80% in Turkey, 85% in Jordan, 99% in Egypt. Figures for those considering themselves to be 'above all, Muslims' were: Iran 61%, Turkey 68%, Jordan 72%, Saudi Arabia 75% and Egypt 79%. These results were also reported in Moadell (2003). The latter set of figures (the 'above all, Muslim' figures) are found only in the presented paper. See also, the recent survey poll at: www.todayonline.com/world/asia/most-malay-msians-see-themselves-muslims-first-poll, where most Malay Malaysians identify themselves as "Muslims first" rather than Malaysians or Malays first, independent pollster Merdeka Centre, amid rising religious conservatism in the country.

57 Saudi Arabia 28%, Turkey 38%, Morocco and Egypt 42%.

58 See survey results at: www.pewresearch.org/fact-tank/2016/07/22/muslims-and-islam-key-findings-in-the-u-s-and-around-the-world/. Note also, however, there is diversity among Muslims themselves as to whether they believe *shari'a* law ought to be implemented. Responses on this question vary widely. Nearly all Muslims in Afghanistan (99%) and most in Iraq (91%) and Pakistan (84%) support *shari'a* law as official law. But in some other countries, especially in Eastern Europe and Central Asia – including Turkey (12%), Kazakhstan (10%) and Azerbaijan (8%) – relatively few favour the implementation of *shari'a* law.

59 Pew Research Center for People and the Press (www.people-press.org), "Among Wealthy Nations . . . U.S. stands alone in its embrace of religion", released 19 December 2002.

60 Turkey is of course officially secular and Kemalism was positively *laïc* in its orientation. The results for Uzbekistan on the other hand may reflect the effect of its decades as part of the Soviet Union and it may be that in the coming generations the feelings of Uzbeks will more closely approximate those of the other countries of Muslim majority noted above.

61 Yavuz (2000) at 21 and 42 (emphasis added).

> Muslims in 14 countries – ranging from Turkey, Pakistan and other predominantly Muslim countries to Uganda and Ghana where Muslims are a relatively small minority were surveyed. . . . In most of these countries support for freedom and a strong Islamic presence in politics go hand in hand.
>
> Support for a religious role in public life among Muslim publics does not necessarily carry the same implications that it might in a nation like the United States, where the separation of church and state has been codified and reinforced over the years. Most importantly, while many Muslim around the world would like to see more religion in politics, this view does not contradict widespread support for democratic ideals among these publics. In fact, in a number of countries, Muslims who support a greater role for Islam in politics place the highest regard on freedom of speech, freedom of the press and the importance of free and contested elections.[62]

Similar conclusions come from the *Gallup World Poll, Special Report: Muslim World* in their report entitled 'Islam & Democracy' (2006).[63] The report states (at page 1):

> A recent in-depth Gallup survey in 10 predominantly Muslim countries, representing more than 80% of the global Muslim population,[64] shows that when asked what they admire most about the West, Muslims frequently mention political freedom, liberty, fair judicial systems, and freedom of speech. When asked to critique their own societies, extremism and inadequate adherence to Islamic teachings were their top grievances.
>
> However, while Muslims say they admire freedom and an open political system, Gallup surveys suggest that they do not believe they must choose between Islam and democracy, but rather, that the two can co-exist inside one functional government.

And, continuing (at page 2),

> Although many Muslims have favourable attitudes toward an inclusive political system, according to Gallup polling, their ideas of self-determination do not require a separation of religion and the state. Poll data show that significant percentages of Muslims cite the importance of the role of Islam in governance. Muslims surveyed indicated widespread support for *Sharia*, Islamic principles that are widely seen as governing all aspects of life from the mundane to the most complex.
>
> Yet, the poll also indicated that support for *Sharia* does not mean that Muslims want a theocracy to be established in their countries. Only minorities in each country say they want religious leaders to be directly in charge of drafting their country's constitution, writing national legislation, drafting new laws, determining foreign policy and international affairs, and deciding how women dress in public or what is televised or published in newspapers.

As Pew and Gallup have noted, such attitudes among Muslims seem to hold not only in environments of Muslim majority but even among minority Muslim populations. Furthermore, these attitudes appear to be not just confined to Muslim populations living in the counties of

62 Pew Research Center for People and the Press (www.people-press.org), "Views of a Changing World, June 2003" (The Pew Global Attitudes Project).

63 Accessible at http://media.gallup.com/worldpoll/pdf/gallupmuslimstudiesislamanddemocracy030607.pdf

64 The countries polled were Egypt, Pakistan, Jordan, Bangladesh, Morocco, Indonesia, Iran, Turkey and Lebanon.

the developing world. On 30 November 2004, *The Guardian* newspaper reported the results of survey of British Muslims conducted by ICM. In this survey, 68% of Muslim women and 46% of men reported praying five times a day, every day, with another 19% of women and 17% of men reporting that they prayed two or more times a day, most days (13% of women and 23% of men reported praying less than once a week or never).[65] These figures suggest a high level of religiosity expressed by religious practice. There was also support, among 61% of those surveyed, for *shari'a* courts being allowed to resolve civil cases within in the Muslim community, so long as the penalties would not contravene British law. So, it seems that a role for, and of, Islam was important for British Muslims. Adding in these results to those we have just seen suggests that among Muslims, religion has mattered and continues to matter.

More interesting even than the headline poll results of the ICM survey in *The Guardian*, however, was the rich range of opinions expressed by participants within roundtable discussions – eight tables, eight subjects, 103 young Muslims – that were arranged as part of *The Guardian* story. By way of example, one can note the following from page 19 of the article. First, from Table (discussion) 5 on 'How the faithful live in a secular society':

> When Asif Dawood, a member of Hizb ut-Tahrir, declared that Islam and democracy were incompatible, there was an uproar at the table, with Mr Yousafazi [a member of Young Citizens in the West Midlands] rejecting the idea outright and insisting that the principles of democracy came out of Islam.
>
> There was an assumption, added Sohaib Saeed Bhutta from the Muslim Association of Britain, that there was such a thing as British Islam, when there were differences "within even Glaswegian Islam".

Second, from Table discussion 6 on 'The widespread perception is that Islam discriminates against women. Why is that so?':

> Sultanah Parvin, a teacher and member of Hizb ut-Tahrir, picked up on this last point: "Islam is not compatible with Western concepts of freedom and choice – they would include the right to wear a miniskirt. From an Islamic point of view we don't agree with that." But Ayisha Ali sees this as a challenge of integration. "You might not want to see people in miniskirts, but that's the right of the country we live in, and it's the law we have to yield to. It is not up to us to come in and tell them how to live".

That there should be such a range of opinions expressed in these discussions is not surprising – it merely reflects what we have already noted about the diversity within 'Muslim contexts'. What it does show, however, is the continued expression of this diversity within the framework of Muslim identity in a Western context.

Prospects for democracy?

In his examination of the prospects for democracy in the Muslim world, Noah Feldman notes the trend mentioned in the empirical studies namely that many contemporary Muslims find the combination of Islamic ideal and democratic values appealing and that, indeed, the

65 *The Guardian*, 30 November 2004 at 17–20.

hunger for Islamic democracy is growing.[66] Feldman makes a distinction between *Islamic* democracy and *Islamist* democracy – the former being a democracy in which 'Islam' develops in tandem and resonates with democratic values, the latter being a usurpation by Islamists of democratic structures for their own ideological and theocratic ends. Feldman sketches out a set of options for Islam in the public sphere in theoretical terms on the one hand, and in practical structures on the other hand. Options for Islam in public sphere include: (i) classical Islamic law, (ii) Islam as the official religion of a secular state, (iii) Islam being the bases for family or personal law only, and (iv) Islam as the symbolic basis for personal legislation. The point here is that the options are richer than a choice between a secular state and an Islamic state.[67] In terms of practical structures (or as he puts it 'How to get an Islamic democracy'), Feldman posits the following practical structures could be used: (i) an Islamic state like Anglican Britain, where Islam is the religion of the state but with equal rights accorded to all citizens, Muslim and non-Muslim; (ii) classical Islamic law as a part of state law (for example, in the way in both contemporary Pakistan and Egypt mention is made of the role of Islamic law in their constitutions). This would be alright, he suggests, so long as the state protects non-Muslims and treats them equally; (iii) Islamic law as the exclusive state law in some codified system along the lines of what the *Mejelle* was attempting; (iv) a constitutional provision that Islamic law shall be the law of the land à la contemporary Saudi Arabia but in this sense making the invocation of Islamic law akin to an invocation of English Common Law, broad and diverse with many opinions being expressed and putting the power of interpreting it in the hands of the judges.[68]

To this, Feldman adds the following principled arguments. First, that a state that embraces religion can still be democratic in the way that Britain is or that the German state of Bavaria is. Second, while it is necessary for a liberal democracy to respect an individual's right to worship and to provide religious liberty for its inhabitants, this is not incompatible with support or even funding for a particular faith.

Feldman adds that an Islamic state can fully respect the moral equality of all its citizens because Islam professes a commitment to equality, as evidenced in theological statements about how all peoples are equal before God. For this, he cites the Qur'anic verse 49:13:

> O mankind! Lo! We have created you male and female, and have made you nations and tribes that ye may know one another. Lo! the noblest of you, in the sight of Allah, is the best in conduct. Lo! Allah is Knower, Aware.[69]

On Feldman's examination, the notion of the basic equality of all people before God, which he finds within Islam, can be used as the starting point for a political democracy that must

66 Feldman (2003) at 6 and 15.

67 Feldman (2003) at 22ff.

68 Feldman (2003) at 54–55.

69 Feldman (2003) at 62. Holy Qur'an, translation of M Pickthall. Other translations of the verse are:

> O mankind! We created you from a single (pair) of a male and a female, and made you into nations and tribes, that ye may know each other (not that ye may despise (each other)). Verily the most honoured of you in the sight of Allah is (he who is) the most righteous of you. And Allah has full knowledge and is well acquainted (with all things). (Translation of Yusuf Ali)
>
> Or
>
> O you men! surely We have created you of a male and a female, and made you tribes and families that you may know each other; surely the most honourable of you with Allah is the one among you most careful (of his duty); surely Allah is Knowing, Aware. (Translation of Shakir)

also embrace basic equality. He concludes by noting, consistent with what we have seen above, that the evidence shows that most Muslims do not want or need religious enforcement by the state, but rather want Islam as a moral guide to keep domestic and foreign polices ethical.[70]

Feldman's analysis is interesting in a least two senses: first, because he theorises about how Islam and democracy can fit together and seeks to make an argument that they can indeed fit, and, second, because he confirms through his analysis some of what we have just seen, namely, that the range of possibilities in terms of democratic models and the 'responses' of Islam to these models are rich and varied. What is implicit in Feldman's analysis, however, is that this fit, or the construction of 'Islamic democracy', is not yet achieved.

Conclusion

At the end of the last chapter, L. Carl Brown's observation, based on his examination of the classical history and heritage of Muslim societies, was cited stating that Muslim history had "rocked along" with a certain indeterminacy in terms of the relationship between religion and politics, leaving this potentially explosive issue unresolved. In looking at the situation in later history and into the contemporary period, we can see that the same indeterminacy obtains inasmuch as there is still not a fixed answer. But the indeterminacy that prevailed in the past that seemed stable is much less stable now. Whereas the past indeterminacy fit the socio-political structures that prevailed, and, indeed, could be seen to have been born out of them, any current indeterminacy is a poor fit for contemporary conditions. What has changed is the nature of political order and institutional structure. It is rather like a challenge to the 'old regime' in both theory and practice. The modern nation-state with all its extensive, controlling, regulating and managing functions is still the basic political unit in operation today, notwithstanding challenges from inside and outside that challenge its hegemony. And the political ideas that go along with the state, ideas of democracy and participation, are the paradigmatic principles for the organisation of political life. These developments were not *sui generis* to Muslim societies. Liberal democracy, of course, was born, painfully, out of a history in Western Europe that was different from the history, taken broadly, of areas of Muslim majority. Yet, directly or indirectly, through colonial infiltration or intellectual adoption – or both – the legacy of Western liberal democracy found its way around the world. In this it became both a challenge and an opportunity and is something with which Muslim, as other, contexts have had to grapple. This grappling continues.

What we have seen is that there is support both for democratic political principles, which are strongly linked to liberal theory, as well as for a place or role or meaning for Islam in politics among Muslims, but no one, and certainly no simple, answer as to how these desires can be harmonised. There seems nothing *immanent* in Islam, given both the varied interpretations of the faith and its traditions and the history of how it has handled – with indeterminacy – the relation of religion and politics, that either provides a system of harmonisation or, the other hand, posits an irresolvable conflict. The interrelationship may be made to work but not in a simple fashion, since there is neither a settled blueprint from classical history nor an obvious conclusion from contemporary debates and viewpoints. But there are debates and there is receptivity. For contemporary Muslim contexts, as opposed to other contexts, these debates are taking place in situations in which both modern political ideas and institutions are known as well as where the heritage and history of Islam and its

70 Feldman (2003) at 228.

texts, models and law(s) are known. And it is within these, thus unique, contexts that transition and liminality are prevailing, as there is both the desire for democracy and for a role for Islam. As Vali Nasr puts it:

> As the example of Iran suggests, the Muslim world is in the midst of a process of change, experimenting with models that, by balancing competing demands of religion and secularism, can create viable ways for these societies to modernize. . . . These states will call upon the cultural resources of religion to address their social and economic needs – but not necessarily in the manner European history suggests.[71]

Having set up our understanding of Muslim contexts, both in historical terms as well as considering some of their contemporary contours, what remains, therefore, is the need for imagination and even a new 'social imaginary'[72] for Muslim contexts that might make sense of the tensions and conflicts, but also opportunities, that come as the religio-legal and political heritage and history, with its indeterminate answer to the relationship of religion and politics, meets new political conditions and new political and legal frameworks, especially in the structure of the modern state. As this discussion makes clear, however, there is much fertile ground for imagination based on a support for democracy and its cognates on the one hand, and of the importance of Islam on the other. As part of this process the old(er) divide of religio-legal authority, on the one hand, and political authority on the other will need to be reworked.

What I will propose next is a new alignment based on the normative usefulness of liberal theory, and in particular on the framework of justice as discourse, in providing fruitful terms for the interaction of religion, law, state and society in Muslim contexts. This new alignment will separate out religion, law and politics as three distinct concepts and reconnect them in a new manner in which they will all be 'public' in a liberal sense.

71 Nasr (2003) at 72. Muslims outside of 'the Muslim world' will also have to deal with these same demands, drawing as they will from the same well of cultural resources and ideas, albeit in different circumstances.

72 I draw the idea of a 'social imaginary' from Charles Taylor's *Modern Social Imaginaries* (Taylor (2004)). Taylor explains this as follows (at 23):

> By social imaginary . . . I am thinking, rather, of the ways people imagine their social existence, how they fit together with others, how things go on between them and their fellows, the expectations that are normally met, and the deeper normative notions and images that underlie these expectations . . . the social imaginary is that common understanding that makes possible common practices and a widely shared sense of legitimacy.

5 Terms of engagement

(Re)imagining religion, law, state and society for Muslim contexts

> You are free; you are free to go to your temples, you are free to go to your mosques or to any other place or worship in this State of Pakistan. You may belong to any religion or caste or creed that has nothing to do with the business of the State. As you know, history shows that in England, conditions, some time ago, were much worse than those prevailing in India today. The Roman Catholics and the Protestants persecuted each other. Even now there are some States in existence where there are discriminations made and bars imposed against a particular class. Thank God, we are not starting in those days. We are starting in the days where there is no discrimination, no distinction between one community and another, no discrimination between one caste or creed and another. We are starting with this fundamental principle that we are all citizens and equal citizens of one State.[1]

> Let's be honest: religion can create community, and it can divide communities. It can lead to searing self-criticism and it can promote a pompous self-satisfaction. It can encourage dissent and conformity, generosity and narrow-mindedness. It can engender both righteous behaviour and self-righteousness. . . . Religion's finest hours have been the times when intense belief led to social transformations, yet some of its darkest days have entailed the transformation of intense belief into the ruthless imposition of orthodoxy.[2]

In this chapter, I attempt to bring together the theoretical framework outlined in Chapters 1 and 2 to the examination of and elaboration of Muslim contexts in Chapters 3 and 4. In so doing, I seek to finalise the argument that I have been developing for the normative usefulness and appropriateness of liberal theory, and justice as discourse in particular, in Muslim contexts, and more specifically for the construction of a framework for relating law, religion, state and society in these contexts. I proceed to do this in three sections. First, I outline some challenges that arise out of liberal theory for Muslim contexts and discuss how these challenges may be addressed generally and within the framework of justice as discourse. These challenges arise in two ways. One set of challenges is, one might say, generic and would arise in any attempt to apply a variety of liberal theory to an environment in which a religious tradition is important. These challenges are captured in the second epigraphic quotation from Dionne, cited just above. Even though this set of challenges is thus not unique

1 Presidential address to the Constituent Assembly of Pakistan by Mohammad Ali Jinnah, first Governor-General and Head of State of Pakistan, on 11 August 1947. Reproduced in *Dawn* (Karachi's English-language daily newspaper), Independence Day Supplement, 14 August 1999.

2 Dionne Jr (2003) at xvi.

to Muslim contexts, I will address it particularly with these contexts in mind. The second set of challenges is particular to Muslim contexts and arises from the fact that liberal theory did not emerge in these contexts. In the second section, I propose an institutional model building from justice as discourse that I will argue is appropriate for a Muslim majority state, and envisage how these principles may be applied practically. In this, the first epigraphic quotation from an address made by Muhammad Ali Jinnah in Pakistan is instructive. Finally, I offer a few thoughts by way of conclusion, noting especially that what I propose here (and the argument that runs throughout this work) calls for Muslim contexts to imagine new possibilities which, while consistent with their heritage, are not based on seeking solutions that are immanent either in Islam as a faith (however so interpreted) or on a set 'Islamic' model from the past.

Challenges to the uses of liberal theory

Issues and challenges from the paradigm of liberal theory

The problem of liberal neutrality

In discussing Rawls and feminism, Elizabeth Brake outlines the heart of the familiar claim for liberal neutrality:

> Liberal neutrality is the doctrine that the state remains neutral between competing conceptions of the good, where an individual's conception of the good is whatever plan of life she has, subject to certain rational constraints. Such conceptions may include, for example, commitment to religious beliefs.[3]

She goes on to assert that the claim to neutrality might not sit well with some comprehensive doctrines, including, significantly, religious outlooks, noting that:

> For instance, a comprehensive doctrine might simply deny that the political sphere is separable [from our morally significant features]: examples of religions that would base law on religious teachings spring readily to mind. Thus the religious believer, who seeks unity of church and state, or a legal system based on the Old Testament, might respond to Rawls that his restriction of the scope of justice does not make the theory either neutral or acceptable to the believer.[4]

Brake identifies an important issue here, which though it has more general application, is salient for Muslim contexts. Whatever Islam means to specific individuals, the key factor that distinguishes Muslim contexts is the reference point of Islam, and like any other religious system Islam is not neutral inasmuch as it will have an outlook about what is morally significant and, therefore, what the best political choices may be. Liberal neutrality may thus be a problem because it posits an uncommitted position in the face of a (potentially) committed outlook. No religious culture or environment where religion is significant may thus readily accept liberal neutrality. In the case of Muslim contexts, this may be felt especially because

3 Brake (2004) at 296. Brake cites Ronald Dworkin's and Will Kymlicka's works reinforcing the liberal requirement of neutrality. See Dworkin (1978) and Kymlicka (1989).
4 Brake (2004) at 299–300.

there has not been any sense of Islam disengaging from worldly affairs. Born in a time of an expanding empire, early Muslim political leaders drew up their sense of the values of the faith to guide the community practically as well as spiritually, whether this was in the time of the Prophet (who combined the role of political and religious leadership) or his successors who, while not being able to unify these authorities as seamlessly in practice, still sought guidance from the faith even for 'worldly' affairs. Additionally, like Jewish law, articulations of Muslim legal traditions dealt with guidance that applied, albeit not always comprehensively, to ritual matters (prayer, washing, dietary rules), to criminal law, to contract and even, inchoately, to administration. In short, the religious law, the *shari'a*, like the other religious values was engaged with the here and now as well as the hereafter.

Thus, the issue, as Michael Cook has noted, is that Islam (and the same may apply to any religion) within certain limits tells people what to believe and how to live, while liberalism, also within certain limits, is about leaving people to work this out for themselves.[5] Cook goes on to claim, however, that Western culture, as broadly secular and liberal, is not necessarily irreligious and in this sense seems readily compatible with a *non-fundamentalist* allegiance to Christianity, Judaism or Islam.[6] This is an important distinction. What Cook helps us to realise is that it is one thing to feel that a faith tradition can speak to and guide an individual in her or his daily life, including in 'worldly' matters, but quite another to think that it must be made to do so by being allied to political decision-making. Some fundamentalists want to construct 'God's kingdom' on Earth and see their religious convictions reflected in political order, but that is only one option even for those who might want to be guided by faith. Thus, while there may be some Muslims (as some of other traditions) that would seek to impose fundamentalist interpretations on their faith, this does not make Islam incompatible with a liberal culture *per se*. Furthermore, as the history of Muslim contexts has shown, there is no clear meaning shared by all Muslims about what the Islamic commitments or attitudes on any particular public issue should be, so there is no simple or clear 'Islamic' alternative to the premise of liberal neutrality on public issues in any case.

On the side of liberal theory, Cook's insight that Western secular and liberal culture is not necessarily irreligious is borne out, theoretically, in the Rawlsian limitation of the commitments to political liberalism to 'constitutional essentials'. While, as mentioned earlier, it is not clear from Rawls exactly what is and is not a constitutional essential, the point to be noted here is that, in Rawls' liberal formulation at least, liberal theory requires an uncommitted stance only up to these essentials; beyond this, liberal neutrality would not be necessary. Additionally, the commitment to neutrality does not have to mean that everything that the state does must be seen to be absolutely neutral. Roger Trigg, for example, suggests that absolute neutrality is impossible to achieve in any case but all that is required to meet the 'liberal neutrality' test is respect for religious liberty and toleration of diversity.[7] Trigg's point that we may never be able to get absolute neutrality is well taken, but his requirements of what is required seem fine if, and only if, one adds to his criteria of respect and toleration a commitment to a type of 'neutrality' on the part of the state (albeit one that may never be completely realised) that Brake outlines.

The idea of liberal neutrality does not, thus, seem to be an insurmountable problem for Muslim contexts. The neutrality may be challenged by potential commitments but there is not a coherent 'Islamic' alternative that stands in opposition to it. There may be the views of

5 Cook (2003) at 114.
6 Cook (2003) at 163.
7 Trigg (2007) at 235.

Muslims, but these inevitably will be highly divergent and perhaps even contradictory. As a political principle, then, state neutrality is an entirely reasonable and even desirable response to these situations. On the other hand, neutrality does not have to mean that religiously committed positions cannot legitimately be held on a wide spectrum of issues. It is only for those matters that will ensure participation that neutrality must apply, though, admittedly, where those lines are drawn is highly significant and may be highly controversial. Justice as discourse may assist in determining where the lines are drawn; as a variant of liberal theory it shares the concern for, and commitment to, neutrality but also circumscribes this neutrality to accommodate the expression of *non-neutral* opinions and reasons and, in particular, religiously parochial reasons.

The contours of secularity

A second and related issue is secularity. As Habermas pointed out, a liberal framework necessarily implies a type of state secularity. This is so because it would violate the liberal principle of neutrality to have pre-set religious commitments on the part of the state. Secularity, therefore, is potentially a challenge for Muslim contexts where levels of religious affiliation are fairly robust. The issue is how the challenge of secularity can sit with religious commitments, and, moreover why those with religious commitments should accept state secularity.

To address this issue, it is important to be clear, however, what the contours and demands of liberal secularity are. Secularity, as we have just noted, need not encompass animosity to religious commitments – which is easy enough – and it need not entail that religious commitments cannot, subject to certain limitations, play a political role or that these commitments must be seen as entirely individual such that there cannot be any collective movement of religious believers. Neither does it mean, therefore, that religious ideas must be seen as having nothing to say to the issues of real-life politics. Unfortunately, however, liberal theory is often believed to require that religion keep silent on matters of public political importance.[8] In part, this impression arises because there are some liberal theorists who appear to support exactly this sort of position. Robert Audi, for example, advocates not just that the state must act on secular rationales, but also out of secular motivations.[9]

As has been seen, however, this position is only one end of a liberal spectrum and other liberal theorists would disagree (including Nicholas Wolterstorff and, indeed, Habermas himself). For instance, other theoretical formulations like that of Gaus explicitly embrace religious voices. What does seem to be required by all liberal theorists is that the state not associate itself in a direct way with any particular religion or set of religious commitments. As a locus for engaging discussion, however, this requirement need not extend, *ipso facto*, to society at large or to all political discussions. An alternative sense of secularity will be necessary in Muslim contexts.

Just as in the case of the general neutrality requirement, this secularity would require only that political decisions that would compel state action not be justified on religious grounds. This secularity seems consistent with the impossibility, within Muslim contexts, of finding a single, agreed Muslim religious outlook in any case. There will always be contested and debated grounds. The issue arises for those who hold religiously inspired positions to accept

8 Trigg seems to make this conflation stating: "A liberal State that stands apart from religion, thinking it is a purely individual matter, is saying that politics must be entirely independent of religion and that religious principles have nothing to say to the real world of political action" (Trigg [2007] at 113).

9 See Audi and Wolterstorff (1997).

that the state should not act explicitly on or out of these grounds, or religious grounds more generally, and in this sense be secular. Of course, there may be many Muslims who are perfectly happy to be privately religious and politically secular, and for this group accepting this requirement would not be controversial.[10] The challenge is for those whose religious convictions may compel political action and commitments. It is here that liberal theory will demand that they accept the limited secularity that precludes state action based on religious principles, while still allowing for religious influence in broader political discussions. It is this space that justice as discourse seeks to carve out. By insisting on a capacious zone of public discourse and by allowing religious reasons to be expressed in it, justice as discourse is permissive of both non-secular discourses and non-secular reasons in public debate, but it keeps these within the bounds of liberal secularity. Those who would seek to act politically out of their Muslim faith need only embrace the idea that theirs is not the only legitimate voice within Muslim contexts, or the only legitimate Muslim voice. This is different from Rawls in two ways. First, it embraces the use of religious reasons *per se* in public reasoning and thus expands the ambit of public reasoning beyond the constraints that Rawls would impose. This would include allowing the expression of what Rawls might consider 'unreasonable' positions. Second, with reference to Muslim contexts, in *The Law of Peoples* Rawls posited through his hypothetical of Kazanistan that Muslim might only be able to be 'decent non-liberals'.[11] Justice as discourse suggests that that characterisation is misleading and that, in fact, there are more liberal possibilities for Muslim contexts than Rawls suggests.

The challenge of democracy

The third major challenge arises from decision-making through a democratic form of government. Democracy and liberal theory run together in part because of liberal neutrality and in part because of the liberal embrace of diversity. Neutrality links to democracy because when the state has no pre-determined commitments, it must seek these from its citizenry and to do this it must hear their views through the mechanisms of democratic participation. The liberal embrace of diversity links to democracy because broad and widespread democratic participation is required actually to capture the diverse views, opinions and outlooks of citizens. Additionally, and crucially, democracy links to liberal theory because it vests sovereignty in the people rather than in any other source of authority and, thus, does not ground itself on pre-determined or defined set of values. Herein lies the challenge: can democracy and truth-claiming traditions like religion co-exist? If they cannot, this would raise a serious problem for liberal theory in Muslim contexts.

At first thought, truth-claiming traditions like religion would seemingly be opposed to democratic forms of decision-making because these could lead to decisions that do not accord with the religious 'truth'. In essence, the problem is that democratic decisions may be 'wrong' in the sense of being religious truth violating. Democracy would only be problematic on these grounds, however, if the religious convictions were to be seen as compelling adherents to reject the moral standing of others as legitimate; that is to say, if the religious tradition was interpreted as providing a truth claim that said that others, whether other Muslims or non-Muslims or those of no religious faith, cannot be tolerated. If, on the

10 As the Commonwealth Commission on Respect and Understanding has noted in their report, there are politically secular Muslims who do not have any great urge to speak in faith-based discussions and can feel voiceless when these are the only term of conversation. See Commonwealth Secretariat (2007) at 21.

11 See Rawls (1999), at 75–76.

other hand, the religious tradition engenders a perspective that others are to be respected, even if they are not correct, then democratic decision-making does not seem problematic. It is thus that Feldman distinguished between 'Islamic democracy' (accepting of the idea of moral equality) and 'Islamist democracy' (convinced of its correctness and not willing to tolerate others).[12] There is, however, a lingering, generic sense of an uncomfortable fit between religious traditions *qua* truth-claiming systems and liberal democracy, which is opposed to accepting any such claim. For liberal democracy to be viable, those of religious convictions must either see their traditions as mandating respect for the opinions of others (say, as part of a common 'Creation') or, at least, of leaving open the possibility that their own truth-claims may be open to question and not something that they can know for sure to be right.

The empirical support for democracy as a system and for democratic values that was noted in the previous chapter, coupled with the discomfort for the enforcement of Islam by the state, demonstrates that within contemporary Muslim contexts some (indeed, most) populations do not see democracy as necessarily incompatible with their religious faith. Whether this is because they recognise the diversity of Muslim interpretations or are simply uncomfortable with the state believing undertaking to define and enforce Islam is not clear. But it does not matter. It may be that both of these are relevant factors given that both are trends link to the religio-legal heritage of Muslim contexts. Moreover, empirical support for democratic decision-making also suggests that there is willingness within these contexts to accept and vest political sovereignty in the people themselves.

It is not clear if these empirical findings also mean an acceptance of the idea that 'Islam', in some essential way, need not be the political master. Yet, justice as discourse would need this demand to be met. It would require that in addition to support for democratic politics as a *method* for political decision-making, that there should also be support for democracy epistemologically, namely a genuine willingness to allow others with their different views to have a say in decisions affecting one's life. Some observers have noted that a certain creative tension exists between support for 'democracy' as the basis for decision-making on the one hand and support for 'religious values' (associated with Islam, of course) to have a guiding role setting policy on the other hand. Additionally, they point out that what these terms mean when they are invoked is not entirely clear: support for democracy seems really to be a vote for 'not autocracy', while the support for religious values/Islam seems to be a desire for 'virtue' (honesty, integrity, etc.) in politics.[13] Thus, whether support for democracy can be read to include a genuine support for popular decision-making including seeing others (i.e. other Muslims and non-Muslims) as moral equals who thereby have a legitimate right to participate in political decision-making is not clear. The expressed support for democracy in opinion surveys and public polls does not conclusively tells us this but it does open the possibility. It does tell us, however, first, that these populations struggle with a connection between *din* and *dawla* and, second, that there are at least elements of a type of liberalism present in their political outlooks. Justice as discourse is particularly well suited to contexts where such a range of opinions, even if potentially conflicting, exists because, unlike other varieties of liberal theory that are more constraining of any appeal to religious ideas in public discourse, it is open to the full range of these outlooks. Justice as discourse would thus allow both the 'we support democracy' and 'we want Islam/the *shariʿa*' opinions to be advanced. In other words, justice as discourse offers a political theory that better fits contexts in which

12 Feldman (2003) at 15–22.
13 See Nelson (2009).

people may wish to rely upon religions ideas and, most significantly, it offers a political theory in which the contradictions, complications and implications of such ideas can be worked out in public discussion.

Challenges arising out of the heritage of Muslim contexts

An 'Islamic' imperative?

At the beginning of his *The Spirit of Islamic Law*, Bernard Weiss asserts:

> Law, it seems, is integral to monotheistic religion. The world's sole creator is necessarily by right its sole ultimate ruler, legislator and judge. All law worthy of that name must therefore originate with him. The human lawgiver is, despite his exalted position within the monotheistic scheme of things, only the mediator of the divine law to mankind. . . . [Such that] Government, too, becomes part of the ideal monotheistic order, for the law is understood to be the embodiment of a social vision that can be realised in this world only if power . . . is placed in the law's service. Accordingly, monotheistic communities inevitably acquire or seek to acquire the character of monotheistic polities.[14]

Weiss' analysis suggests a type of monotheistic imperative that runs from the basic premise of monotheism (that there is one God) through to law and government. Weiss contends that this pattern was classically represented in Judaism, with its most recent manifestation being Islam.[15] If Weiss is correct about the classical pattern and its political imperative, then it seems basically impossible to reconcile this model with the three requirements of liberal theory just presented. This pattern is not neutral because it would be based on realising the divine will, it is not secular as its source would be unapologetically religious and sacred, and it is not democratic, both in terms of citizen participation, which would be essentially irrelevant, and in terms of the source of political sovereignty, which would lie with God not the people. In short, if the classical pattern represents the practical political imperative of monotheism, then any environment that draws its inspiration or values from a monotheistic tradition such as Islam, or even more generally where the monotheistic tradition is inherently important, could not really accept a liberal system without admitting stark inconsistency.

There are two issues with Weiss' classical pattern: first, a theoretical concern about his reading of what an Islamic imperative would be and, second, that history has evidenced a more complex situation than he describes. Interestingly, Weiss himself acknowledges these complexities. Although he says that "Muslim history places the revelation of Islam's law in the context of a polity based in Medina and portrays Muhammad as, like Moses, both prophet and ruler",[16] he goes on to note:

> Though the seeds of the new Islamic order were planted in the time of the prophet Muhammad, its full maturation required the labors of subsequent generations of

14 Weiss (1998) at 1.

15 Weiss asserts that Islam is a more complete and autonomous representation of the classical pattern than is Christianity in part because Islam presented itself as the possessor of a law unique in itself, while Christianity saw itself emerging out of Judaism and the law of Moses (Weiss, 1998 at 1).

16 Weiss (1998) at 3.

> Muslims. The building up of the Islamic polity was largely the achievement of the first caliphal dynasty, that of the Umayyads. . .[17]

And, moreover,

> Without denying the rootedness of the Islamic polity in the time of Muhammad, modern Western scholarship *has come to see the period after Muhammad and the first conquests as more decisive* for the building up of the polity and the law . . . the Umayyad caliphate and its successor, the Abbasid caliphate . . . would do for Islam what the Davidic kingdom had done for the religion of Israel, that is, provide the political context necessary for the development of genuine law.[18]

So, Weiss takes a theoretical, and idealised, classical pattern which, as we have tried to suggest, contains within it a certain political imperative, but then recognises, albeit in a somewhat hesitant way, that the real driver for the development of the law was not the imperative of the classical pattern alone but rather the practical requirements of the political system of the early dynasties (and, so we might reasonably extrapolate, the political systems after these early dynasties). While Weiss would like to see a consistent theoretical thread in the classical pattern that just gets worked out later on, the events of history have shown that this is too simplified an account. The way in which both political and legal principles were established does not suggest that there was a single master narrative or pattern – certainly not at a conscious level – that animated the actors involved in establishing the political order, on the one hand, or articulating the *shari'a* on the other. Indeed, while the Muslim polities may have been the sites for the development of the legal rules of the *shari'a*, the legal elaboration proceeded largely outside of, and was not linked to, political authority. Thus, Weiss' neat connection from a monotheistic premise through law into government and the political order might seem to make sense in theory but it was not lived practice in any such clear-cut way. This may be as much the case for Islam as other monotheistic traditions. In any case, the result is that the lived experience of these traditions, Islam included, appears open to greater political arrangements than the theoretical imperative contained in Weiss' argument seems to admit.

Weiss' historical analyses have also been challenged by other scholars such as Abdulaziz Sachedina,[19] Asma Asfaruddin[20] and L. Carl Brown.[21] Sachedina's investigation is an attempt to mine the sources of Muslim tradition for a greater range of theoretical possibilities than Weiss' classical pattern admits. Sachedina acknowledges the pattern of the prophet being sent as both a lawgiver and an organiser, and thus that in the prophetic order political and religious authority were united as a matter of principle and of fact. He further asserts that among the Abrahamic traditions, Islam has been in his view that most conscious of its earthly agenda, or as he puts it, "Islam has been a faith in the realm of the public."[22] The medium for realising this agenda was the *shari'a*, which could be called upon to regulate human affairs through its comprehensive reach. However, as we saw, Sachedina further posits that

17 Weiss (1998) at 5.
18 Weiss (1998) at 4 (emphasis added).
19 Sachedina (2006).
20 Asfaruddin (2008).
21 Brown (2000).
22 Sachedina (2006) at 6.

the *shari'a* provides the paradigm of a civil religion by a separation of jurisdictions on all its laws, a principle he calls 'secularity' (*sifa madaniyya*). This separation of jurisdictions is found in a division of topics within the classic texts of Islamic law (the *fiqh*) between those regulating the relationship of humans and God (*ibadat*), on the one hand, and those regulating the relationship of humans to other humans (*mu'amalat*), on the other. Sachedina finds that the human–God relationship is beyond the state, for here only God can judge and demand explanations for behaviour. Thus, worldly political authority has no role to play in enforcing these aspects of *shari'a* and, *a fortiori*, for imposing sanctions or penalties upon people for breaches of an individual's responsibilities to God. At the human–human level, the state and its courts may, however, become involved but here the requirements for justice, Sachedina contends, generate an ethic of civic equality and mutual responsibilities. His overall conclusion, therefore, is that Islamic heritage must guide rather than govern, because Islam recognises humans as equal in creation and, in their relationships with each other, in need of guidance, not governance, from religion.

The significance of recalling Sachedina's analysis here is that we can see in it a markedly different reading of the requirements of the 'Islamic tradition' at a theoretical level. While recognising much of the same heritage as Weiss, Sachedina's conclusion about what this heritage must result in practically is substantially different. Gone is the strict logic from the premise of monotheism to a monotheistic polity with religion seeking dominion over government. Instead, we have a (potential) zone of civic equality and mutual responsibility, with the state stepping out of the enforcement of religious norms that exist to regulate the relationship between the individual and God, where Islam guides but does not govern. Sachedina's model, therefore, seems compatible with liberal perspectives, even though it is not quite fully satisfying. Nonetheless, it opens up a sense of 'Islamic heritage' that is not locked in Weiss' imperative and through an ethic of civic equality and mutual responsibility offers real liberal possibilities.

What Sachedina's distinction between guidance and governance appears to amount to is this: Islam, and in particular its articulation through the *shari'a*, cannot provide all the political principles or all the public policy needed for a Muslim society and perhaps was never meant to do so, but it can provide a moral and ethical direction that can guide Muslims both in asserting an ethic of civic equality and mutual responsibilities and in working out politically what this ethic means. Justice as discourse can help give meaning to this conception of the role of Islam. It eschews the idea that Islam in any interpretation should be called upon to furnish a framework of governing principles, indeed, it explicitly denies that any such principles should be justified on the basis of their 'Islamic credibility.' However, it also allows religious ideas to enter into public political debate and therefore to influence, shape and even guide public policy, so long as no religious conception is permitted, by itself, to dictate or determine public policy.

Asfaruddin, through an examination of early texts provides a different challenge to Weiss' outlook. She states that:

> None of the pre-modern sources – the Qur'an, *hadith*, historical works, exegeses – refers to the recurrent fundamental Islamist terms of '*al-Dawla al-Islamiyya*' (the Islamic state), '*al-Hukma al-Islamiyya*' (the Islamic Government) or '*al-hakimiyya*'.[23]

23 Asfaruddin (2008) at 183–184.

Instead of these terms, the early discourses used the term *ummah* for the community of Muslims and their polity, though, importantly, Jews and Christians were also themselves *ummahs*. The term *dawla* or state, she claims, was first used for the Abbasids and Fatimids to justify their particular polities. Moreover, she states that:

> There is no evidence at all in the early sources that the Companions [of the Prophet] invoked a supposedly divinely mandated blueprint for an 'Islamic Government' or an 'Islamic State' in the election of the Prophet's first successor.[24]

In a similar vein, L. Carl Brown points out a difference in practice that followed after the early years. While Christianity, he argues, chose to wrestle with the problem of political loyalty ("of what to render unto Caesar and what to God, of who is entitled to speak for Christendom, who decides on religious orthodoxy, and who enforces that orthodoxy"):[25]

> Islam largely abstained from this effort, clung consistently to the model of the God-ordained early *ummah*, accepted implicitly that later government did not live up to this standard (but largely avoided asking either why or what could be done) and bridged the gap between ideal and reality by accepting the bleak necessity for government however bad . . . but at the same regarding that government as largely irrelevant to the individual believer's task of living according to God's plan. . .[26]

It was thus that there resulted a separation between political ideal and political reality and a *de facto* (though never idealised) compartmentalisation between politics and religion.

Considering these different analyses makes clear that it is not possible to present a simplified notion of an Islamic political pattern or an Islamic political alternative – whether constructed on idealised terms or out of historical experience. Furthermore, it is not possible to present an 'Islamic' tradition that is inevitably in opposition to liberalism and, specifically, to justice as discourse as a liberal framework.

A Western conceit?

Might liberal theory, however, as something that developed in the West, be too alien and too much of a misplaced cultural import to work in Muslim contexts given their different heritages, such that any member of the liberal family would be either inappropriate, or rejected outright, simply because of its Western progeny? This, however, is a significant challenge today given the claims presented by some groups who assert that they can explain what Islam or Islamic government means and equally what it rejects.

A challenge on these grounds would depend on the argument that there is something essential about the categories 'the West' and 'Muslim contexts'. As was argued earlier, however, this is a false premise. Not only has there been much interaction in general but, more importantly for our purposes, the political ideas that underpin liberal theory have also been present within Muslim contexts for a long time. A contemporary call, therefore, for the normative usefulness of liberal theory in Muslim contexts would not be introducing ideas

24 Asfaruddin (2008) at 184.
25 Brown (2000) at 63.
26 Brown (2000) at 63.

or concepts that are completely alien, unknown or unrecognisable. Indeed, the quotation from Muhammad Ali Jinnah with which this chapter begins evidences at least some familiarity with both Western history and liberal ideas. Liberal theory may not have originated in Muslim contexts but to say that it would be so alien as to be irrelevant overstates the consequences of this fact. It also fails to recognise that through colonisation and the spread of intellectual ideas, liberalism has had a long-standing presence in Muslim contexts.[27] Finally, such a position seems to suggest that majority Muslim environments are incapable of being liberal and thereby to limit these populations to being at most, in the words of Rawls, a decent, *non*-liberal people. Why this must be accepted is not clear.[28] In proposing justice as discourse for Muslim contexts, therefore, one is able to draw upon Muslim contexts' existing familiarity with, and at least early reception of, liberal ideas. Moreover, one is further able to participate and advance discussions within these contexts that have sought to mine liberal theory to meet the needs of Muslim contexts. For example, within Muslim history there have been thinkers that have taken up what could be characterised as liberal arguments. A notable example is Ali Abd al-Raziq (d. 1966), the Azharite shaykh who in his work *al-Islam wa Usul al-Hukm* ('Islam and the Principles of Government'), argued that religious and political authority could be and should be separated. Abd al-Raziq, and others like him, was a Muslim, indeed a shaykh, speaking about secularism, but the idea he was advocating was still not organic to his society. For his views, Abd al-Raziq was severely criticized, cast out of the '*ulama*, removed from his position as a judge and ended up living his remaining days in seclusion.[29] Does Abd al-Raziq's fate mark not just a personal tragedy but also the death of an idea? To reach this conclusion would mean that the type of thoughts Abd al-Raziq had ended with him. But this is not the case because one can look at the contemporary work ideas of An-Na'im or Sajoo, discussed earlier, to see the continuation of this line of thought.[30]

The artistic and physical heritage of Muslim contexts also has something to tell us here. The interaction with scholarly traditions of 'the West' is evidenced in illustrated manuscripts. The cover image of this book, for example, depicts Pythagoras dressed in characteristically 'Eastern' style in the idiom of traditional Muslim societies. Pythagoras is, one might say, not portrayed as foreign but as a familiar figure and teacher. Another similar example comes from a thirteenth-century manuscript of the *Mukhtar al-Hikam wa Mahasin al-Kalim* ('Choice Judgements and Improving (or Fine) Sayings') by al-Mubashshir b. Fatiq al-Qa'id. In an illustrated manuscript of this text,[31] the image of Socrates and two students again in an Eastern style of dress poignantly signals that an awareness of Western thinkers and thought has indeed be part of the intellectual heritage of Muslim contexts for centuries. Additionally, examples from the architectural heritage suggest that Muslim contexts in the past did not reject influences from other contexts. The great Umayyad mosque in Damascus, built in the eighth century, a large and still-emblematic structure, did

27 For example, in Niall Ferguson's analysis, among the important features that the British left behind where they governed were the Common law, the limited night watchman state and the idea of liberty. See Ferguson (2003) at xxiii.

28 An argument that I have tried to make in Jamal (2010).

29 See a discussion of Abd al-Raziq in Yared (2002).

30 For a collection of writings that are taken to express a liberal temper, see Kurzman (1998).

31 Image and description available at: http://digitool.haifa.ac.il/R/2BM25TN7QPCSXVMLTYH2QD15RD1GT4CVKQQRIG3CIJS277EQY9-01060?func=search-simple-go&local_base=GEN01&find_code=WTI&request=Socrates%20and%20two%20pupils%20(ca.%201200-1250)%20%5Bdigital%20image%5D. Original manuscript in the Topkapi Saray Museum.

not destroy the arch of the ancient Roman Temple of Jupiter, but incorporated it into the mosque complex. Indeed, even influences from other religions were maintained, such as a shrine to St John the Baptist a revered figure in Christianity that is inside the prayer area of the Umayyad mosque. Similarly, in the Qusayr Amra (Little Castle of Amra) in Jordan, a red limestone structure located about 80 kilometres east of the city of Amman and again built in the eighth century under the Umayyads, one can find Byzantine-style fresco portraits and paintings of figures representing the disciplines of philosophy, history and poetry, with their names inscribed in Greek. They appear to illustrate the Umayyads' view of themselves building upon the traditions of the ancient ('Western') world.

The point of mentioning these examples from the manuscript and architectural traditions is simply to point out that the argument saying that ideas or influences from the West cannot have any standing in Muslim contexts rejects the evidence of rich interactions that have occurred throughout history which defy a simple bifurcation of West and Islam.

Islamically unredeemed?

To say that some form of liberalism is familiar enough in Muslim contexts is one thing; it may still lack cultural credibility. One objection to using any variety of liberal theory, therefore, is that it does not have an 'Islamic' pedigree and that, as such, it will not have standing as a viable option among Muslim populations. This relates to a tension that Bowering notes has existed throughout much of Muslim history between "the authority of theological 'Islamic' sources as opposed to philosophical 'non-Islamic' sources or, put another way, faith versus reason."[32] An example of this debate comes from a famous quotation of the philosopher Abu Yusuf Ya'qub ibn Ishaq al-Kindi (ca. 800–870 CE; al-Kindi). In the first section of his *On First Philosophy*, al-Kindi chastises those who, even at his time, criticised the use of 'non-Islamic' sources saying:

> We must not be ashamed to admire the truth or to acquire it, from wherever it comes. Even if it should come from far-flung nations and foreign peoples, there is for the student of truth nothing more important than the truth, nor is the truth demeaned or diminished by the one who states or conveys it; no one is demeaned by the truth, rather all are ennobled by it.[33]

Frank Vogel has elucidated this point in his study of Egypt's legal structure when he noted that there is:

> a common enough impression among believing Egyptians that their laws are Islamically unredeemed, and, even if theoretically acceptable as *siyasa* [roughly 'political'] measures, are in this case merely taken from the West and wholly inspired by secular considerations . . . [L]aws that *do not conflict* with God's law will never arouse the same religious enthusiasm as do laws that *apply* God's law.[34]

Vogel's notion of things being 'Islamically unredeemed' is important in two ways. First, it is important practically, since being Islamically unredeemed might be said to mean that

32 Bowering (2015) at 27.
33 See 'Al-Kindi' in the *Stanford Encyclopedia of Philosophy*: https://plato.stanford.edu/entries/al-kindi/.
34 Vogel (1999) at 539–540 (emphasis in original).

liberal ideas would not be accepted 'on the Muslim street'. Second, being Islamically unredeemed might result in a principled rejection of the possibility of drawing upon liberal theory because it would be associated with an outlook and political programme that is perceived as being hostile to the heritage of Muslim contexts. Edward Kessler, discussing dialogue between Muslims and Jews, has articulated this issue, noting:

> Today we face not so much a clash of civilizations as a clash of ignorance. The downward spiral is obvious. Inaccurate or incomplete knowledge about the 'other' allows room for prejudice and sets off a cycle of mistrust, suspicion and anger. Consequent insularity, and an exclusivism in turn, causes boundaries to be drawn closer and tighter so we are left with an 'us' versus 'them' tension.[35]

Thus, the questions are whether liberal theory is, in fact, 'Islamically unredeemed' because it lacks an Islamic pedigree and, if it is, what are the consequences of this situation for the usefulness of liberal theory in Muslim contexts?

In discussing Islamic law and human rights, Mohammed Fadel says: "While liberalism and Islam are philosophically incompatible as comprehensive theories of the good . . . [e]lsewhere I have argued that [Rawlsian] public reason is legitimate from the perspective of Islamic theology, ethics and law."[36] Fadel proceeds in his argument both to outline "accepted doctrines of Islamic law" that are compatible with public reason while also noting that some of these doctrines still seem to be up for debate, at least among contemporary scholars. For example, he notes that "Numerous modern Muslims have proposed theories that would *justify departing from classical* [i.e. *fiqh*-based] *doctrine* regarding the necessity of the obligation of *hudud* [strong criminal] penalties"[37] and later notes that, for example:

> prominent figures such as Selim el-Awa – widely recognised to be an important Islamist legal scholar – have rejected the *traditional* criminalisation of apostasy, arguing that it is fundamentally inconsistent with Islam's commitment to free acceptance of religious truth based on rational conviction.[38]

What Fadel's analysis shows is that: (i) there continues to be debate and diversity of opinion about the content of the 'classical heritage', here represented by the "classical doctrines of Islamic law"; and (ii) contemporary scholars, like Fadel himself, are struggling to generate new, and possibly Islamically redeemed, answers in light of contemporary developments and theories (such as, in his particular case, the norms of international human rights).

Justice as discourse offers itself as another such response. Like Fadel's approach, it embraces liberal theory (though not just of the Rawlsian variety) and in addition it embraces, indeed relies upon, the variety of opinions about the 'classical heritage'. Unlike Fadel, however, it does not seek to justify the appropriateness of liberal theory (whether in the form of Rawls' 'public reason' or in other formulations) against the perspectives of 'Islamic theology, ethics and law', but rather in light of the diversity of opinions among Muslims today and in the history of Muslim contexts and encourages debate and discussion about precisely what these

35 Kessler (2008) at 13.

36 Fadel (2007); accessible at http://ssrn.com/abstract=98177

37 Fadel (2007) at note 11 (emphasis added). He gives as an example of this trend the work of Khaled Abou el Fadl.

38 Fadel (2007) at 14 (emphasis added).

perspectives *are*. It is a 'liberal' idea that does not impose any one variety of 'liberalism' upon Muslim contexts.

An answer to the challenge that liberalism is unacceptable as a framework for political decision-making because it is not Islamically redeemed, then, is that neither liberalism nor what it means to be Islamically redeemed is always clear (the quote from Al-Kindi given above exemplifying this debate). Liberal theory, as we have seen, encompasses a variety of perspectives in its different versions. To be Islamically redeemed is similarly unclear both because of the *continued* debate over the classical Islamic tradition, something that is expressed, for better or worse, *par excellence* in the varied schools and doctrines of Islamic law; and it is not clear because the terms of what would therefore constitute a redemption are not certain. In short, to reject the role that liberal theory may usefully play for Muslim contexts because it is 'not Islamic' begs fixed definitions of fluid concepts. This conclusion does not, however, enable us to judge the practical applicability of any aspect of liberal theory on the 'Muslim street' – assessing this would ultimately be an empirical exercise – but it does allow us to answer the objection that liberal theory would necessarily be useless because it is, or at least might be characterised as, 'Islamically unredeemed'.

Liberal individualism vs. the Ummah

One of the strongest critiques of what we might call the 'classical' theory of liberalism has been the communitarian critique. Communitarians (such as Michael Sandel, Alasdair MacIntyre, Robert Putnam, Charles Taylor, Amitai Etzioni)[39] charge that liberalism is a conception of social life that cut us off from our 'life in common' and in communities leaving us individually isolated and, thus, atomised. Classical liberalism is criticised for conceiving of us as individuals who construe ourselves independently when in truth we are socially and communally constituted and our group identities matter, both in an ontological sense and in terms of practical politics. The communitarian critique of classical liberal theory has also informed critical legal theory, including feminist and critical race theories and queer theory which have emphasised socially connected perspectives taking into account our positions as being embedded within social groups (whether chosen or not) that may be defined by socio-economic circumstances, sex/gender, race or sexual orientation. Thus, classical liberalism is held to be both descriptively inaccurate because we are not completely self-constituting, and philosophically undesirable because it impoverishes our social and political lives and hampers our self-actualisation by undermining what we get from our life in community. A liberalism premised on an (atomised) individualism, therefore, will be particularly inappropriate for Muslim contexts which are characterised by a rich though ill-defined sense of community, namely the *ummah*, which links all Muslims.

This conflict, however, is not as irreducible as it first appears. The first of the possibilities for resolving it comes from within liberal theory itself. The communitarian critique has, as we have seen, shaped contemporary liberal theory. The 'new' liberal theory now takes more seriously the claims of community and the role of communities in helping to shape the individual. In short, the sharp divide between 'liberal' and 'communitarian' outlooks has been moderated and nuanced within the liberal family. While liberalism still is concerned

39 Sandel (1984) and Sandel (1988) are good representations of the liberal-communitarian debate and the communitarian critique of liberalism, respectively. One can also see MacIntyre (1985), Taylor (1989) or Putnam (2000) for communitarian perspectives.

that community life not suppress the needs and aspirations of the individual, it does broadly acknowledge that individual needs may be at least partially shaped by community.

Second, since liberal theory is open to change, the rich notion of the *ummah* may engender more evolution of its perspectives. The unifying sense of community in the concept of the *ummah* may enrich further those aspects of the existing of liberal theory and liberal politics that take community life seriously. Justice as discourse, by permitting public discourses to be initiated by groups that have a religious character, whether organised as political parties or in other forms of civil society associations, may contribute to this reassessment. At the same time, liberalism's concern not to override the individual may also, in turn, challenge a too-heavy reliance on the community in Muslim contexts. The commitments of justice as discourse, therefore, aim to provide maximal space for discussions about both the political values of liberalism and the requirements of religion including what the political implications, if any, of the notion of the *ummah* may be. Thus, if undertaken sincerely, dialogue on these lines might develop a further bridge between liberalism and the *ummah*, enriching an understanding of both. Justice as discourse seeks to be facilitative of this dialogue. It only insists that no one group, even if, for example, it calls itself 'Islamic' or 'Muslim,' be taken to be representative of the opinions of all Muslims.

The macro challenges: pluralism and sovereignty

All of the challenges here raised can be resolved into two key macro issues. The first is pluralism. The existence of religious, ethnic or cultural plurality itself is not pluralism; the former may be a fact, but the latter is an attitude and, hence, an option both for any society at large and for its institutions. A proper liberalism, it might be said, does not demand simply admitting plurality but rather accepting pluralism. Similarly, any religious articulation that would squelch religious plurality by imposing orthodoxy and orthopraxy would fail to be 'liberal'. As we noted in earlier chapters, the lived experience of most of Muslim history demonstrates its 'liberal' credentials on this test because of the irrepressible plurality which has prevailed and which has been a leitmotif of the tradition. But these liberal credentials do not necessarily lead to an ethic of pluralism more broadly within Muslim majority contexts. To find pluralism compatible with Muslim contexts, we can note, first, that while there may be some Muslims who would seek to impose rigid interpretations on their faith, there are also Muslims who would not make these claims and, in fact, accept and support the diversity of Muslim outlooks. This is because, as Carl Ernst points out, it is not possible to speak about what Islam (Christianity, Judaism, etc.) 'says' in an essential way but rather we must understand it through the voices of Muslims (Christians, Jews, etc.).[40] Second, and relatedly, we must recall that since there is virtually no one 'Islamic' answer to any question, a plurality-enhancing choice is available in Muslim contexts. And it is precisely the diversity that has existed through history that would make plurality-limiting choices appear to wrong-step the history of Muslim contexts.

Be this as it may, however, the challenge to embrace and adopt pluralism positively as a value still remains. In his assessment of the prospects of Rawlsian political liberalism in non-western societies, M. F. Bilgin concludes that:

40 This is why the emphasis in this study has been on the thoughts, opinions and the historical legacy of Muslims as defining the nature of Muslim contexts.

> in these [Western] countries the political culture has taken a certain form that might be branded as reasonable pluralism. Therefore, if the political establishments in non-Western societies act in similar fashion, it should be possible to expect similar consequences. Political liberalism is the normative source at hand that could guide those societies to this ideal.[41]

Bilgin's analysis is not specific to Muslim contexts (he considers non-Western societies generally), but one may argue that it provides good reasons for coming to a similar conclusion specifically for Muslim contexts. If the political establishments in Muslim contexts 'act in similar fashion', then liberal theory becomes an available and possible normative source for their acts, and a reading of the heritage of Muslim contexts has real pluralism-enhancing choices waiting to be seized. In both a theoretical sense as well more practically, therefore, Muslim heritage has elements that seem to open it up to choices that can indeed be pluralism-enhancing. A recognition of authentic religious diversity and the validity of other communities of belief (at least among the *ahl al-kitab*), the tradition of diffused religious authority in the absence of a church, the acceptance of some range of legal diversity and the separate jurisdictions of political and religious authority were aspects that developed in the heritage of Muslim contexts over time as part of its own, fluid, evolution and there is no reason to believe this development has stopped. In essence, therefore, Muslim schools of thought are largely organised amorphously and organically and with rather diffuse structures of authority. Indeed, embracing pluralism would appear to be the option best suited to the realities of this history and to the on-going diversity of interpretation of Muslim contexts. Justice as discourse seeks to safeguard against any limitation of the diversity of Muslim voices by asserting that no one voice be allowed to claim exclusive 'Islamic' authenticity or be recognised by state structures, such as legislatures, courts and state bureaucracies, as having any such authenticity. In addition, justice as discourse is specifically open to the promotion of multiple expressions of Muslim opinion and to have these compete for popular support. Finally, justice as discourse is committed to facilitating these expressions by leaving discursive politics open to hearing religious (and, of course, non-religious) voices on their own terms.

The second macro issue is the question of political sovereignty. In embracing democratic politics, liberal theory also embraces the idea that political sovereignty rests with the people within a polity, primarily in their role as citizens. What Weiss asserted, however, was that a monotheistic tradition such as Islam would see ultimate sovereignty vested in the divine, with the human lawmaker simply exercising a derivative role. Doing what God wants would, of course, commit our political order to determining the divine will, which is an effort that has taken various forms in the three great monotheistic traditions of Judaism, Christianity and Islam. While Christianity developed its structures of corporate churches, in the cases of Judaism and Islam understanding the divine will fell mainly, and normatively, to the religio-legal scholars who did not operate under a church.[42] For Islam's '*ulama*, even when grouped together into general schools of thought, this history has meant a set of traditions

41 Bilgin (2007) at 376.

42 Though, of course, the case of Shia Islam was somewhat different historically because of the roles of the Imams. That said, there is only one Shia community today that has its living Imam present, namely the Nizari Shia Ismaili Muslims who hold that His Highness Prince Karim Aga Khan is their 49th Imam in direct lineal descent from the Prophet Muhammad. Other Shia communities either draw their leadership from religious scholars or from other leaders who do not have the status of hereditary Imams and who are themselves usually expected to be learned in religious matters and so follow a pattern that is more akin to the Sunni traditions.

that has been characterised by, to revive Hallaq's phrase, 'ubiquitous plurality'. In turn, this means that there has been no way of definitively determining or explaining the divine writ, such that an appeal to divine sovereignty has needed to be mediated through the diverse voices that have been recognised as expressing – though never absolutely – the divine will. The precise nature of the divine will has, thus, always remained ineffable even to those apparently most qualified to determine it and who have made its understanding their vocation; it is a moving referent rather than a fixed trope, engendering not a seamless outlook but rather variant options of the nature of Islam. Indeed, it is a widespread feature of the written legal opinions (*fatawa*) that after the exposition of the legal position they will typically end with the phrase "but God knows best".

As a result, any appeal to divine sovereignty has always had to mean, in fact, an appeal to opinions that could not even be secured by an overriding corporate authority which could pronounce canonically. It is thus that, until today, opinions and even schools of thought are associated with individual scholars themselves and even when these scholars occupy certain offices (like the Shaykh of the Al-Azhar in Egypt, a position that is considered one of the most senior among the Sunni '*ulama*), their opinions are still challengeable both by other scholars as well as by ordinary, 'lay', Muslims. A good practical example of this comes from the *Munir Report*,[43] which states:

> Therefore the question immediately arises: What is Islam and who is a *momin* or Muslim? We put this question to the '*ulama* and we shall presently refer to their answers to this question. But we cannot refrain from saying here that it was a matter of infinite regret to us that the '*ulama* whose first duty should be to have settled views on this subject, were hopelessly disagreed among themselves.[44]

Picking up this point later, the Report continues:

> the claim that a certain person or community is not within the pale of Islam implies on the part of the claimant an exact conception of what a Muslim is. The result of this part of the inquiry, however, has been anything but satisfactory, and if considerable confusion exists in the minds of our '*ulama* on such a simple matter, one can easily imagine what the difference on more complicated matters will be.[45]

Which leads to the report's conclusion:

> Keeping in view the several definitions given by the '*ulama*, need we make any comment except that no two learned divines are agreed on this fundamental. If we attempt our own definition as each learned divine has done and that definition differs from that given by all others, we unanimously go out of the fold of Islam. And if we adopt the definition given by any one of the '*ulama*, we remain Muslims according to the view of that *alim* [sing. of '*ulama*] but *kafirs* [unbelievers] according to the definition of everyone else.[46]

43 Officially: Punjab, *Report of the Court of Inquiry constituted under the Punjab Act II of 1954 to enquire into the Punjab Disturbances of 1953*, Lahore, 1954.

44 At 205.

45 At 211.

46 At 218.

In the face of this long-standing historical reality, there is no 'Islam' to which political sovereignty can be given outside of the thoughts and conceptions of Muslims, which can shape and reshape the collective ethos of Muslim contexts. Once this is recognised, then the liberal option of vesting political authority in the people becomes not just possible but compelling. Islam's meaning would best be plumbed by considering the various points of views of its adherents under political principles that are premised on securing broad participation – precisely the perspective of liberal theory. It is only in this way, after all, that anything like a broadly shared view of an Islamic way might be determined. Necessarily then, political sovereignty would lie with the people, as Muslims, rather than with an abstracted Islam because the latter would inevitably have to reflect only a small slice of the diversity that has characterised the former, and it would be a slice that could not in any sense be held to reflect an authentic or correct Islam in any case.

Transitional character of Muslim contexts

Emphasising their continuing development, Sajoo calls Muslim societies 'transitional' in that they are going through a phase of tremendous change and rearticulating their values in both a post-colonial context and one in which theoretical structures that had been developed in pre-modern social orders have now to face the reality of new structures, such as the modern nation-state.[47]

Abdou Filali-Ansary's analysis helps to draw out the point when he says:

> What happened in the nineteenth century was the transformation of the medieval settlement into a system in the modern sense of the word. The duality of fact and norm was inverted, as *sharia*-bound societies were confused with fully legitimate Muslim communities and deemed to be fully realisable through voluntary political action. . . . We therefore see how the confusion between a 'model' and a historical system could arise and spread among Muslims at a time when they were confronted by the challenge of modern ideas.[48]

Filali-Ansary's argument then is about a lost sense of actual history (facts) and the replacement of these facts by an Islamic norm, which was not the actual lived experience. As a result, a Muslim political ethic was defined, epistemologically, through the construction of an idealised model developed in response to modern conditions. In this, Filali-Ansary's observation reiterates the point made by Zubaida about the new environment ushered in by the modern state structure. This new environment extended to the incorporation of law, whereby the broad *shari'a* with its moral and ethical nature was codified by the new states.

The upshot of these processes has been the formulation of an Islamist alternative that sits in real tension, both theoretically as well as practically, with liberalism and the principles of neutrality, democracy and secularity.[49] The broader, and more specifically Muslim, context

47 See Sajoo (2004).

48 Filali-Ansary (1999) at 23.

49 As Filali-Ansary has also noted, the idea of secularism did not develop in Muslim societies internally, or autonomously. Muslim societies did not go through the same historical trajectory that lead to the development of the doctrine of secularism organically. On the contrary, this idea has often either been imposed (through colonial administration), or imported by the state (Turkey is a paradigm example). See Filali-Ansary (1996) as well as Agrama (2010).

of the challenges of liberal theory may, thus, be understood in light of the development of this alternative norm. Critically though, this Islamist alternative must not be understood as representing an inherent Muslim (or, indeed, Islamic) rival structure or set of principles stemming out of the history of Muslim societies. It is only one choice available in a situation where there is no one coherent and universal set of principles that emerges as the 'Muslim model'. Moreover, such a perspective rejects the historical heritage because the lived experience of Muslim contexts has witnessed diverse alternative structures in fact, including, as we have seen, in the substantial plurality of legal outlooks that emerged in these contexts over time.

As a result, there remains the possibility of arguing for a framework for Muslim contexts that is in harmony with the principles of liberal theory. To do this more concretely, we need to add to the response to the theoretical challenges of neutrality, secularity and democracy a formulation in practical political terms how Muslim contexts may be structured today, which is based on a richer and informed sense of how these contexts have developed over time. It is to this that we may now turn.

Defining a practical political model

In undertaking to define justice as discourse as a practical political model of liberal theory for Muslim contexts, I have in mind a country of Muslim majority. Real-life examples could include Pakistan, Indonesia, Tunisia or Morocco. While I imagine this model for a notional state, keeping in mind these real-world examples is useful. I outline what I think justice as discourse would offer at the level of constitutional law, at the level of non-constitutional law and, finally, at the level of discursive political debate.

Constitutional law

The requirement of liberal neutrality vis-à-vis religious convictions is, at a minimum, expressed in the need to be free from what John Keane refers to as "ecclesiastical diktat", namely the capacity of any religious organisation or officials to dictate matters of policy. This, in turn, seems to have at least two implications. The first would be the absence of any state established religion in constitutional terms. This means more specifically that the state should have no express faith commitment or, at least, that no such commitment becomes a defining source for policy or the action taken in the name of the states by executive, bureaucratic and judicial officials. Some might see this as a principle whose absence is not, in fact, an impediment to a liberal model and cite the example of the UK, with its established churches of England and of Scotland. Other Western European examples the Netherlands, Sweden, Denmark, etc. –functioning liberal states but with established churches, might also be cited. Taking the UK as a working example, the reason that the presence of the established churches, though upsetting to some, does not inhibit the functioning of the liberal state is because the representatives of the churches do not get to decide matters of public policy. The British case is perhaps particularly 'messy' because senior bishops of the Church of England still sit, *qua* bishops, in the House of Lords and, thus, are part of the parliamentary decision-making process. Nonetheless, neither of the established churches can settle a matter of public policy through internal church discussions, and in this way Britain may still be said – albeit not uncontroversially – to be 'secular' in a manner that is consistent with liberalism. Justice as discourse demands more than this, however, especially for Muslim contexts. It seeks to prevent any constitutional establishment of religion for two reasons.

The first is, absent the system of churches, it is not possible to choose corporate bodies that can realistically act as constitutional representatives for Muslims. The second reason is that any reference to Islam as an established tradition would raises the question of which interpretation(s) of the faith are being invoked. Asking the state to choose an interpretation would undermine the diversity that has been ubiquitous in Muslim history and thereby undermine the heritage of Muslim contexts.

Second, and allied to the question of established churches, justice as discourse would permit no reference to religious texts, doctrines or sources as the bases for laws. This means that there should not be constitutional references to Islam, the Qur'an or Islamic law (in any of its versions) as being the bases for the laws of the land in any general way. So, for example, the invocation of premises such as that "the Injunctions of Islam as laid down in the Holy Qur'an and Sunnah shall be the supreme law and source of guidance for legislation to be administered through laws enacted by the Parliament and Provincial Assemblies, and for policy making by the Government", found in the Constitution of the Islamic Republic of Pakistan[50] or that "Islam is the Religion of the State. Arabic is its official language, and the principal source of legislation is Islamic Jurisprudence (Sharia)" as found in the Constitution of Egypt,[51] must be avoided. The reasons for this are two-fold and emerge out of liberal theory and Muslim contexts themselves: first, provisions like this would require a determination of what Islam (or the injunctions of the Qur'an and Sunna or the meaning and content of the Islamic *shari'a*, etc.) means, requires and demand, even though there exists no process or tradition to define the tenets of Islam, in any determinative way. Indeed, provisions that would compel such definition would run afoul of the interpretive diversity that has been an irresolutely obstinate fact of both liberal theory and the history of Muslim contexts, including of the history of Muslim legal traditions. Second, if such limiting definitions were offered, the shaping and re-shaping of both liberalism and the contours of Muslim values in changing political conditions would be stifled.

If we are to take seriously, as we must, the importance of religious convictions in Muslim contexts and the conception of religion as not being separable from worldly life, however, then as a corollary to a constitutional system that does not seek to impose Islam, there must also be guarantees that the state will not seek to do the alternative, that is to impose an areligious or anti-religious orthodoxy. This would also, in its own way, require restrictive definitions that raise a no-less-problematic issue. The secular space liberal theory demands cannot be allowed to become so radically *laic* that it allows no room for the expression of religious ideas. That, too, would compromise liberalism's commitment to diversity. To guarantee this balance, one might rely upon the type of language found in the US Constitution, requiring a 'free exercise' clause – a provision to prevent the state from restricting the exercise of religion by its citizens.[52] In Muslim contexts, this sort of provision would embrace the idea that liberal theory, and certainly justice as discourse, need not be linked to a radical secularity and that it can accommodate and allow the expression of religious convictions and in addition embrace the importance of these sorts of expressions in the nexus of *din* and *dunya*.

50 (Part I, Article 2). See www.nrb.gov.pk/constitutional_and_legal/constitution/ for the text of the Constitution.

51 Being Chapter One, Article 2 of the Constitution. See www.egypt.gov.eg/english/laws/Constitution/chp_one/part_one.asp for the text of the Constitution. Several other examples could be given of similar types of provisions.

52 Article 9 of the European Convention of Human Rights contains like-minded provisions. See *Convention for the Protection of Human Rights and Fundamental Freedoms*, accessible at http://conventions.coe.int/Treaty/Commun/QueVoulezVous.asp?NT=005&CL=ENG

This also decouples the normative aspects of liberal theory, so conceived, from the predictive aspects of secularisation theory.

Non-constitutional law

Keeping out references to Islam or Islamic law at the constitutional level alone will not, however, be sufficient to establish justice as discourse and guarantee that the diversity of normative positions within Muslim contexts can be expressed. Reference in non-constitutional law is equally a concern. In personal law, some states – such as contemporary Pakistan – have allowed for legal diversity between the different schools of Islamic law. Thus, in applying Islamic law they make two concessions: that it should apply only to Muslims, and that Muslims may choose to invoke any school of Islamic law to govern them. Such provisions may seem to provide an acceptable application of Islamic law on the one hand, while allowing the state to avoid having to define it on the other. In addition, this sort of provision may have the merit in the eyes of some observers of embracing a vision of legal pluralism.

But there is, for justice as discourse, an inherent problem with these arrangements. For example, we can imagine that, within certain limits, we might have different rules for inheritance, or for capacity to marry, or for the grounds and terms of divorce and allow particular juridical traditions and interpretations to define these rules. If it turns out that these differences continue to rest on judges needing to choose among the schools or opinions of Islamic law – e.g. to determine shares of inheritance, capacity to marry, the right to divorce or similar issues – we would once again be in the position of state officials having to decide what Islam, in some version, says. Thus, divorce granted in accordance with Islamic law, though a non-constitutional provision, would require similarly problematic decisions to be made.

When we turn to other areas of law, such diversity appears even more problematic. Criminal law is an obvious example. Different definitions of what constitutes a crime, what evidence must be provided to prove it or what punishments it will attract if proved are difficult to maintain within one legal system. Even if some crimes were considered only to be so if committed by Muslims (here seeking to make into state crime what in other language we might call sins), it would be rather ridiculous to have a patchwork of different criminal rules based on the religion of the individual. The same may apply to other areas of law as well, for example in insurance law or contracts. If one school of Islamic law recognised a certain type of contract as valid and another did not, or if one school found certain types of insurance arrangements to be acceptable and other did not – and these sorts of differences do exist – then the allowing of some and not others would not only mean a confusing array of contract options but also require the state to decide what an authentic reading of Islamic law, or the Islamic law of some school, would require. Provisions invoking Islam, its texts, sources or its laws thus would lead us back to the same dilemma: a doctrinaire definition of 'Islamic' requirements would be necessary.

To be clear, this is different from judges who may be Muslim having a sense of 'Islam' as part of their personal moral makeup and therefore informing their decision-making. We argued earlier that in such situations judges would be required to provide non-religiously-based reasons for their judgments. Here we encounter a different issue, namely, judges being *compelled* to interpret *legislative* language that invokes Islam or some form of Islamic law. It is thus that justice as discourse limits religious reasoning in legislative language (and, as we will be discussed below, in judicial pronouncements) but would welcome this reasoning in broader political discussion, as elaborated next.

Political debate

With the above caveats, religious voices, that is to say those who might be inspired even in part by their religious convictions, should be allowed to express themselves in public discourse and debates, including legislatives debates in state institutions and in civil society. Thus, religiously-grounded or affiliated political parties could exist and express themselves publicly as representing a normative position that is linked (though likely in diverse ways) to their religious convictions. So too could religiously affiliated institutions of civil society, such as NGOs and advocacy groups or newspapers. In addition, legislative representatives should be permitted to argue in deliberations from positions coming from religious convictions, and would always bear in mind that speaking too parochially may be more or less politically efficacious, depending on the issues and context. Indeed, justice as discourse encourages this plurality of debate.

In providing this extensive space for religious voices in political discussions broadly defined, justice as discourse distinguishes itself from Rawls' and, to a lesser extent, Habermas' theories. It is much more in line with the principles espoused by Weithman and Gaus and the outlook advanced by Levison. Moreover, justice as discourse will allow for the desire that Islam have a public political role – that is, that it may be deliberated in the public sphere – which as we noted in the survey reports many Muslims express in different locales, though it will insist that this desire and the sense of 'Islam' that may be invoked be expressed in all of its diversity. Finally, justice as discourse embraces the possibility (perhaps better, the likelihood) that permitting political debate on these lines will result in a constantly 'hot' politics of the type envisaged by Robert Unger.[53]

Judges, state executives and civil servants

While plurality of debate is to be encouraged in all spheres, limits would have to be in place for those occupying state offices, be these in the executive or judicial branches of government (though less so in the legislative, as has just been discussed). Persons in these offices may have religious convictions, of course, but should not justify decisions taken *qua* public office holder. This would mean, as was noted above, that judges could not justify decisions on reasons derived from their individual religious convictions (or any religious convictions) and that state officials, whether in the executive or civil service, could not justify actions on these same grounds. If a state official justified her or his actions on a religious grounding, it would be tantamount to declaring that a religious tradition required certain state action and this declaration would be anathema to both justice as discourse and the heritage of Islam. It is important to note that this is a different reason for this restriction from that which was offered for a similar restriction in the political theory of Rawls and Habermas discussed earlier. Both Rawls and Habermas, the latter more clearly, place limits or requirements on what state officials can do. These requirements seemed to have in mind a particular concern for comprehensibility. Thus, Rawls and Habermas both envisaged a requirement that in public political debate religious reasons must be translated to be comprehensible to those from outside the particular religious tradition. These requirements (found in Rawls' proviso and in Habermas' theory generally) would then make some religious speech politically acceptable. The position articulated here is not persuaded that religious speech would necessarily be so incomprehensible and, thus, that we need have the same concern for its translatability or that that religious speech should necessarily be more obtuse than other forms of speech. Justice as discourse is, therefore, different from both Rawlsian and Habermasian liberalism in where and how it limits religious speech and the invocation of religious reasons.

53 Unger (2007).

It is also different from some liberal ideas of secularity in being willing to allow political speech within public debate to be 'unsecular.' The secularity envisaged by justice as discourse, however, stands in opposition to the phenomenon of *etatization* noted in Zubaida's work. Unlike the contemporary realities of some countries of Muslim majority that have sought to incorporate 'Islamic law' into their constitutions (for example, Pakistan and Egypt or Iraq and Afghanistan),[54] justice as discourse demands an anti-*etatization* of Islam or of Islamic law, precisely because *etatization* will inevitably require the state to choose which version of Islam or Islamic law to apply and, in so doing, will counteract the heritage of diverse interpretations of the faith and of the *shari'a*. While this stance may be at variance from the recent *etatization* model, it is not inconsistent with the broader historical tradition in which the state was not the locus – at least not the main locus – and not a locus in any sort of authoritative way of either Islam or its laws.

Bader's models revisited

Veit Bader made practical, institutional suggestions about methods by which religious diversity can be accommodated within a structure that respects liberal tenets and it thus useful to revisit Bader's model and compare it to justice as discourse. To recall, Bader's preferred model was nonconstitutional pluralism (NCP)[55] and this model included disestablishment with some measure of legal pluralism (e.g. in family law) and the institutionalisation of organised religions. The advantage of this model in Bader's view was that it better allows for the religious pluralisation of society as compared to an alternative nonestablishment and private pluralism (NEPP), which "declares a strict legal separation of the state from all religions as well as a strict administrative and political separation".[56]

Bader's favoured NCP model and his NEPP alternative show that part of the evolution of liberal theory has meant that liberal principles may work with different institutional models, including those that recognise a religious heritage. Indeed, justice as discourse demonstrates this as well but while NCP would depend on some sort of corporate structure of organised religion(s) with which the state could interact, justice as discourse does not. An NCP model would falter in precisely the conditions in which justice as discourse would flourish: a society without an institutionalised religious body to act as a representative, in a tradition, like that of Muslim contexts, that has never known a sort of church structure and in which, on

54 For instance, for Afghanistan see www.mfa.gov.af/Documents/The%20Constitution.pdf
Extracts are as follows:

Preamble
We the people of Afghanistan:

1. With firm faith in God Almighty and relying on His mercy, and Believing in the Sacred religion of Islam . . .

Article One
Afghanistan is an Islamic Republic independent, unitary and indivisible state.

Article Two
The religion of Afghanistan is the sacred religion of Islam.
Followers of other religions are free to perform their religious rites within the limits of the provisions of law.

Article Three
In Afghanistan, no law can be contrary to the sacred religion of Islam and the values of this Constitution.

55 Bader (2003).
56 Bader (2003) at 271.

the contrary, religious authority has never rested unambiguously with a hierarchical clerical establishment but rather with diffuse theologian-jurist-scholars who have been respected for their learning, rather than their position. For Muslim majority environments, an NCP model does not, therefore, much improve the situation from a state determination of the religious tradition. Representative corporate bodies may add some diversity but would still invite selected individuals to make problematic decisions about what Islam means.

Justice as discourse may, in fact, be closer to the NEPP model that Bader rejects in insisting in legal and administrative separation of the state from religion. Where it differs from NEPP is in embracing the participation of religious voices in the broader context of political discussions and allowing these voices to influence public policy in this way. NEPP seems at best agnostic on the role of religious reasons in general political debate, and at worst deeply suspicious of these influences as having the potential to breach, to use the language of American constitutional writings, the 'wall of separation' between church and state. Justice as discourse has no such qualms, subject to the limitations expressed above. Finally, while justice as discourse shares the Bader's priority for democracy concern, it emphasises that in Muslim contexts mediating this priority through organised religious groups or representatives is unworkable and detrimental.

The bridge from politics to law: Menski's kite

One question that still requires elaboration is how the political model just discussed will sit with the heritage of Muslim legal traditions. To address this question of the bridge between politics and law, we can turn to the analysis of different legal regimes and the nature of law offered by Werner Menski after his review of various 'non-Western' legal systems.

Menski posits that:

> law as a global phenomenon is only the same all over the world in that it is everywhere composed of the same basic constituents of ethical values, social norms and state made rules but appears in myriad culture-specific variations.[57]

From this, he develops a graphical kite with religion/ethic/morality at one corner of the kite, society at another corner of the kite, the state at the third corner and international law at the 'tail-end' corner of the kite – hence laws are created by the state, by society and through values and ethics and with international influences.[58] For our purposes, the reason why this kite is interesting is that it both helps to explain a Muslim legal culture in which, as we have seen, legal norms were formulated through a discourse of values and ethics coming from the faith and grounded in a practice of (largely) non-state social actors, and by the state itself: sometimes in a manner consistent with these values and ethics, sometimes in areas where the norms of the faith were seemingly absent, and sometimes in an attempt to shape these values and ethical norms to meet state needs. Secondly, and even more importantly, the image of the kite outlines the relationship that we have to be concerned with, namely the relationship of religion to the state and to society. While Menski appears to offer his kite as descriptive,[59] we can now see that its values for Muslim contexts may also be normative. The kite keeps law a fluid developing system, something which is consistent with the

57 Menski (2006) at 610.
58 Menski (2012) at 81ff.
59 I would venture to say, however, that Menski's kite is not meant just as descriptive model but also as a model with which he finds normative comfort.

historical traditions of Muslim legal developments and also faithful to these traditions normatively by keeping the law separated, though not disconnected, from the state. The space within Menski's kite would capture a public domain informed by ethics/religion/morality, encompassing society (and I would add civil society) and linked to but not circumscribed by the state, and with law generated out if it. The kite thus conceived also offers a conceptual framework upon which we can rest justice as discourse. While all versions of liberal theory are concerned to allow ethics and values to be expressed, some versions, as we have seen, limit expressions which have a religious basis. Menski's kite, however, recognises religion as part and parcel of the corner of ethics and morality, a conception that justice as discourse shares. As such, justice as discourse wants to allow religion, as much as other sources of ethics and values, to be expressed politically. Furthermore, and again like Menski's kite, justice as discourse recognises, and more importantly allows, the law to be formed at least in part by religious values and, importantly, recognises that our understandings of justice are always developing.[60] Other versions of liberalism are very concerned about religious arguments and reasoning affecting the law seeking to keep these away from 'constitutional essentials' or at least requiring 'translation'. Menski's model, however, embraces this influence, as does justice as discourse.

The overall argument and conclusion

While there is nothing immanent that connects liberal theory and Muslim contexts, there are strong arguments for the normative usefulness of liberal theory in those contexts and particularly of justice as discourse as a variety of that liberal theory. The first of these is that liberal theory asks how we can deal with diversity and posits a possible answer. Second, in dealing with this question, liberal theory takes religion and religious diversity seriously, neither ignoring nor denigrating religious belief. Both of these factors are, thirdly, relevant to Muslim contexts because these contexts exhibit diversity and are contexts in which religious sentiments are salient. Fourth, given its relevance, the use of some form of liberal theory to deal with issues around the role of Islam in public and political discourse and in the shaping of law is something that can be imagined, notwithstanding the different social and historical developments in the West (where liberal theory emerged) and Muslim contexts. Thus, both recognise that there can and may well be legal as well as political implication of religious arguments.

This exercise will need to be imaginative in a rich sense of the term: to consider possibilities without adopting an attitude that we have necessarily to look for either sources of liberalism in Muslim heritage or to find an 'Islamic' answer that will justify, or fully redeem, liberal theory. While not minimising the cultural importance of things being 'Islamically redeemed' in Muslim contexts, the content of what an Islamic redemption would entail is not clear, and the long-standing but also on-going diversity of 'Islamic' answers within Muslim heritage means that searching for one answer simply will not be a viable option. This, in turn, means that a key challenge is for this diversity to be embraced by Muslims. One way of achieving this end would be for Islam to have a role in the politics of Muslim contexts, but not in the formal mechanisms and structures of the state or in the justifications of the decisions of its officials. Such a secular – in the sense of denominationally uncommitted – space

60 Menski cites Jacques Derrida, who called justice something that is always in the making (literally *à venir*) (Menski, 2012) at 73.

could be described as both thin or thick:[61] it would be a thin space because it would sheath only the formal structures of the state and the justifications of state officials acting as such, and it would be thick because it would allow, outside of these limits, a large space to be filled by individuals, groups and civil society organisations and even legislative fora (with possibly religious religiously-motivated political parties). Justice as discourse is proposed as a framework to achieve this end. Unlike some other varieties of liberal theory, justice as discourse aims to provide the broadest possible space for discourses of value and in particular of religious values in public political discussions. This is especially important in Muslim contexts because of the significance of the religious heritage in these contexts. This framework would mean that politics was always kept 'hot' and agitated by contentious normative claims that would come from religious diversity, including *intra*-Muslim religious diversity. This, however, is no bad thing. As Roberto Unger has argued, it is only in this way that we can constantly throw open new institutional possibilities and new means of our own self-understanding.[62] Too often in the analysis of religious communities and their relationship with liberalism, *intra*-religious diversity appears to get missed. This leads either to a conception that religious communities cannot be liberal, even if they can be decent (as in Rawls' *The Law of Peoples*) or to arguments that worry that liberalism carries with it its own autocracy which, if imposed on religious traditions, can do violence to the practices and worldviews of these traditions.[63] In both cases, however, the value and advantage of a form of liberal theory to meet the needs of religious contexts which have been characterised by internal diversity, like Muslim contexts, is missed in a constructed opposition between liberal values on the one hand and religious values on the other.[64] It is precisely in the face of this dichotomy that a more nuanced understanding of the interaction between religious commitments and liberal theory is required, sensitive to the diversities that both contain, and especially to the great value that plurality-sensitive and pluralism-enhancing liberal theory has for religious contexts that have been and are interpretationally diverse, like Muslim contexts.

It is this space that justice as discourse fills. Justice as discourse recognises that the language and culture of 'Islam' has been and continues to be a salient trope in Muslim contexts and it recognises that while the pre-modern Islamic state was justified by and operated through law,[65] the *shari'a* is not some "brooding omnipresence" that can be invoked in a word.[66] In short, justice as discourse recognises that, especially for Muslim contexts, the range of influences and factors highlighted by Menski's kite is important. Unlike other varieties of liberal theory – and, in particular, Rawls' political liberalism – justice as discourse thus responds to this broader Menskian conception of the sources of law by allowing a

61 I am indebted to David Little of Harvard Divinity School for an engaging conversation during which he helped me to see these perspectives of secular 'thinness' and 'thickness'.

62 See Unger (2007) and in particular the section entitled 'Religion: the self awakened'. Similarly, one can see Unger (1986) and Unger (1996), which are more specifically legal.

63 See Spinner-Halev's (2008) piece in which he claims (at 554) that:

> Rawls worries that advocates of comprehensive views of religion will want to impose their views on others, but in fact it is his comprehensive view of justice that is in danger of imposing itself on religion. Liberal views of justice are much more imperialistic than most religions.

64 Some scholarship is recognising the problem with these overly neat dichotomies. For example, Ayelet Shachar argues that we must recognise the multiple affiliations of those with religious communities, for instance, as religious believers and women, and how these multiple afflictions challenge an understanding of ourselves as undifferentiated citizens (e.g, just belonging to a religious community or just being women, rather than having both affiliations simultaneously). See Shachar (2008).

65 Feldman (2008) at 7.

66 Feldman (2008) at 10.

greater role for ethical values and social norms in political decision-making and as sources of political authority. Since in Muslim contexts much of the basis of these values and norms is likely to be derived from or developed in dialogue with conceptions of 'Islam' and its legal expressions, justice as discourse affords religious reasons an enhanced position in political processes and in the influence of these processes on the development of legal outcomes, and vice versa. At the same time, justice as discourse emphasises that the content of ethics, values and social norms in Muslim contexts has always been contested and subject to myriad expressions. As such, the state cannot presume formally to adopt any one articulation of these values. Justice as discourse thus posits political arrangements of the kind that Anver Emon describes as follows: "No single Muslim voices will be empowered by the state; rather the state will provide an equal playing field for all voices to be heard, thereby contributing to debate and dialogue . . ."[67]

At first thought, there may be in the minds of many no obvious fit and much tension in the invocation of liberal theory to meet the needs of Muslim contexts. This chapter has sought to address key tensions that might exist from liberalism's demands for neutrality, secularity and democratic politics as they relate to environments in which religion in general has a significant influence, and more particularly for Muslim contexts. It has been argued that these seeming conflicts can be resolved and, moreover, that these factors, which are important elements in liberal theory, offer much to Muslim contexts because by embracing and adopting these principles, the long-standing plurality inherent within Muslim contexts can be drawn upon in political decision-making.

The second major goal of this chapter has been to suggest how – as a more practical political exercise – justice as discourse as a particular version of liberal theory might be applied for the benefit of Muslim contexts. In this effort, the argument has been that both constitutional and non-constitutional law must be kept apart from the explicit invocation of any religious principles, as must the reasoning of courts. However, in broader zones of public discourse at further length from the 'state', such as in civil society organisations, media debates, political party discussions and electoral politics (where such exist) religious expressions and religious reasons should be given broad room to operate, though recognising that any attempt to mediate these expressions through representative corporate bodies is problematic and antithetical.

Finally, drawing upon Menski's analysis of how law is influenced and constructed in (primarily) 'non-Western contexts', this chapter has reasserted the framework of justice as discourse to argue that this particular version of liberal theory is appropriate for Muslim contexts because it allows for the ethics, values and norms of 'Islam' – in their varied expressions – to inform the great challenge of drawing upon Muslim heritage(s) to meet present needs.

67 Emon (2006) at 354.

Conclusion

This work began with the hope of addressing a particular challenge which faces Muslim contexts. This challenge emerges as Muslims attempt to relate their heritage, and in particular the conceptions of political, religious and legal authority, to contemporary conditions.

As we noted, on the one hand, there is view that Islam speaks in terms that require obedience and enforcement and which dictate how Muslim societies should be arranged. While this position is often associated with Islamist/fundamentalist groups, it is a view that can be derived from some academic analyses as well. Noel Coulson, for example, states the following:

> [Islamic] Law, therefore, does not grow out of, and is not moulded by, society as is the case with Western systems. Human thought, unaided, cannot discern true values and standards of conduct; such knowledge can only be attained through divine revelation, and acts are good or evil exclusively because God has attributed this quality to them. In the Islamic concept, law precedes and moulds society; to its eternally valid dictates the structure of State and society must, ideally, conform.[1]

Opposing this outlook are positions which question the desirability or practicality of an 'Islamic polity'. As part of this questioning, these alternative perspectives also seek to debate the 'dictates' of Islam (or more specifically Islamic law), thus throwing open the whole issue of establishing an 'Islamic normativity'.

In entering into this debate and the search for principles by which Muslims might bring their heritage to bear on their current political circumstances, this study has noted the importance of the establishment of the modern state as the basic unit of political organisation for Muslim societies. Within the pre-modern empires, the sultanates, emirates, etc., Muslims mainly lived in a *de facto* separation between political authority on the one part and religio-legal authority on the other part. This separation allowed for 'state' and religion to interact without the latter, in particular, losing its independent authority or the variety of its voices. However, the relationship between political and religio-legal authority waxed and waned and never achieved either an institutional or, more significantly, a normative stability such that 'furry edges' usefully accommodated not only different institutional arrangements but different normative interpretations, reflected, for example in the different schools of law and the variety of opinions within and between these schools. With the advent of the modern state, the indeterminacy of this sort (which characterised Muslim history) became

1 Coulson (1964) at 85.

a serious issue. In many cases, as states have asserted themselves in the face of this indeterminacy, the interpretational and normative diversity which existed within the religio-legal heritage, while not entirely extinguished, has been marginalised through attempts at control and codification. This, however, is a relatively new phenomenon in Muslim experience and represents a departure from a religio-legal tradition that has been, in the main, tremendously plural. The situation of the modern state, therefore, requires Muslims to think about how to draw upon their traditions in new contexts and this reality has informed the analysis in this study.

In developing the idea of justice as discourse as a way to address this challenge, this study has deliberately posited that a broadly liberal framework provides the appropriate philosophical perspective for Muslim contexts despite the concerns that may be raised about the appropriateness of relying on theoretical perspectives that developed largely outside of Muslim contexts. To some, relying on liberal theory in Muslim contexts may seem not just inappropriate but positively unwise; indeed, it may seem to insult the heritage of these contexts to import a framework which developed within a markedly different political, legal and religious context. Moreover, liberal theory may seem a particularly bad fit for contexts in which (i) there is a vital sense community – i.e., the *ummah* – given the association of liberal theory with an emphasis on individual versus communal identities, and (ii) where religious outlooks are important given the association of liberal theory with 'secularism' (and, in the minds of some perhaps, a hostility to religious belief).

I have attempted to answer these concerns in the preceding chapters by making a series of points. First, while one must indeed acknowledge that liberalism did not grow from Muslim contexts, it does not follow from this that it cannot be normatively useful for these contexts. In fact, many of the conditions out of which a liberal perspective did emerge in Western Europe were stimulated by the issues of how to deal with religious disagreements and religion's role in public life. One might, thus, see liberal theory as addressing precisely the questions that are being encountered in Muslim contexts today. Additionally, as has been discussed, it is not as if liberal ideas have not been received to some extent in Muslim contexts so the idea that they are entirely 'alien' is historically inaccurate. Second, as has been noted, liberal theory is really a family of positions within which there are different views about the appropriate role for religious reasoning. All of these positions, even ones that would be most restrictive of the role of religious sentiments in public life, take the question of religion seriously. This perspective too is appropriate for Muslim contexts where religious belief is a significant factor. Third, and more importantly, the answers that justice as discourse offers to the question of religion's appropriate place in public life are also highly relevant to Muslims. As we have seen, Muslim contexts are, and have been, very diverse and in particular for our purposes diverse in their understandings of norms of Islam. Thus, while these environments share common sources of inspiration, these have been interpreted in myriad ways over centuries. As a result, the *ummah* has never represented a monolith of normative opinion. Justice as discourse *qua* liberal theory embraces this plurality and fosters an ethic of pluralism – that is to say, a commitment to allowing the expression of the diversity of opinions in Muslim contexts. It is thus that justice as discourse allows no claim to be promoted as more 'Islamic' than another. Moreover, justice as discourse also recognises that historically part of what allowed the diversity of Muslim opinions to be expressed was their organic development within a social milieu, which the political authorities of the time were denied the legitimacy of prescribing normative orthodoxy. It is because of this that justice as discourse, like other varieties of liberal theory, emphasises the necessity of a secular, but normatively porous, state. Fourth, contemporary information about opinions in Muslim contexts emphasises and confirms that while people in these societies continue to hold religious beliefs to a significant degree and to see these as important, they are hesitant to see them enforced by the state. Thus, justice as discourse which insists that the state remain formally neutral to religious beliefs (by, *inter alia*, not declaring itself a religiously-orientated state, not justifying legislation or judicial decisions on religious grounds or not invoking religious conceptions as part of its positive law), balances the desire that religious views can speak to, but not dictate, public policy. It is here also that justice as discourse departs from the Rawlsian and Habermasian versions of liberal theory, which would, in their own ways, impose certain fetters on the expression of religious sentiments in public discourse. Drawing on the critiques of these approaches (by Elshtain, Weithman and others) and upon formulations like that of Gaus that seek to construct some more expansive, justice as discourse abandons these constraints in favour of allowing broad expression of religious sentiments and religious reasons in public discussion. Where Rawls and others have seen the need, with all good intentions, to subtract certain types of reasoning from our public deliberations for mutual comprehensibility or stability, justice as discourse adopts the position of addition asserting that it is through addition that the challenge of diversity – and in particular the challenge of diversity for contemporary Muslim contexts – can best be addressed. Finally, while the notion of the *ummah* provides Muslims with a notional sense of collective identity and fraternity, it does not and has not ever provided a shared interpretation of the 'Islamic impulse'. Opinions about what Islam means have been not only diverse and varied among Muslims but they have also been, by and large, individual because Muslim communities (albeit with some notable exceptions in some interpretations and at some times in history) have no church-like institutions of normative orthodoxy, or at least not those that have been able to act with the same type of authority as Christian churches. Calder puts this point succinctly:

> Islam, by contrast, does not have such a system of authority. There has never been a council in Islam and there are no clearly articulated hierarchies. In fact, we cannot find a single Muslim (or Sunni) creed that is believed in by all Muslims. There are probably hundreds of Muslim creeds; certainly dozens can be found in, for example, the university library at Manchester.[2]

Hence, situating individual versus corporate opinion at the heart of public discourse in Muslim contexts is not to destroy the *ummah* but to affirm its pluri-vocality and to recognise that this is not new.

It remains to acknowledge what remains undone. Political principles of the type articulated here can only be useful if they are applied. There are a variety of existing liberal regimes in the world today, which express their liberalism in ways that vary considerably. This is, of course, the result of the choices made by these societies in light of their particular historical, cultural and social circumstances, and such choices are constantly being re-considered and adjusted. If the ideas expressed in this work are to be applied in Muslim contexts, then they too will have to be thought of in the light of specific national circumstances. Furthermore, this work cannot pretend to be the final word on political principles for how Muslim contexts address the 'challenge of pluralism'. At best, what is presented here might be an

2 Calder (2000) at 68.

initial offering though, it is hoped, one on novel terms. It might cause reflection on at least three questions: (i) Is liberal theory compatible in any sense with Muslim contexts (though this is an old debate among Muslims, scholars and otherwise)?; (ii) Does justice as discourse represent a version of liberal theory that is normatively useful in and for Muslim contexts?; and (iii) If justice as discourse is to be used as a principled framework in Muslim contexts, in what specific institutional forms should it be implemented? If the terms of any future debate are, however, enriched because of this study and, in particular, if the viability of a form of liberal theory for Muslim contexts is taken seriously as something that is valuable in light of the heritage of these contexts themselves, then the work presented here will have some value. Moreover, while this study invites the discussion to continue, and indeed, fully expects that it must do so, what it posits are new terms of engagement for Muslim contexts. These terms of engagement are about recognising, affirming and capturing the inherent plurality of Muslim contexts as these has been expressed in historical as well as contemporary terms. This affirmation has real implications especially in light of current discourses and debates. It means clearly that assertions that define Islam closed, ahistorical terms must be shown up as untenable. Simultaneously, it recognises the importance of religion within Muslim contexts. It thus advances the idea of justice as discourse to provide a theoretical and principled basis upon which the significance but also diversity of expressions of Islam in myriad forms may be brought to contribute to the political and legal needs of Muslim contexts today. In doing this, this study also asserts the capacity of Muslim contexts to be open to concepts, like liberal theory, that originated in other environments, abjuring the understanding of these contexts that would reject ideas whose origins lie in different milieu as *per se* unfit or unacceptable. Finally, by advancing a liberal theory-informed conception, this study responds to those offer up only obscurantist visions of the possibilities for Muslim contexts with an alternative that it contends can be truer to the intellectual and cultural experience of the past of Muslim contexts but still rich in modern discussion and debate.

These debates and discussions are both for today and for the future; the process must necessarily continue as Muslim contexts address their changing circumstances. As the term 'discourse' in the phrase 'justice as discourse' has sought to emphasise, considering the relationship of law, religion and state for Muslim contexts is not about searching for answers in the sense of settled conclusions, or at least not answers that can be expected to be applicable to all circumstances or to endure indefinitely. Instead, to reiterate, what is proposed is that justice should be thought of more as a verb than as a noun. The terms of the discourse, however, should be understood to be aligned to the plurality of the experience of Muslim contexts as well as to a range of perspectives and ideas coming from different environments that can be normatively useful in and for these contexts.

Bibliography

Works cited

Abou el-Fadl, Khaled M. (2002) *The Place of Tolerance in Islam*. Boston, MA: Beacon Press.

Adamson, Peter (2015) "Al-Kindi" in Edward N. Zalta, ed., *The Stanford Encyclopaedia of Philosophy*, Spring 2015 ed. (accessible at: https://plato.stanford.edu/archives/spr2015/entries/al-kindi).

Aga Khan, His Highness (1982) Speech at the Foundation Ceremony of the Ismaili Jamatkhana and Centre, Burnaby, B.C., Canada, 26 July 1982 (accessible at: http://ismaili.net/speech/s820726.html).

Agrama, Hussein Ali (2010) "Secularism, Sovereignty, Indeterminacy: Is Egypt a Secular or a Religious State?" 52(3) *Comparative Studies in Society and History*, 495–523.

Ahmad, Feroz (2000) "Ottoman Perceptions of the Capitulations 1800–1914" 11(1) *Journal of Islamic Studies* 1.

Ahmed, Eqbal (1995) "Islam and Politics" in Mohammad Ashgar Khan, ed., *Islam, Politics and the State: The Pakistan Experience*. London: Zed Books.

Ahmed, Laila (1992) *Women and Gender in Islam: Historical Roots of a Modern Debate*. New Haven, CT: Yale University Press.

Ahmed, Shahab (2016) *What Is Islam: The Importance of Being Islamic*. Princeton, NJ: Princeton University Press.

Anderson, Benedict (1991) *Imagined Communities: Reflections on the Origin and Spread of Nationalism*, rev. ed. London: Verso.

An-Na'im, Abdullahi Ahmed (1996) *Towards an Islamic Reformation*. Syracuse, NY: Syracuse University Press.

An-Na'im, Abdullahi Ahmed (2008a) "Shari'a in the Secular State: A Paradox of Separation and Conflation" in Peri Bearman, Wolfhart Heinrichs and Bernard G Weiss, eds., *The Law Applied: Contextualising the Islamic Shari'a – a Volume in Honor of Frank E Vogel*. London: IB Tauris.

An-Na'im, Abdullahi Ahmed (2008b) *Islam and the Secular State: Negotiating the Future of Shari 'a*. Cambridge, MA: Harvard University Press.

An-Na'im, Abdullahi Ahmed (2013) "Complementary, Not Competing, Claims of Law and Religion: An Islamic Perspective" 39 *Pepperdine Law Review*, 1231–1256.

An-Na'im, Abdullahi Ahmed (2015) "Islamic Politics and the Neutral State: A Friendly Amendment to Rawls?" in Tom Bailey and Valentina Gentile, eds., *Rawls and Religion*. New York: Columbia University Press.

Arkoun, Mohammed (1995) "The State, the Individual, and Human Rights: A Contemporary View of Muslims in a Global Context" in Azim Nanji, ed., *The Muslim Almanac: A Reference Work on the History, Faith and Culture and Peoples of Islam*. New York: Gale Research Inc.

Asad, Talal (2003) *Formations of the Secular: Christianity, Islam, Modernity*. Stanford, CA: Stanford University Press.

Asfaruddin, Asma (2008) *The First Muslims: History and Memory*. Oxford: Oneworld.

Aslan, Reza (2005) *No God But God: The Origins, Evolution and Future of Islam*. New York: Random House.

As-Sadr, Muhammad Baqir (2003) *Lessons in Islamic Jurisprudence*, trans. & intro. by Roy P. Mottahedeh. Oxford: Oneworld.

Audi, Robert and Wolterstorff, Nicholas (1997) *Religion in the Public Square: The Place of Religious Convictions in Political Debate*. New York: Rowman and Littlefield Publishers Inc.

Augusti, Eliana (2011) "From Capitulations to Unequal Treaties: The Matter of an Extraterritorial Jurisdiction in the Ottoman Empire", 4 *Journal of Civil Law Studies*, 285.

Ayubi, Nazih N. (1991) *Political Islam: Religion and Politics in the Arab World*. London: Routledge.

Bader, Veit (1999) "Religious Pluralism: Secularism or Priority for Democracy" 27(5) *Political Theory*, 597–633.

Bader, Veit (2003) "Religious Diversity and Democratic Institutional Pluralism" 31(2) *Political Theory*, 265–294.

Bailey, Tom and Gentile, Valetina, eds. (2015) *Rawls and Religion*. New York: Columbia University Press.

Bartrum, Ian (2014) "Nonpublic Reasons and Political Paradigm Change" 85(2) *St. John's Law Review*, 473–494.

Beem, Christopher (1998) *Pluralism and Consensus: Conceptions of the Good in the American Polity*. Chicago: Centre for the Scientific Study of Religion.

Berkes, Niyazi (1964) *The Development of Secularism in Turkey*. London: Hurst.

Bhargava, Rajeev (2011) "States, Religious Diversity, and the Crisis of Secularism" *Open Democracy*, 22 March 2011 (accessible at: www.opendemocracy.net/rajeev-bhargava/states-religious-diversity-and-crisis-of-secularism-o).

Bhargava, Rajeev (2013) "Can Secularism Be Rehabilitated?" in Bruce Berman, Rajeev Bhargava and André Laliberté, eds., *Secular States and Religious Diversity*. Vancouver: UBC Press.

Bilgin, M. F. (2007) "The Prospect of Political Liberalism in Non-Western Societies" 10(3) *Critical Review of International Social and Political Philosophy*, 359–376.

Bilgrami, Akeel (2003) "The Clash Within Civilisations" 132(3) *Daedalus*, 88–93.

Black, Anthony (2001) *The History of Islamic Political Thought*. Edinburgh: Edinburgh University Press.

Bonotti, Matteo (2015) "Political Liberalism, Free Speech and Public Reason" 14(2) *European Journal of Political Theory*, 180–208.

Bowen, John R. (2005) "Islamic Norms, Pluralism and Principles: A Challenge for Political Theory and Legal Change" (unpublished paper; on file with the author).

Bowering, Gerhard (2015) *Islamic Political Thought*. Princeton, NJ: Princeton University Press.

Bowers, Michaelle and Kurzman, Charles, eds. (2004) *An Islamic Reformation?* Lanham, MD: Lexington Books.

Brake, Elizabeth (2004) "Rawls and Feminism: What Should Feminists Make of Liberal Neutrality?" 1(3) *Journal of Moral Philosophy*, 293–309.

Brown, L. Carl (2000) *Religion and State: The Muslim Approach to Politics*. New York: Columbia University Press.

Brown, Nathan (1997) "Shari'a and State in the Modern Middle East" 29 *International Journal of Middle Eastern Studies*, 359–376.

Cahen, Claude (1960-) s.v. "Dhimma" in *Encyclopaedia of Islam*, 2nd ed. Leiden: Brill.

Calder, Norman (1993) *Studies in Early Islamic Jurisprudence*. Oxford: Clarendon Press.

Calder, Norman (2000) "The Limits of Islamic Orthodoxy" in Farhad Daftary, ed., *Intellectual Traditions in Islam*. London: IB Tauris.

Calder, Norman (2010) *Islamic Jurisprudence in the Classical Era*. Cambridge: Cambridge University Press.

Calo, Zachary R. (2014) "Religion Human Rights, and Post-Secular Legal Theory" 85(2) *St John's Law Review*, 495–520.

Carter, Stephen (1994) *The Culture of Disbelief: How American Law and Politics Trivialize Religious Devotion.* New York: Anchor Books.
Casanova, José (1994) *Public Religions in the Modern World.* Chicago: University of Chicago Press.
Casanova, José (2009) "The Secular and Secularisms" 76(4) *Social Research*, 1049–1066.
Christiano, Thomas (2000) "Waldron on Law and Disagreement" 19 *Law and Philosophy*, 513–543.
Commonwealth Commission on Respect and Understanding (2007) *Civil Paths to Peace.* London: Commonwealth Secretariat.
Connolly, William (2000) *Why I am Not a Secularist.* Minneapolis, MN: University of Minnesota Press.
Cook, Michael (2003) *Forbidding the Wrong in Islam.* Cambridge: Cambridge University Press.
Coulson, Noel (1964) *A History of Islamic Law.* Edinburgh: Edinburgh University Press.
Coulson, Noel (1968) "Islamic Law" in J. D. M. Derrett, ed., *An Introduction to Legal Systems.* London: Sweet & Maxwell.
Crone, Patricia and Hinds, Martin (1986) *God's Caliph: Religious Authority in the First Centuries of Islam.* Cambridge: Cambridge University Press.
Daftary, Farhad (1989) *The Ismailis: Their History and Doctrines.* Cambridge: Cambridge University Press.
D'Agostino, Fred (1996) *Free Public Reason: Making It Up as We Go.* New York: Oxford University Press.
Dimock, Susan (2002) "Liberal Neutrality" 34 *The Journal of Value Inquiry*, 189–206.
Dionne, E. J. Jr. (2003) "Foreword" in Hugh Heclo and Wilfred M. McClay, eds., *Religion Returns to the Public Square: Faith and Policy in America.* Washington, DC: Woodrow Wilson Centre Press & Johns Hopkins University Press.
Dutton, Yasin (2002) *The Origins of Islamic Law: The Qur'an, the Muwatta and Medinan 'Amal.* London: Routledge.
Dworkin, Ronald (1978) "Liberalism" in Stuart Hampshire, ed., *Public and Private Morality.* Cambridge: Cambridge University Press.
Eberle, Christopher J. (2002) *Religious Convictions in Liberal Politics.* Cambridge: Cambridge University Press.
Eberle, Christopher J. (2015) "Respect and War: Against the Standard View of Religion in Politics" in Tom Bailey and Valentina Gentile, eds., *Rawls and Religion.* New York: Columbia University Press.
Eldemn, Ehdem (2006) "Capitulations and Western Trade", in Suraiya N. Faroqhi (ed), *The Cambridge History of Turkey*, vol III at 290. Cambridge: Cambridge University Press.
Elshtain, Jean Bethke (2003) "Against Liberal Monism" 132(3) *Daedalus*, 78–79.
Emon, Anver (2006) "Conceiving Islamic Law in a Pluralistic Society: History, Politics and Multicultural Jurisprudence" *Singapore Journal of Legal Studies*, 331–355.
Ernst, Carl W. (2003) *Following Muhammad: Rethinking Islam in the Contemporary World.* Chapel Hill, NC: UNC Chapel Hill Press.
Estlund, David (2000) "Jeremy Waldron on Law and Disagreement" 99(1) *Philosophical Studies*, 111–128.
Fadel, Mohammed (2007) "Public Reason as a Strategy for Principle Reconciliation: The Case of Islamic Law and International Human Rights" Toronto: University of Toronto Legal Studies Series, Research Paper No 981777, April 2007 (accessible at http://ssrn.com/abstract=98177).
Fadel, Mohammed (2008) "The True, the Good and the Reasonable: The Theological and Ethical Roots of Public Reason in Islamic Law" 21 *Canadian Journal of Law and Jurisprudence*, 5.
Feldman, Noah (2003) *After Jihad: America and the Struggle for Islamic Democracy.* New York: Farrar, Strauss & Giroux.
Feldman, Noah (2008) *The Fall and Rise of the Islamic State.* Princeton, NJ: Princeton University Press.

Ferguson, Niall (2003) *Empire*. London: Penguin.
Filali-Ansary, Abdou (1996) "The Challenge of Secularisation" 7(2) *Journal of Democracy*, 76–80.
Filali-Ansary, Abdou (1999) "Muslims and Democracy" 10(3) *Journal of Democracy*, 18–32.
Flores d'Arcais, Paolo (2009) "Eleven Theses Against Habermas" *The Utopian*, 12 February 2009 (accessible at www.the-utopian.org/2009/02/000062.html).
Foster, Nicholas H. D. (2014) "Commerce, Commercial Law and Legal Transformation" 7 *Journal of Comparative Law*, 214.
Frye, Northrop (1982) *The Great Code: The Bible and Literature*. New York: Harcourt, Brace and Jovanovich.
Gaus, Gerald F. (2009) "The Place of Religious Belief in Public Reason Liberalism" in M. Dimova-Cookson and P. Stirk, eds., *Multiculturalism and Moral Conflict*. New York: Routledge.
Gaus, Gerald F. (2013) "On Theorizing About Public Reason" 9(1) *European Journal of Analytical Philosophy*, 64–85.
Gaus, Gerald F. and Vallier, Kevin (2009) "The Roles of Religious Conviction in a Publicly Justified Polity: The Implications of Convergence, Asymmetry and Political Institutions" 35(1–2) *Philosophy & Social Criticism*, 51–76.
Geertz, Clifford (1971) *Islam Observed: Religious Developments in Morocco and Indonesia*. Chicago, IL: University of Chicago Press.
Gellner, Ernst (1981) *Muslim Societies*. Cambridge: Cambridge University Press.
Gellner, Ernst (1994) *Conditions of Liberty: Civil Society and Its Rivals*. New York: Allen Lane.
George, Robert P. (1993) *Making Men Moral: Civil Liberties and Public Morality*. Oxford: Oxford University Press.
Gill, Graeme (2003) *The Nature and Development of the Modern State*. New York: Palgrave Macmillan.
Government of Punjab (1954) *Report of the Court of Inquiry Constituted Under the Punjab Act II of 1954 to Enquire Into the Punjab Disturbances of 1953*, Lahore.
Habermas, Jurgen (1989) *Structural Transformation of the Public Sphere: An Enquiry Into a Category of Bourgeois Society*, trans. by Thomas Burger. Cambridge, MA: MIT Press.
Habermas, Jurgen (1995) "Reconciliation Through the Public Use of Reason: Remarks on John Rawls's Political Liberalism" 92(3) *Journal of Philosophy*, 109–131.
Habermas, Jurgen (2006a) "Religion in the Public Sphere" 14(1) *European Journal of Philosophy*, 1–25.
Habermas, Jurgen (2006b) "Secularization as a Twofold and Complementary Learning Process" in Joseph Cardinal Ratzinger (Pope Benedict XVI) and Jurgen Habermas, *Dialectics of Secularization: On Reason and Religion*. San Francisco, CA: Ignatius Press.
Habermas, Jurgen (2006c) "Religious Tolerance: The Pacemaker for Cultural Rights" in Lasse Thomassen, ed., *The Derrida-Habermas Reader*. Edinburgh: Edinburgh University Press.
Habermas, Jurgen (2009) "Again Religion and the Public Sphere: A Response to Pablo Flores d'Arcais" *The Utopian*, 12 February 2009 (accessible at www.the-utopian.org/2009/02/000063.html).
Haidar, Hamid Hadji (2008) *Liberalism and Islam: Practical Reconciliation Between the Liberal State and Shiite Muslims*. London: Palgrave Macmillan.
Haider, Najam (2014) *Shia Islam: An Introduction*. Cambridge: Cambridge University Press.
Hallaq, Wael (2001) *Authority, Continuity and Change in Islamic Law*. Cambridge: Cambridge University Press.
Hallaq, Wael (2005) *The Origins and Evolution of Islamic Law*. Cambridge: Cambridge University Press.
Hallaq, Wael (2005–2006) "What Is Sharia?"12 *Yearbook of Islamic and Middle Eastern Law*, 151–180.
Hallaq, Wael (2009) *Shariʿa: Theory, Practice and Transformations*. Cambridge: Cambridge University Press.

Hanafi, Hassan (2002) "Alternative Conceptions of Civil Society: A Reflective Islamic Approach" in Sohail Hashmi, ed., *Islamic Political Ethics: Civil Society, Pluralism and Conflict*. Princeton, NJ: Princeton University Press.
Harris, Jose (2006) "Development of Civil Society" in R. A. W. Rhodes, S. A. Binder and B. A. Rockman, eds., *The Oxford Handbook of Political Institutions*. Oxford: Oxford University Press.
Hasan, Riaz (2002) *Faithlines: Muslim Conceptions of Islam & Society*. Oxford: Oxford University Press.
Hay, Colin (2006) "(What's Marxist About) Marxist State Theory" in C. Hay, M. Lister and D. Marsh, eds., *The State: Theories and Issues*. New York: Palgrave Macmillan.
Heffner, Robert (2000) *Civil Islam: Muslims and Democratization in Indonesia*. Princeton, NJ: Princeton University Press.
Hodgson, M. G. S. (1974) *The Venture of Islam: Conscience and History in World Civilization*. Chicago: University of Chicago Press.
Holmes, Stephen (1998) "Jean Bodin: The Paradox of Sovereignty and the Privatisation of Religion" in J. Roland Pennock and John W. Chapman, eds., *NOMOS XXX (Religion, Morality and the Law)*. New York: New York University Press.
Holy Qur'an (Pickthall translation).
Holy Bible (King James version).
Imber, Colin (1997) *Ebu's Su'ud: The Islamic Legal Tradition*. Stanford, CA: Stanford University Press.
Inglehart, Ronald F. (2017) "Changing Values in the Islamic World and the West: Social Tolerance and the Arab Spring" in Mansoor Moaddel and Michele Gelfand, eds., *Values and Political Action in the Middle East*. New York: Oxford University Press.
Jamal, Arif A. (2001) "Principles in the Development of Ismaili Law" 7 *Yearbook of Islamic and Middle Eastern Law*, 115–126.
Jamal, Arif A. (2010) "Moving Out of Kazanistan: Liberal Theory and Muslim Contexts" in Gabriele Marranci, ed., *Muslim Societies and the Challenge of Secularization: An Interdisciplinary Approach*. Dordrecht, The Netherlands: Springer.
Jamal, Amaney and Tessler, Mark (2008) "The Democracy Barometers: Attitudes in the Arab World" 19(1) *Journal of Democracy*, 97–110.
Jessop, Bob (2006) "The State and State-Building" in R. A. W. Rhodes, S. A. Binder and B. A. Rockman, eds., *The Oxford Handbook of Political Institutions*. Oxford: Oxford University Press.
Johnson, Robert (2004) "Kant's Moral Philosophy" in Edward N. Zalta, ed., *The Stanford Encyclopaedia of Philosophy*, Spring 2004 ed. (accessible at http://plato.stanford.edu/archives/spr2004/entries/kant-moral/).
Kalanges, Kristine (2012) *Religious Liberty in Western and Islamic Law: Toward a World Legal Tradition*. Oxford: Oxford University Press.
Kalanges, Kristine (2014) "Sharia and Modernity" in Rudolph Peters and Peri Bearman, eds., *The Ashgate Research Companion to Islamic Law*. Aldershot: Ashgate.
Kause, Sharon R. (2008) *Civil Passions: Moral Sentiment and Democratic Deliberation*. Princeton, NJ: Princeton University Press.
Keane, John (1998) "The Limits of Secularism", *The Times Literary Supplement*, 9 January 1998.
Keddie, Nikki R. (1994) "The Revolt of Islam, 1700–1993: Comparative Considerations and Relations to Imperialism" 36(3) *Comparative Studies in Society and History*, 463–487.
Keddie, Nikki R. (2003) "Secularism and It Discontents" 132(3) *Deadalus*, 14–30.
Kelsay, John (2002) "Civil Society & Governance in Islam" in Sohail Hashmi, ed., *Islamic Political Ethics: Civil Society, Pluralism and Conflict*. Princeton, NJ: Princeton University Press.
Kennedy, Hugh (1986) *The Prophet and the Age of the Caliphates: The Islamic Near East From the Sixth to the Eleventh Century*. London: Longman.
Kessler, Edward (2008) "Renovating a Jewish-Muslim Bridge" (Spring) *Harvard Divinity Bulletin*, 10–13.

Khan, Mohammad Ashgar, ed. (1995) *Islam, Politics and the State: The Pakistan Experience*. London: Zed Books.
Kurzman, Charles (1998) *Liberal Islam: A Sourcebook*. New York: Oxford University Press.
Kymlicka, Will (1989) "Liberal Individualism and Liberal Neutrality" 99(4) *Ethics*, 883–905.
Ladd, John (1988) "Politics and Religion in America: The Enigma of Pluralism" in J. Roland Pennock and John W. Chapman, eds., *NOMOS* XXX *(Religion, Morality and the State)*. New York: New York University Press.
Lægaard, Sune (2008) "Moderate Secularism and Multicultural Equality" 28(3) *Politics*, 160–168.
Lægaard, Sune (2013) "Secular Religious Establishment: A Framework for Discussing the Compatibility of Institutional Religious Establishment With Political Secularism" 3(2) *Philosophy and Public Issues*, 119–157.
Lambton, A. K. S. (1980) *Theory and Practice in Medieval Persian Government*. London: Vaorium Reprints.
Lapidus, Ira M. (1996) "State and Religion in Islamic Society" 151 *Past and Present*, 3–27.
Lapidus, Ira M. (2002) *A History of Islamic Societies*, 2nd ed. Cambridge: Cambridge University Press.
Levinson, Sanford (1992) "Review: Religious Language in the Public Square" 105(8) *Harvard Law Review*, 2061–2079.
Lewis, Bernard (1988) *The Political Language of Islam*. Chicago, IL: University of Chicago Press.
MacIntyre, Alasdair (1985) *After Virtue: A Study in Moral Theory*, 2nd ed. London: Duckworth.
Madelung, Wilferd (2004) *The Succession to Muhammad*. Cambridge: Cambridge University Press.
Mahmood, Saba (2003) "Questioning Liberalism, Too" *Boston Review* (accessible at: https://bostonreview.net/archives/BR28.2/mahmood.html).
March, Andrew F. (2013) "Rethinking Religious Reasons in Public Justification" 107(3) *American Political Science Review*, 523–539.
Masud, Khalid (2002) "The Scope of Pluralism in Islamic Moral Traditions" in Sohail Hashmi, ed., *Islamic Political Ethics: Civil Society, Pluralism and Conflict*. Princeton, NJ: Princeton University Press.
Menski, Werner (2006) *Comparative Law in a Global Context: The Legal Systems of Asia and Africa*, 2nd ed. Cambridge: Cambridge University Press.
Menski, Werner (2012) "Plural Worlds of Law and the Search for Living Law" in Werner Gephart, ed., *Rechtsanalyse als Kulturforschung*. Frankfurt am Main: Vittorio Klostermann.
Moadell, Mansoor (2003) "The Worldviews of Islamic Publics: Findings From the Values Surveys in Egypt, Iran, Jordan Morocco, Saudi Arabia and Turkey vs. Americans" a paper presented to the Department of Government, Harvard University, October 2003 (on file with the author).
Moadell, Mansoor (2004) "The Worldviews of Saudi Citizens vs. Other Islamic Countries and Americans: Findings From Values Surveys" (accessible at www.psc.isr.umich.edu/research/tmp/moaddel_capitol-hill-may04.pdf).
Modood, Tariq (2008) "Multicultural Citizenship and the Anti-Sharia Storm" *Open Democracy*, 14 February 2008 (accessible at: www.opendemocracy.net/article/faith_ideas/europe_islam/anti_sharia_storm).
Moors, Annelise (1999) "Debating Family Law: Legal Texts and Social Practices" in Margaret Merriweather and Judith Tucker, eds., *Social History of Women and Gender in the Modern Middle East*. Boulder, CO: Westview Press.
Mottahedeh, Roy P. (1995) "The Islamic Movement: the Case for Democratic Inclusion" (Spring) 4 *Contention: Debates in Society, Culture and Science*, 107–127.
Mottahedeh, Roy P. (2000) *The Mantle of the Prophet: Religion and Politics in Iran*. Oxford: Oneworld.
Movsesian, Mark L. (2011) "Religious Legal Theory Symposium: Introduction" *Faculty Publications*, 397–406 (Paper 94, St John's University) (accessible at: http://scholarship.law.stjohns.edu/faculty_publications/94).

Nasr, Vali (2003) "Lessons From the Muslim World" 132(3) *Daedalus*, 67–72.
Nelson, Matthew J. (2009) "Dealing With Difference: Religious Education and the Challenge of Democracy in Pakistan" 43(2) *Modern Asian Studies*, 591–618.
Nichols, Joel A. and McCarty, James W. III (2014) "When the State Is Evil: Biblical Civil (Dis) Obedience in South Africa" 85(2) *St. John's Law Review*, 593–626.
Norris, Pippa and Inglehart, Ronald (2004) *Sacred and Secular: Religion and Politics Worldwide*. Cambridge: Cambridge University Press.
Panjwani, Farid (2005) "The 'Islamic' in Islamic Education" 7(1) *Current Issues in Comparative Education*, 19–29.
Pasternak, Lawrence, ed. (2002) *Immanuel Kant: Groundwork of the Metaphysic of Morals in Focus*. London: Routledge.
Perry, Michael J. (1991) *Love and Power: The Role of Religion and Morality in American Politics*. New York: Oxford University Press.
Perry, Michael J. (1997) *Religion in Politics: Constitutional and Moral Perspectives*. Oxford: Oxford University Press.
Putnam, Robert (2000) *Bowling Alone: The Collapse and Revival of the American Community*. New York: Simon & Schuster.
Qureshi, Emran (2006) "Toward a New Cold War" (Spring) *Harvard Divinity Bulletin*, 12–14.
Rawls, John (1987) "The Idea of an Overlapping Consensus" 7(1) *Oxford Journal of Legal Studies*, 1–25.
Rawls, John (1993) *Political Liberalism*. New York: Columbia University Press.
Rawls, John (1997) "The Idea of Public Reason Revisited" 64(3) *University of Chicago Law Review*, 765–807.
Rawls, John (1999) *The Law of Peoples*. Cambridge, MA: Harvard University Press.
Raz, Joseph (1986) *The Morality of Freedom*. Oxford: Oxford University Press.
Rehman, Javaid (2005) *Islamic State Practices, International law and the Threat From Terrorism*. Oxford: Hart Publishing.
Rizzo, H., Abdel-Latif, A. and Meyer, K. (2007) "The Relationship Between Gender Equality and Democracy: A Comparison of Arab Versus Non-Arab Muslim Societies" 41(6) *Sociology*, 1151–1170.
Roy, Olivier (1994) *The Failure of Political Islam*. Cambridge, MA: Harvard University Press.
Royle, Edward (1974) *Victorian Infidels: The Origins of the British Secularist Movement 1791–1866*. Manchester: Manchester University Press.
Ruskola, Teemu (2011) "Where Is Asia? When Is Asia? Theorizing Comparative and International Law" 44 *UC Davis Law Review*, 879–896.
Sachedina, Abdulaziz (2006) "The Role of Islam in the Public Square: Guidance or Governance?" ISIM Paper 5. Amsterdam: Amsterdam University Press.
Sadurski, Wojciech (1990) *Moral Pluralism and Legal Neutrality*. Dordrect, The Netherlands: Kluwer Academic Publishers.
Sajoo, Amyn B. (2004) *Muslim Ethics: Emerging Vistas*. London: IB Tauris.
Sandel, Michael J. (1984) "The Procedural Republic and the Unencumbered Self", 12(1) *Political Theory*, 81–96.
Sandel, Michael J. (1984) *Liberalism and Its Critics*. Oxford: Blackwell.
Sandel, Michael J. (1988) *Liberalism and the Limits of Justice*. Cambridge: Cambridge University Press.
Sandel, Michael J. (1994) "Political Liberalism" 107(7) *Harvard Law Review*, 1765–1794.
Schacht, Joseph (1964) *An Introduction to Islamic Law*. Oxford: Clarendon Press.
Schacht, Joseph (1965) *Origins of Muhammadan Jurisprudence*. Oxford: Clarendon Press.
Sen, Amartya (1998) "Secularism and Its Discontents" in Rajeev Bhargava, ed., *Secularism and Its Critics*. New Delhi: Oxford University Press.
Shachar, Ayelet (2008) "Privatising Diversity: A Cautionary Tale From Religious Arbitration in Family Law" 9(2) *Theoretical Inquiries in Law*, 573–589.

Solum, Lawrence B. (1993) "Constructing an Ideal of Public Reason" 30 *San Diego Law Review*, 729–762.

Spierings, Niels (2014) "Islamic Attitudes and the Support for Gender Equality and Democracy in Seven Arab Countries, and the Role of Anti-Western Feelings" 3(2) *Multidisciplinary Journal of Gender Studies*, 423–456.

Spinner-Halev, Jeff (2008) "Liberalism and Religion: Against Congruence" 9(2) *Theoretical Inquiries in Law*, 553–572.

Stout, Jeffrey (2004) *Democracy and Tradition*. Princeton, NJ: Princeton University Press.

Sunstein, Cass R. (1996) "On the Expressive Function of Law" 144 *University of Pennsylvania Law Review*, 2021–2053.

Taylor, Charles (1989) *Sources of the Self: The Making of Modern Identity*. Cambridge: Cambridge University Press.

Taylor, Charles (1995) *Philosophical Arguments*. Cambridge, MA: Harvard University Press.

Taylor, Charles (1998) "Modes of Secularism" in Rajeev Bhargava, ed., *Secularism and Its Critics*. New Delhi: Oxford University Press.

Taylor, Charles (2004) *Modern Social Imaginaries*. Durham, NC: Duke University Press.

Taylor, Charles (2007) *A Secular Age*. Cambridge, MA: Harvard University Press.

Taylor, Charles (2011) "Why We Need a Radical Redefinition of Secularism" in Eduardo Mendieta and Johnathan Vanantwerpen, eds., *The Power of Religion in the Public Sphere*. New York: Columbia University Press.

Trigg, Roger (2007) *Religion in Public Life: Must Faith Be Privatised?* Oxford: Oxford University Press.

Unger, Roberto (1986) *The Critical Legal Studies Movement*. Cambridge, MA: Harvard University Press.

Unger, Roberto (1996) *What Should Legal Analysis Become?* London: Verso.

Unger, Roberto (2007) *The Self Awakened: Pragmatism Unbound*. Cambridge, MA: Harvard University Press.

Van den Boogert, Maurits H. (2004) "Consular Jurisdiction in the Ottoman Legal System in the Eighteenth Century", in Maurits H. Van den Boogert and Kate Fleet eds., *The Ottoman Capitulations: Text and Context*. Roma: Istituto per l'Oriente C.A. Nallino.

Vatikiosis, P. J. (1957) *The Fatimid Theory of State*. Lahore: Orientalia Publishers.

Vikor, Knut (2005) *Between God and the Sultan*. London: Hurst & Co.

Vogel, Frank (1999) "Conformity With the Shari'a and Constitutionality Under Article 2: Some Issues of Theory, Practice and Comparison" in Eugene Cotran and Adel Omar Sherif, eds., *Democracy, the Rule of Law and Islam*. London: Kluwer Law International.

Waldron, Jeremy (1999) *Law and Disagreement*. Oxford: Oxford University Press.

Waldron, Jeremy (2012) "Two Way Translation: The Ethics of Engaging With Religious Contributions in Public Deliberation" 63 *Mercer Law Review*, 845–868.

Weber, Max (1978) *Economy and Society: An Outline of Interpretive Sociology, Volume 1*. G. Roth and C. Wittich, eds. Berkeley, CA: University of California Press.

Weiss, Bernard (1998) *The Spirit of Islamic Law*. Athens, GA: University of Georgia Press.

Weithman, Paul J, ed. (1997) *Religion and Contemporary Liberalism*. Notre Dame, IN: University of Notre Dame Press.

Weithman, Paul J. (2002) *Religion and the Obligations of Citizenship*. Cambridge: Cambridge University Press.

Welchman, Lynn (2002) "Islamic Law: Stuck With the State" in Andrew Huxley, ed., *Religion, Law and Tradition: Comparative Studies in Religious Law*. London: Routledge.

Wittgenstein, Ludwig (2001) Philosophical Investigations, the German text, with a revised English translation trans. by G. E. M. Anscombe, 3rd ed. London: Blackwell.

Yared, Nazik Sabra (2002) *Secularism and the Arab World: 1850–1939*. London: Saqi Books.

Yavuz, M. Hakan (2000) "Cleansing Islam From the Public Sphere" 54(1) *Journal of International Affairs*, 21–42.

Zubaida, Sami (2003) *Law and Power in the Islamic World*. London: IB Tauris.
Zubaida, Sami (2005) "Islam and Secularisation" 33(3) *Asian Journal of Social Science*, 438–448.
(No author) (2004) "Young, Muslim and British" *The Guardian*, 30 November, 17–20.

Works consulted

Ahdar Rex J., ed. (2000) *Law and Religion*. Aldershot: Ashgate.
Al-Attas, S. M. N. (1993) *Islam and Secularism*. Kuala Lumpur: ISTAC.
Ansari, M. T. (2001) *Secularism, Islam and Modernity*. New Delhi and London: Sage Publications.
Arkoun, Mohammed (2002) *The Unthought in Contemporary Islamic Thought*. London: IB Tauris.
Audi, Robert (2000) *Religious Commitment and Secular Reason*. Cambridge: Cambridge University Press.
Bader, Veit (2003) "Taking Religious Pluralism Seriously: Arguing for an Institutional Turn" 6(1) *Ethical Theory and Moral Practice*, 3–22.
Bader, Veit (2007) *Secularism or Democracy? Associational Governance of Religious Diversity*. Amsterdam: Amsterdam University Press.
Bellamy, Richard (2000) *Rethinking Liberalism*. London: Pinter.
Bellamy, Richard and Hollis, Martin, eds. (1999) *Pluralism and Liberal Neutrality*. London: F. Cass.
Berkey, Jonathan Porter (2003) *The Formation of Islam: Religion and Society in the Near East, 600–1800*. Cambridge: Cambridge University Press.
Carrol, James (2003) "Why Religion Still Matters" 132(3) *Daedalus*, 9–13.
Carter, Stephen (1998) *The Dissent of the Governed: A Meditation on Law, Religion and Loyalty*. Cambridge, MA: Harvard University Press.
Carter, Stephen (2000) *God's Name in Vain the Wrongs and Rights of Religion in Politics*. New York: Basic Books.
Charfi, Mohamed (1998) *Islam et liberté – le maltendu historique*. Paris: Editions Albion Michel.
Coles, Robert (1999) *The Secular Mind*. Princeton, NJ: Princeton University Press.
Cooper, John, Nettler, Ronald and Mahmoud, Mohamed, eds. (1998) *Islam and Modernity: Muslim Intellectuals Respond*. London: I.B. Tauris.
Crimmins, James E. (1990) *Religion, Secularization and Political Thought: Thomas Hobbes to J.S. Mill*. London: Routledge.
Crone, Patricia (2004) *God's Rule: Government and Islam*. New York: Columbia University Press.
Durkheim, Emile (2001) *The Elementary Forms of Religious Life*, trans. by Carol Cossman. Oxford: Oxford University Press.
Dworkin, Ronald (1977) *Taking Rights Seriously*. Cambridge, MA: Harvard University Press.
Dworkin, Ronald (1986) *Law's Empire*. Cambridge, MA: Harvard University Press.
Dworkin, Ronald (2000) *Sovereign Virtue*. Cambridge, MA: Harvard University Press.
Edge, Peter W. (2002) *Legal Responses to Religious Difference*. Hague: Kluwer Law International.
Edge, Peter W. and Harvey, Graham, eds. (2000) *Law and Religion in Contemporary Society: Communities, Individualism and the State*. Aldershot: Ashgate.
Engineer, Ashgar Ali (1999) *Essays in Contemporary Politics of Identity, Religion and Secularism*. New Delhi: Ajanta Books International.
Esposito, John and Tamimi, Azam (2000) *Islam and Secularism in the Middle East*. New York: New York University Press.
Esposito, John, and Voll, John, eds. (2001) *Makers of Contemporary Islam*. Oxford: Oxford University Press.
Farrow, Douglas (2004) *Recognizing Religion in Secular Society: Essays in Pluralism, Religion and Public Policy*. Montreal: McGill-Queens University Press.
Galston, William (2002) *Liberal Pluralism*. Cambridge: Cambridge University Press.
George, Robert P. (2001) *The Clash of Orthodoxies: Law, Religion and Morality in Crisis*. Wilmington, DE: ISI Books.

Habermas, Jurgen (2002) *Religion and Rationality: Essays on Reason, God and Modernity.* Cambridge, MA: MIT Press.
Hadden, Jeffrey K. and Shupe, Anson (1989) *Secularization and Fundamentalism Reconsidered.* New York: Paragon House.
Hashemi, Nader (2005) "Rethinking the Relationship Between Religion, Secularism and Liberal Democracy: Toward a Democratic Theory for Muslim Societies" Thesis, PhD (University of Toronto). [Now see Hashemi, Nader (2009) *Islam, Secularism and Liberal Democracy: Toward a Democratic Theory for Muslim Societies.* New York: Oxford University Press].
Heclo, Hugh (2003) "An Introduction to Religion and Public Policy" in Hugh Heclo and Wilfred M McClay, eds., *Religion Returns to the Public Square: Faith and Policy in America.* Washington, DC: Woodrow Wilson Centre Press & Johns Hopkins University Press.
Heft, James L., ed. (1999) *A Catholic Modernity: Charles Taylor's Marianist Award Lecture.* Oxford: Oxford University Press.
Jan, Tarik, et al. (1998) *Pakistan Between Secularism and Islam: Ideology, Issues, Conflict.* Islamabad: Institute of Policy Studies.
Janis, Mark W. and Evans, Carolyn, eds. (2004) *Religion and International Law.* Leiden: Martinus Nijhoff.
Kennedy, Duncan (2003) "Two Globalizations: Law & Legal Thought, 1850–1968" 36(3) *Suffolk University Law Review*, 631–679.
Kepel, Gilles (2002) *Jihad: The Trial of Political Islam.* Cambridge, MA: Harvard University Press.
Khalidi, Rashid (2004) *Resurrecting Empire: Western Footprints and America's Perilous Path in the Middle East.* Boston, MA: Beacon Press.
Madeley, John T. S., ed. (2003) *Religion and Politics.* Aldershot: Dartmouth Publishing Company.
Mallat, Chibli (1993) *The Renewal of Islamic Law.* Cambridge: Cambridge University Press.
Marquand, David and Nettler, Ronald, eds. (2000) *Religion and Democracy.* Oxford: Blackwell.
Martinich, Aloysius P. (1992) *The Two Gods of Leviathan: Thomas Hobbes on Religion and Politics.* Cambridge: Cambridge University Press.
McClay, Wilfred M. (2003) "Two Concepts of Secularism" in Hugh Heclo and Wilfred M. McClay, eds., *Religion Returns to the Public Square: Faith and Policy in America.* Washington, DC: Woodrow Wilson Centre Press & Johns Hopkins University Press.
Metcalf, Barbara (1996) *Making Muslim Space.* Berkeley, CA: University of California Press.
Modood, Tariq (1997) *Church, State and Religious Minorities.* London: Policy Studies Institute.
Modood, Tariq (1998) "Anti-Essentialism, Multiculturalism and the 'Recognition' of Religious Groups" 6(4) *Journal of Political Philosophy*, 378–399.
Nadeem, Azhar Hasan (2002) *Pakistan: The Political Economy of Lawlessness.* Oxford: Oxford University Press.
Neusner, Jacob (2003) *God's Rule: The Politics of World Religions.* Washington, DC: Georgetown University Press.
O'Dair, Richard and Lewis, Andrew, eds. (2001) *Law and Religion.* Oxford: Oxford University Press.
Peach, Lucinda J. (2002) *Legislating Morality: Pluralism and Religious Identity in Lawmaking.* New York: Oxford University Press.
Perry, Michael J. (1988) *Morality, Politics, and Law: A Bicentennial Essay.* New York: Oxford University Press.
Perry, Michael J. (1993) "Religious Morality and Political Choice: Further Thoughts – and Second Thoughts – on *Love and Power*" 30 *San Diego Law Review*, 703–728.
Perry, Michael J. (1994) *The Constitution in the Courts: Law or Politics?* New York: Oxford University Press.
Perry, Michael J. (1997) *Religion in Politics: Constitutional and Moral Perspectives.* New York: Oxford University Press.

Perry, Michael J. (2003) *Under God? Religious Faith and Liberal Democracy.* Cambridge: Cambridge University Press.
Raikka, Juha (2000) "The Place of Religious Arguments in Civic Discussions" 13(2) *Ratio Juris*, 162–176.
Sadurski, Wojciech, ed. (1992) *Law and Religion.* Aldershot: Dartmouth Publishing.
Sohail, Khalid (2001) *From Islam to Secular Humanism.* Toronto: Abbeyfield Publishers.
Soroush, Abdolkarim (2000) *Reason, Freedom & Democracy in Islam.* Oxford: Oxford University Press.
Stark, Rodney and Finke, Roger (2000) *Acts of Faith: Explaining the Human Side of Religion.* Berkeley, CA: University of California Press.
Tamimi, Azzam S. (2001) *Rachid Ghanouchi: A Democrat Within Islamism.* New York: Oxford University Press.
Taylor, Charles (1989) *Sources of the Self: The Making of Identity.* Cambridge, MA: Harvard University Press.
Taylor, Charles (1995) *Liberal Politics and the Public Sphere – Discussion Paper 15.* London: London School of Economics, Centre for the Study of Global Governance.
Thieman, Ronald, ed. (2005) *Religion in Public Life: A Dilemma for Democracy.* Cambridge: Harvard University Press.
Thierstein, Joel and Kamalipour, Yahya R., eds. (2000) *Religion, Law, and Freedom: A Global Perspective.* Westport, CN: Praeger.
Tushnet, Mark (1991) "The Limits of the Involvement of Religion in the Body Politic" in James E. Woods and Derek Davis, eds., *The Role of Religion in the Making of Public Policy.* Waco, TX: Baylor University.
Waldron, Jeremy (1993) "Religious Contributions in Public Deliberation" 30 *San Diego Law Review*, 817–848.
Watson, Alan, ed. (1996) *Law, Morality, and Religion: Global Perspectives.* Berkeley, CA: University of California Press.
Weithman, Paul J. (1991) "The Separation of Church and State: Some Questions for Professor Audi" 20(1) *Philosophy and Public Affairs*, 52–65.
Weithman, Paul J. (2016) *Rawls, Political Liberalism and Reasonable Faith.* Cambridge: Cambridge University Press.
Westerlund, David, ed. (1996) *Questioning the Secular State: The Worldwide Resurgence of Religion in Politics.* New York: St. Martin's Press.
World Peace Through Law Center (1973) *Religion and the Law: The World's Great Religions, The World's Great Law Systems.* Washington, DC: World Peace Through Law Center.

Websites

BBC News Article – 'West-Muslim Divide'
http://news.bbc.co.uk/1/hi/world/europe/6142308.stm (last accessed 20 August 2017)
BBC News Report – 'What the World Thinks of God: Survey Results'
http://news.bbc.co.uk/1/shared/spl/hi/pop_ups/04/world_what_the_world_thinks_of_god/html/1.stm (last accessed 20 August 2017)
Constitution of Afghanistan
http://president.gov.af/en/afghan-constitution-2/ (last accessed 20 August 2017)
Constitution of Egypt
www.egypt.gov.eg/english/laws/Constitution/chp_one/part_one.aspx (last accessed 20 August 2017)
Constitution of Iran
www.iranonline.com/iran/iran-info/Government/constitution-1.html (last accessed 20 August 2017)

Constitution of Iraq
www.wipo.int/edocs/lexdocs/laws/en/iq/iq004en.pdf (last accessed 20 August 2017)
Constitution of Pakistan
www.pakistanconstitutionlaw.com (last accessed 20 August 2017)
Cover Illustration: Socrates and Two Pupils
http://digitool.haifa.ac.il/R/2BM25TN7QPCSXVMLTYH2QD15RD1GT4CVKQQRIG3CIJS277EQY9-01060?func=search-simple-go&local_base=GEN01&find_code=WTI&request=Socrates%20and%20two%20pupils%20(ca.%201200-1250)%20%5Bdigital%20image%5D (last accessed 20 August 2017)
European Convention on Human Rights
http://conventions.coe.int/Treaty/Commun/QueVoulezVous.asp?NT=005&CL=ENG (last accessed 20 August 2017)
Gallup Polls
http://media.gallup.com/worldpoll/pdf/gallupmuslimstudiesislamanddemocracy030607.pdf (last accessed 20 August 2017)
Karl Marx's Writings ('On the Jewish Question')
http://marx.eserver.org (last accessed 20 August 2017)
Most Malay Malaysians See Themselves as Muslims First
www.todayonline.com/world/asia/most-malay-msians-see-themselves-muslims-first-poll (last accessed 20 August 2017)
Muslims and Islam: Key Findings in the US and around the World (Michael Lipka)
www.pewresearch.org/fact-tank/2016/07/22/muslims-and-islam-key-findings-in-the-u-s-and-around-the-world/ (last accessed 20 August 2017)
Pew Centre Reports and Opinion Polls
www.people-press.org (last accessed 20 August 2017)
Speech of His Highness the Aga Khan
http://ismaili.net/speech/s820726.html (last accessed 20 August 2017)
The Divide Over Islam and National Laws in the Muslim World (Jacob Poushter)
www.pewglobal.org/2016/04/27/the-divide-over-islam-and-national-laws-in-the-muslim-world/ (last accessed 20 August 2017)
The Utopian (Pablo Flores d'Arcais and Jurgen Habermas articles – 12 February 2009)
www.the-utopian.org/2009/02/000062.html (last accessed 20 August 2017)
University of Michigan Research (Mansoor Moaddel)
www.psc.isr.umich.edu/research/tmp/moaddel_capitol-hill-may04.pdf (last accessed 20 August 2017)
University of Toronto Faculty of Law Research Papers (Article of Mohamed Fadel)
http://papers.ssrn.com/sol3/papers.cfm?abstract_id=981777 (last accessed 20 August 2017)

Index

Abbasids 72–73, 80
Abd al-Raziq, Ali 113
Abou el-Fadl, Khaled 89
absolutisms 29
Abu Bakr 70
Afghanistan 1–2
Aga Khan, Karim 92
Ahmed, Eqbal 82
Ali b. Abi Talib 67, 70
Anderson, Benedict 64
An-Na'im, Abdullahi 35–37, 113
anti-perfectionism 42
Arkoun, Mohammed 85
Asad, Talal 47
Asfaruddin, Asma 110, 111–112
Asharites 79
Audi, Robert 9, 10, 20, 40, 106

Bader, Veit 34–35, 125–126
Bayhaqi 80
Beem, Christopher 8
Berkes, Niyazi 88
Bhargava, Rajeev 38, 49
Bilgin, M. F. 117–118
Black, Anthony 68, 71–72, 78, 80
Bowen, John 87
Bowering, Gerhard 66, 114
Brake, Elizabeth 104
Brennan, William 43, 55
Brown, L. Carl 82, 102, 110, 112
bureaucratic authorities and justice as discourse 51–53

Calder, Norman 59, 77, 132
caliphal authority 70–72, 84–85
caliphal state 72–73
Capitulations 87, 90
Carter, Stephen 2
Casanova, José 9, 46, 47–48, 67
civic reason 35–37
civility, duty of 13
civil society and justice as discourse 53–54
clerical authority 61
codification process 87
colonialism: codification and 87–88; experience of 85–86, 87
communitarian critique of liberal theory 116–117
comprehensive doctrines 7–8, 12–13
consocial position 21–22
constitutional law and justice as discourse framework 121–123
Cook, Michael 105
Coulson, Noel 130

D'Agostino, Fred 37
dawla 93
debate, political, in justice as discourse framework 124
democracy: challenges of, in Muslim contexts 107–109; opinions of 95–99; 'priority for' 34–35; prospects for 99–102
democratic societies 12–13, 31
deprivatisation of religion 84, 86
dhimmis 92n39
din 91–95
discourse 133; *see also* justice as discourse framework
discourse ethics 32–33
discursive political sphere 5
diversity: justice as discourse, liberal theory and 40–42; liberal and theological responses to 9–10; of Muslim contexts 59–62, 99; overview 7–9; Rawls' political liberalism and 10–13; responses to and critiques of Rawls 13–19; *see also* pluralism
'domain of the political' 13
dunya 91–95
dynasties, establishment of 71–73

'East' and 'West,' relationship between 65–66, 112–114
Eberle, Christopher 15, 30
Egypt 122
Elshtain, Jean Bethke 15, 40
Emon, Anver 88, 129

Ernst, Carl 59, 61, 64, 117, 132
etatization of Islamic law 88–91
executive authorities and justice as discourse 51–53

Fadel, Mohammed 115
Fatimids 79, 94, 118n41
Feldman, Noah 50, 99–100, 108
Filali-Ansary, Abdou 48, 120
fiqh 75, 77, 89–91
Frye, Northrop, *The Great Code* 62

Gallup World Poll, 'Islam & Democracy' report 98
Gaus, Gerald 30, 37, 106
Geertz, Clifford 59–60
geography of Muslim presence 59
al-Ghazzali 63, 80

Habermas, Jurgen 2, 4, 16, 22–26, 32–33, 106
Hallaq, Wael 68, 78, 90–91, 94
Hanafi, Hassan 63–64
Harris, José 53–54
Hasan, Riaz 60
Heffner, Robert 86
Hodgson, Marshall 72, 73
Holmes, Stephen 41

Ibn Muqaffa 72
(re)imagination, use of term 5
imagined communities 64
Imams 70
Imber, Colin 75
impartiality 44
implementing justice as discourse 51–55, 56–57
indeterminacy of relationship between religion and politics 101–102, 130–131
Ingelhart, Ronald 95
Iran, constitution of 89
Iranian Revolution 1
Iraq, constitution of 2
'Islamically unredeemed,' liberal theory as 114–116
Islamic democracy 100, 108
'Islamic' imperative and liberal theory 109–112
Islamic law: development of 73–78; reworking 87–91; *shari'a* 67–68, 75–76, 78, 88–91, 96
Islamist democracy 100, 108
Ismailis 79, 92, 118n41

judicial authorities and justice as discourse 51–53
juridical plurality 96

justice as discourse framework: alternatives to 34–38; argument of 6; classical liberal theory and 40–45, 115–116; constitutional law and 121–123; construction of 30–33; contribution of 5; democracy and 108–109; goal of 55–56; implementing 51–55, 56–57; judges, state executives and civil servants in 124–125; Menski's kite and 126–127; Muslim contexts and 4–5; non-constitutional law and 123; overview 3–4, 38–39, 40, 127–129, 131–132; political debate and 124; as practical political model 121–126; requirements of 51; secular and 45–51

Keane, John 121
Keddie, Nikki 82
Kelsay, John 90
Kennedy, Hugh 69
Kessler, Edward 115
Khan, Mohammad Ashgar 63
al-Kindi, Abu Yusuf Ya'qub ibn Ishaq 114

Ladd, John 29–30, 40
Lapidus, Ira 82
law: bridge from politics to 126–127; constitutional 121–123; (re)imagining for Muslim contexts 103–104; non-constitutional 123; role of 3; *see also* Islamic law; politico-legal legacy of Muslim contexts
legislative provisions and justice as discourse 53
Levinson, Sanford 16, 124
liberalism: of reasoned respect 14; standard approach of 10–11, 14, 26, 40
liberal theory: communitarian critique of 116–117; diversity and 7–9, 40–42; evolution of 40; limits and 44–45; in Muslim contexts 65–66, 127–129, 131–132; neutrality and 42–44; normative commitment to pluralism of 9–10; as range pf positions 7; religion and 6; *see also* Rawls' theory
liberal theory, challenges to uses of: democracy 107–109; individualism and Ummah 116–117; 'Islamic' imperative 109–112; neutrality 104–106; non-Islamic pedigree of theory 114–116; pluralism and sovereignty 117–120; secularity 106–107; transitional character of Muslim contexts 120–121; Western conceit of theory 112–114
limits on public role of religion, justice as discourse and liberal theory 44–45

al-Mamum 78–79
March, Andrew 44–45

Marx, Karl, *On the Jewish Question* 10
Masud, Kahlid 89
Menski, Werner 68, 126
Moadell, Mansoor 96
monotheistic imperative and liberal theory 109–112
Moors, Annelies 74
Mottahedeh, Roy 73, 82
Muawiya b. Abu Sufayn 71
Muhammad: authority and roles of 67–69; death of and succession to 69–70
Munir Report 119
Muslim contexts: challenges facing 1–3, 130; decline of Ottoman Empire and 84–87; democracy in 107–109; diversity of 59–62, 99; (re)imagining religion, law, state and society for 103–104; lessons from heritage of 81–83; liberal theory in 65–66, 127–129, 131–132; overview 4, 58–59; pluralism in 59–62, 117–118, 132–133; sameness of differences in 62–66; 'social imaginary' for 102; terms of engagement for 103–104, 133; transitional character of 120–121; use of term 59–62; *see also* justice as discourse framework; liberal theory, challenges to uses of; politico-legal legacy of Muslim contexts
Muslimness 64
Mutazilites 79

Nasr, Vali 102
nation-state *see* state
neutrality: justice as discourse, liberal theory and 42–44; problem of 104–106
non-constitutional law and justice as discourse framework 123
Norris, Pippa 95–96

offices of state, in justice as discourse framework 124–125
Ottomans 80–81, 84, 87–88
overlapping consensus 18–19

Pakistan 89, 122
Pew Global Attitudes Surveys 97, 98
pluralism: challenge of 2; of comprehensive doctrines 8; in Muslim contexts 59–62, 117–118, 132–133; nonconstitutional 34; nonestablishment and private 34; normative commitment to 9–10; Rawls on 7, 11–12; *see also* diversity
political authority *see* politico-legal legacy of Muslim contexts
'political Islam' 1
political reasons and justice as discourse 54–55
political sovereignty and liberal theory 118–120
politico-legal legacy of Muslim contexts: development of law 73–78; early dynasties 71–73; Muhammad 67–69; power, law and religion 78–81; succession to Muhammad 69–70
politics: bridge to law from 126–127; discursive political sphere 5; indeterminacy of relationship between religion and 101–102, 130–131; state, religion and 91–95; zone of 55
post-secular society 25
Principle of Public Justification 30, 37
'priority for democracy' 34–35
public policy decisions: comprehensive doctrines and 12–13; religion and 9–10
public reason: expanded 30, 37–38; Na'im on 35–37; Rawls on 11–12, 13, 19
public sphere: defined 2; options for Islam in 100; secularism in 46–47

Qureshi, Emran 85, 86

Rawls, John: on constitutional essentials 56–57, 105; *The Law of Peoples* 107; on neutrality 44; on pluralism 7; *Political Liberalism* 3–4, 10–13
Rawls' theory: Gaus and 30; Habermas and 22–26; Ladd and 29–30; responses to and critiques of 13–19; theologically-oriented alternatives to 19–21; Weithman and 26–29; Wolterstorff and 21–22
Rehman, Javaid 88
religion: appealing to, as practical authority 49; constitutional establishment of 121–123; deprivatisation of 84, 86; *din* 91–95; discursive political sphere and 5; diversity in 40–42; importance of 96–98; indeterminacy of relationship between politics and 101–102, 130–131; liberal theory and 6; limits on public role of 44–45; power, law and 78–81; public policy decisions and 9–10; role for, in public discourse 2–3, 13–19; as source of comprehensive doctrines 8; *see also* Muslim contexts
responsible citizenship, conditions of 26–29
Rightly Guided caliphs 67, 70

Sachedina, Abdulaziz 93, 110–111
Safavids 79, 81
Sajoo, Amyn 86, 93, 113, 120
Saljuqs 80
Sandel, Michael 28–29, 38
schools of Islamic law 76, 78
secular: defined 3, 45–46; *dunya* 91–95; justice as discourse framework and 45–51
secularization 47–49
secularism 45–47
secularity 106–107, 110–111
Sen, Amartya 50

shari'a 67–68, 75–76, 78, 88–91, 96
Shia tradition 70, 76, 79–80, 92
sovereignty, political, and liberal theory 118–120
standard approach of liberalism 10–11, 14, 26, 40; *see also* justice as discourse framework
state: caliphal 72–73; *dawla* 93–94; defined 52; establishment of, as basic institution of political organization 86, 130–131; (re)imagining for Muslim contexts 103–104; Islamic law and 88–91; offices of, in justice as discourse framework 124–125; religion, politics and 91–95; religious character of nation-states 41–42
Stout, Jeffrey 49
Sunni tradition 70, 76

Taylor, Charles 2, 41–42, 45, 46, 102n71
terms of engagement for Muslim contexts 103–104, 133
theologically-oriented positions 19–21
transitional character of Muslim contexts 120–121
translation requirement 24–26, 32
Trigg, Roger 105

'ulama 74–76, 77–78, 79, 80–81
Umayyads 71–72
ummah 64–65, 67, 68–69, 116–117, 132
Unger, Robert 124, 128
usul al-fiqh 76–77

Vallier, Kevin 30, 37
Vogel, Frank 114–115

Waldron, Jeremy 15, 49
Weber, Max 52
Weiss, Bernard, *The Spirit of Islamic Law* 109–110, 118
Weithman, Paul 4, 14, 16, 18–19, 26–29, 40, 124
Western conceit of liberal theory 112–114
Western powers, domination of Muslim societies by 85–86
'whole truth' frameworks 11, 13, 18, 26
Wittgenstein, Ludwig 65
Wolterstorff, Nicholas 9, 10, 14, 17, 20, 21–22, 40
World Values Survey 95

Yavuz, M Hakan 97–98

Zubaida, Sami 48, 71, 88